On PERSECUTION,
IDENTITY & ACTIVISM

Aspects of the Italian-American Experience
From the Late 19th Century to Today

By
CRISTOGIANNI BORSELLA

Dante University Press
Boston

Library of Congress Cataloging-in-Publication Data

Borsella, Cristogianni, 1979-
  On persecution, identity & activism : i.e. "Italian-Americans" : aspects
of the Italian-American experience from the late 19th century
to today / by Cristogianni Borsella.
  p. cm.
  Includes bibliographical references and index.
  ISBN 0-937832-41-3 (pbk : alk. paper)
    1. Italian Americans—Social conditions.
    2. Immigrants—United States—Social conditions.
    3. Italian Americans—Ethnic identity.
    4. Italian Americans—Cultural assimilation.
    5. Italian Americans—Civil rights.
    6. Discrimination—United States.
    7. Persecution—United States.
    8. Racism—United States.
    9. United States—Ethnic relations.
    10. United States—Race relations.

 I. Title. On persecution, identity, and activism. II. Title
    E184.I8B675 2005
    305.85'107309—dc22
                        2005022981

Dante University Press
www.danteuniversity.org
PO Box 812158
Wellesley MA 02482

This book is dedicated to those downtrodden, powerless Italian-Americans who were persecuted and killed on account of their ethnic background. I've heard their cries.

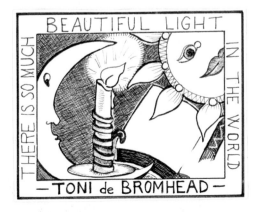

THERE IS SO MUCH BEAUTIFUL LIGHT IN THE WORLD

— TONI de BROMHEAD —

Contents

Preface 6
Part I: Italian-Americans: The Third Most Persecuted Minority
    In U.S.History 8
    Chapter One 13
        Section A: *Chinese-Americans* 14
        Section B: *Japanese-Americans* 16
        Section C: *Hispanic-Americans* 17
        Section D: *Irish-Americans* 22
        Section E: *Jewish-Americans* 24
    Chapter Two 37
        Section A: *Backgrounds of a Marginalized Group* 39
        Section B: *Timeline of Tears* 52
            Era of Physical Attacks 52
            Era of Americanization 88
            Era of Sociological Statistics 106
            Era of Heightened Media Defamation 113
        Section C: *Conclusion* 128
Part II: Italian-Americans: *In-between* on Arrival 130
    Chapter Three 132
    Chapter Four 136
        Section A: *Identity & Assimilation* 138
        Section B: *Erroneous and Antiquated Racial Beliefs* 143
        Section C: *"Are Italians White?"* 146
        Section D: *Forging a " Wog" Identity Down Under* 157
        Section E: *Conclusion* 159
Part III: *Italian-Americans Unite* 164
    Chapter Five 165
        Section A: *Italian-Americans vs. Mafia TV* 165
        Section B: *Italian-Americans and the Columbus Day*
                Controversy 175
        Section C: *Conclusion* 186
    Chapter Six 189

Epilogue..193
Appendices to Chapter 2, Section B....................195
Appendix I (Executions 1873-1899) 195
Appendix II (Executions 1900-1920)....................197
Appendix III (Executions 1921-1941)...................206
Appendix IV (Executions 1942-1962) 215
Works Cited 219
Endnotes..235
Index 254

Preface

I wrote this book with both love and resentment guiding my pen—love for those who remember and respect history and resentment for those who ignore and disdain it. Though some understand (even if vaguely) that the Italian experience in America was characterized by hardships, many others (including well read historians) do not. By ignoring the historical record, such people trivialize the incredible odds Italians faced on their journey to becoming fully assimilated Americans. Thus a prime reason for writing this book was to educate others (Italians and non-Italians alike); I wanted to gather in one collection a wealth of anti-Italian incidents so that when I tell people "Italians are the third most persecuted minority in U.S. history," and they proceed to look at me like I have two heads, I'll be able to say, "Here, read my book." I also wanted to show the reader the hidden danger behind stereotypes, particularly the "Mafia" stereotype and how it was responsible for the lynching of eleven Italians in New Orleans. I strove to achieve all this in the first part of the book.

Part Two gets into the concept of race as it has pertained to Italian-Americans through the years; here I tried to convey the historical "in-betweenness" of Italian-Americans (i.e. their long time status as a racially ambiguous group). I used online correspondences between myself and others to show, that the "whiteness" of Italian-Americans continues to be heatedly debated. I also strove to prove that being "ethnic" and "white" at the same time is more of a contradiction than a reality. For example, many Americans today do not consider Latinos "white," yet many Latinos have European backgrounds; even more perplexing, the original "Latin" tribe, language, and race all sprung forth from Italy in ancient times—Rome itself is located in the "Latin" province, and Italians were once regarded as "Latins" in this country—yet today, regardless of their diverse and often swarthy complexions, Italian-Americans are merely "white." If this does not prove that race is a social construct, I do not know what does.

The third and final part of the book deals with modern Italian-American activism and how it is important for Italian-Americans to combat media defamation so that the severe bigotry of the past (in the form of anti-Italian persecution and discrimination) is not repeated. I have in this section provided more of my online letters—ones that were written and sent in protest to various persons. (The two main targets of modern Italian-American activism have been the media and those with anti-Columbus Day agendas.)

Hopefully I have achieved all of my objectives in writing this book, on the Italian-American experience.

Cristogianni Borsella

Part I
Italian-Americans: The Third Most Persecuted Minority in U.S. History.

1: Family of Italian migrant workers.

2: Elderly Chinese-American man walking hand in hand with the next generation.

3: Japanese-Americans.

4: A Japanese-American contingent evacuated from Los Angeles.

5: Hispanic-American family.

6: An Irish-American lad.

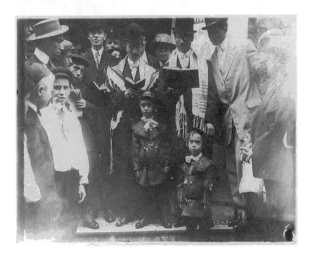

7: Jewish-Americans.

8: The lynching of Leo Frank.

Chapter One

*You persecute the people, tyrannize over them, and
kill them. You try to put a path between us and some
other nationality that hates each other. This is why I
am here today on this bench for having been the oppressed class.*

Nicola Sacco

(speaking to the Court before he and
Bartolomeo Vanzetti were sentenced to die)

As the title of Part I clearly suggests, it is the purpose of chapters one
and two to establish that Italian-Americans have experienced a
great deal of suffering on their path to assimilation. Far from setting
it in stone that Italian-Americans are "the third most persecuted minority in
U.S. history," the title of this section was intended primarily to grip the
reader's attention and to force one to think. In this first chapter, specific non-
Italian groups are afforded ample space so that the reader can attain a general knowledge of the oppression that they have been subjected to, and so he
or she can compare the degree of persecution they suffered to the level the
Italians endured. Due to the virtual genocide of American Indians and the
enslavement of blacks, it should be universally accepted that these two
groups are, respectively, the first and second most persecuted minorities;
thus, there will be no mention of them here.

Based on the number of discriminatory accounts and nativist outbursts,
the only groups that can seriously contest the third slot of victim hood (besides Italian-Americans) are the Chinese-, Japanese-, Hispanic-, Irish-, and
Jewish-Americans. A historical background and description of injustices

committed will be provided for each group. The Italian-Americans will be dealt with in the next chapter. Let it first be known, however, that it is not the goal of this book to lessen the degree to which other groups have suffered. I, the author, am merely going on my own personal knowledge of the oppression other minority groups have faced, and ultimately I am attempting to enlighten my readers by showing just how much Italian-Americans have been persecuted themselves.

A. Chinese-Americans

Sixty-three thousand Chinese were living in the United States by the year 1870. Ninety-nine percent of them were located on the West Coast. This, then, is the region in which the overwhelming majority of anti-Chinese incidents took place (Sung, 1967: 42).

Prior to 1876, Chinese immigrants were regarded, by and large, as nonthreatening creatures from another world. Although they did not mix socially with their white (or non-Chinese) contemporaries, they were often described as industrious, efficient, and indispensable workers, in addition to being clean and cheerful in disposition (Sung, 1967: 27). However, the "distant admiration" white people had for the Chinese took a swift turn south in 1876, along with the U.S. economy.

It is a sad legacy for both capitalism and the human condition that, when an economic "panic" occurs, scapegoating begins. It happened in 20th century Germany, and it happened more than once in 19th century America. When the Panic of 1876 came around everyone was hit hard, even those in the "Golden State." The bottom fell out of the market and ruined lives up and down the economic ladder. As this was occurring, the political climate in California was worsening, and popular disgust mounted for the state's incompetent officials. The stage was being set for a demagogue like Dennis Kearney to come along (Sung, 1967: 40-1).

Like many at the time, Dennis Kearney was deep into mining stocks. And like many, he lost practically everything in 1876. Angry over the situation he now found himself in, Kearney chose to play the "race card," and in so doing, he chose to transfer all blame over to the Chinese. Though seemingly illogical to a rational mind, this made perfect sense to Dennis Kearney and his ilk. After all, *white people* had lost their money, their homes, their jobs, et cetera. Soon, one of the leading San Francisco newspapers, the *Chronicle*, was championing Kearney in an effort to boost sales (Sung, 1967: 41).

With ignorance and a newfound publicity on his side, Dennis Kearney spoke out against Chinese immigration. He and his followers accused the Chinese of being in cahoots with the land and rail monopolies and of subsisting on slave wages in order to take over "white jobs." (These charges, by the way, were conveniently disproved *after* the Chinese exclusion laws were put in place.) At the end of every speech that Kearney gave he barked, "The Chinese must go!" Following that slogan many white Californians were moved to violence, thus contradicting their originally positive view of Chinese immigrants. Chinese people were now being described as clannish, dangerous, deceitful, and vicious (Sung, 1967: 42-3). In at least ten more years the newly arrived Italian immigrants would be described in the same way, with the same words.

The following is a list of anti-Chinese incidents that occurred (Sung, 1967: 43-6):

Spring 1876: Chinese were driven out of small towns and their quarters were burned; some killed and injured.

June 1876: An anti-Chinese attack was made in Truckee, CA.

March 1877: Six Chinese farmers were attacked and five killed. The killer admitted to being under orders from the CA Workingmen's Party (founded by Dennis Kearney).

July 1877: A large-scale riot broke out. Chinese were not safe to walk the streets for months. Some were the victims of shootings and arson.

1878: All the Chinese denizens of Truckee were driven out of town.

1880: A rioting mob destroyed every Chinese business and home in Denver. The Chinese victims were actually placed in jail for their own protection. One Chinese was killed in the fray and several white men were wounded.

1885: Twenty-eight Chinese were massacred in Rock Springs, WY. Others were wounded and hundreds driven out.

1886: Another massacre occurred, this time in Log Cabin, OR.

As one can apparently see, mob violence against the Chinese essentially began in 1876. The economic panic of that year was, for many whites, reason enough to persecute the Chinese—to make this highly visible minority population the target of their misplaced rage. However, there was a xenophobic feeling in existence prior to 1876 as well, even amidst all those nice compliments white folks gave the Chinese at first. To prove this, one of the bloodiest lynching happened five years before the Panic of 1876. In 1871 (twenty years before the lynching of 11 Italians in New Orleans) a pack of white ruffians stormed into Chinatown and killed 21 Chinese, fifteen of whom were lynched in the streets; Chinese homes and shops were thoroughly pillaged before the riot's end (Sung, 1967: 48).

The fact that the Chinese had to endure such cruel attacks was not unique to their particular group however. Virtually all immigrating and non-Anglo-Saxon peoples went through a period of persecution. What *was* unique to them was the Chinese Exclusion Act, passed in 1882, which, in effect, barred them from entering the country. Never before was the U.S. government so blatant in proclaiming that it did not want a certain group coming into the nation. Even so, other groups deemed "undesirable," such as Southern and Eastern Europeans, were also prevented from entering the nation *en masse* under the infamous Immigration Restriction Act of 1924. To this day, it is still not easy for someone from Italy, for example, to become a U.S. citizen.

B. Japanese-Americans

The story of anti-Japanese sentiment in the United States parallels the Chinese experience in that both groups were persecuted primarily on the West Coast, both came from East Asian societies, they were considered one and the same by white racists who subscribed to "Yellow Peril" dogma, and, although ironic, both groups were originally welcomed for the cheap labor they provided.

It was during the first few years of the twentieth century that demands were made to end Japanese immigration. Much like the anti-Chinese period twenty years before, economic and racial factors were behind the xenophobia now affecting the Japanese community. Racists and the organizations to which they belonged (like "The Native Sons of the Golden West") put enough pressure on California's legislature to get a resolution passed in 1905, which urged Congress to stop Japanese immigration. What was finalized two years later was the so-called "Gentlemen's Agreement" between the United States and Japan. Under this plan, the Japanese government voluntarily stopped issuing passports to both skilled and unskilled workers (Simpson and Yinger, 1965: 92). The Gentlemen's Agreement did curtail Japanese immigration, but to the dismay of the racists, it failed to stop it altogether (Hosokawa, 1969: 94).

Indubitably, the most tragic chapter in Japanese-American history came right after the attack on Pearl Harbor. The same people who wanted the Japanese out of the country decades earlier were now given the ammunition they needed to go after them again. These rabble-rousers wasted no time in expressing how disloyal and untrustworthy Japanese-Americans were. Even if the government did not believe such outright lies, it implicitly heeded the words of the hate-mongers, and was thus responsible for one of the greatest injustices in U.S. history—the relocation and internment of an entire ethnicity (Simpson and Yinger, 1965: 93).

When the roundup of Japanese-Americans was completed, 117,116 had been evacuated from their homes and interned. This comprised the entire Japanese population living on the West Coast; approximately 70,000 of them were American citizens (Hosokawa, 1969: 259, 334). This was in all honesty one of America's darkest hours.

Many people erroneously believe, however, that Japanese-Americans were the only ones during the Second World War to go through this. They are mistaken. Bill Hosokawa is flat out wrong when he states in his book *Nisei: The Quiet Americans* that "only those of Japanese extraction were evacuated [and interned]" (265). Although there were not nearly as many Italians *interned* as Nisei, tens of thousands did in fact have their civil liberties violated during World War II. To those who would deny the suffering Italian-Americans faced when compared to the larger-scale Japanese ordeal, the question must be asked: Just because less people had their civil liberties violated vis-à-vis internment, is it less of an injustice?

In November 2001, *A Review of the Restrictions on Persons of Italian Ancestry During World War II* was published by the U.S. Department of Justice. In it are the following findings of congressional investigation (pp. iv-v): "The freedom of more than 600,000 Italian-born immigrants in the United States and their families was restricted during World War II by Government measures that branded them 'enemy aliens' and included carrying identification cards, travel restrictions, and seizure of personal property...more than 10,000 Italian-Americans on the West Coast were forced to leave their homes and prohibited from entering coastal zones. More than 50,000 were subjected to curfews...thousands of Italian-American immigrants were arrested, and hundreds were interned in military camps." One can ascertain from these figures that, overall, there were more people of Italian ancestry who had their civil rights violated than Japanese.

C. Hispanic-Americans

Historically and culturally, Americans of Hispanic descent are probably more similar to Italian-Americans than any other group. Both are descended from peoples who spoke Latin-based languages (sometimes collectively referred to as "Italic"), both groups are overwhelmingly Roman Catholic by faith, and both have been on the receiving end of an inordinate amount of persecution. The frequent clash between "Latin" and "Anglo" cultures in the United States (one a minority culture, and the other a dominant culture) has often precipitated violence. "Latinity" has been and continues to be associated with weakness in our still very Anglo-oriented society. (The trepidation both Anglos and Latins have for one another could partly be due to a rivalry, dating back to the Age of Exploration, between two forces—one which sought to "Anglicize" the New World, and the other which sought to "Latinize" it. We are not going to get into that here however.)

Generally speaking, anti-Hispanic behavior has been and continues to be stimulated by many of the same prejudices that roused anti-Italian sentiment—that "these people" do not care about this country; that they have no intention of staying and becoming citizens (they just want to make their money and go home); that there are too many of them coming into the nation; they do not speak the English language (none of them do); they are all poor, and thus filthy, criminal, ignorant, deceitful, etc. While one must concede that this is stereotyping in its harshest form, it is true that many Hispanic newcomers (like their Italian predecessors) are poor and do not speak English fluently. (*But so what!* This is nothing to be ashamed of. America was not built by pick-wielding wealthy aristocrats.) It is also true that most northern Europeans who fit the above description (as being poor and not able to speak English well) have rarely been persecuted so severely on account of their background. Once I had heard mention of a Scandinavian immigrant who was not included in a group of "white men" (of Anglo-Saxon descent) in the labor camps of Minnesota, but this I believe was an exception. It is important to remember that Latin people are much more "visible" in society than Nordic ethnics. Hispanics and Italians are therefore much easier targets to locate.

Ethnic slurs, which have been commonly hurled at both the Italian and Hispanic groups, such as "dago" and "greaseball," prove that they were, at least at one time, even considered one and the same by many Anglos. Since their backgrounds were so similar (culturally, linguistically, spiritually, and even ethnically), racists could not resist dehumanizing them with the same words. Indeed, like their Italian cousins, Hispanics have had to endure a gargantuan amount of racist hostility through the years.

When, predominantly, Spanish-speaking territories were annexed to the United States, Uncle Sam treated the Hispanics (especially the *mestizo* or "mixed blood" variety) just as harsh as the Spanish Crown had treated them.

The only difference was now they had to learn a new language and new customs if they were going to succeed and be a part of the new country they now found themselves in. Because of their differences with the White Anglo-Saxon Protestant (or "WASP") majority, Hispanic-Americans were forced into taking a subservient role in society and were even segregated against in parts of the southwest. This "status quo" lasted, for the most part, up until the mid-1960s and the start of the *Chicano* movement (Moore, 1970: 148-156).

Although Puerto Ricans and other Latin Caribbean and Central American groups have been the victims of great prejudice and discrimination, when considering which individual group suffered the largest degree of anti-Hispanic oppression, and which one through their fight for civil rights "paved the way" for other Spanish-speaking people to stand up for themselves, it becomes clear that the story of Hispanic persecution in the United States is largely a *Chicano* or Mexican-American one.

Below is a list pertaining to the ill treatment of Hispanics in the United States ("Hispanic American Timeline"):

1912: The Mexican ambassador to the U.S. issues a formal protest over the lynchings and murders of Mexican-Americans in California and Texas.

1926: Non-Hispanics attack rioting Puerto Ricans in Harlem.

1943: Year of the racially motivated "Zoot Suit Riots" in southern California. Hundreds of U.S. soldiers and sailors roam the streets of Hispanic neighborhoods looking for their target: Mexican-American men wearing zoot suits. When they are found, they are beaten and their suits are torn off.

1954: The Supreme Court recognizes in the pivotal case of *Hernandez v. Texas* that Hispanics are a distinct group, that they suffer a great deal of discrimination, and that they are not treated as "whites." This opened the door for Hispanic Americans to legally attack discrimination aimed at them. (*Hernandez v. Texas* was also the first Supreme Court case to be argued by Mexican-American lawyers.)

1954-1958: Thousands of United States citizens of Mexican ancestry are arrested and detained during "Operation Wetback" —a government effort to deport illegals.

1966: Police brutality prompts hundreds of Puerto Ricans to riot in Chicago.

1970: In a scuffle between the police and demonstrators, during an antiwar protest in Los Angeles, Ruben Salazar— (not involved in the fight) was killed by police.

It is important to note that the maltreatment of migrant workers did not end in the 1960s when Cesar Chavez fought "the system." Physical abuse against them persists to this day, often because their impoverished environment is an eyesore for the rest of the community in which they live. In my own town of Riverhead, New York, two alleged white supremacists were each found guilty of two counts of attempted murder and assault in the September 17, 2000, beatings of two Hispanic day laborers. The workers were lured to an abandoned basement with the promise of work, and there they were nearly beaten to death with shovels, a post-hole digger, and a knife ("Man Guilty of Beating"). Luckily, they were able to escape. In 2003, another hate crime occurred in which a migrant family's home was firebombed. Fortunately, no one was killed in this case either ("FBI Joins Long Island Firebombing Probe"). There can be no doubt that modern anti-Hispanic violence mirrors anti-Italian violence of the past, though on a smaller scale.

The Long Island community of Farmingville (the town where the beatings and the bombing took place) and its local anti-immigrant group, "Sachem Quality of Life," has been at the center of a national debate on immigration in recent years. It is thought by many that Sachem Quality of Life—through its association with right-wing groups like the John Birch Society and American Patrol (the latter listed as a "hate group" by the Southern Poverty Law Center) —has contributed nothing but enmity to the already tense atmosphere that exists between Hispanic day laborers and the greater community. On the one hand there is the white middle-class that makes up most of Farmingville's population, and on the other there are the day laborers who congregate in motley clusters on busy suburban streets looking for work, much to the chagrin of many white passers-by. Again, their apparent poverty renders them "eyesores" ("Latino Laborers Targeted").

Sachem Quality of Life's haranguings parallel what has been said of practically every other foreign-born group; thus, the group's banter is *nativist* at its very core. Members of this group "complain that the day laborers that gather each day along Farmingville's main street to wait for work evade taxes and crowd Americans out of the labor market." They accuse them of "dragging down property values, raising the crime rate and endangering children." They even go as far as to call these workers "invaders" (though many of them have come here legally). Looking at the immigration issue from a privileged perspective, Sachem Quality of Life's attention is not focused on the disturbing fact that the day laborers often work twelve or more hours per day, that their wages are often withheld, and that many of them live in crowded yet overpriced housing (conditions that were all too common for Italian laborers last century). In many ultra-conservative communities attention is being shifted away from the realistic plights affecting Hispanic day laborers to the *alleged* plight society must suffer on account of this population ("Latino Laborers Targeted"). This, to me, is the true crime being committed.

Treated as an inconvenience by the Farmingville community, the migrants are also accused of groping women outside the local 7/11, where they frequently assemble in search of work. This kind of complaint against swarthy Latin immigrants is nothing new. The same thing was reported in newspapers about Italians, a century ago. From the *Brooklyn Standard Union* (April 1906) came the following reports:

April 29, 1906: KICKED BY ITALIAN; WOMAN WILL MAKE NO COMPLAINT Maggie MCNAMARA, of 20 Flushing Avenue, was removed to the Cumberland street hospital yesterday afternoon suffering from contusions of the abdomen, which, she said, were caused by an Italian who kicked her. She refused to make a complaint and was later taken home in an ambulance.

April 30, 1906: ITALIANS HUG WOMEN AND FIGHT POLICE While Capt. PINKERTON and Detective HOLLAND, of the Bedford Avenue station, were standing in front of the station house last night several young women who were passing were stopped by two Italians who, it is alleged, tried to hug them. The captain and HOLLAND ran up and grabbed hold of the two men, who, not knowing they were in the hands of the police, put up a lively fight. They were finally subdued and landed in the station house. In the Lee Avenue Court today the hearing was adjourned.

The above is just a sample of the numerous reports that came out of newspapers on a daily basis, identifying Italian perps by their nationality. The level of racism in these articles is much greater than what can be found in legitimate papers today. One can imagine the massive protests that would be mounted if headlines read: "A Boisterous Gang of Puerto Ricans Abduct Woman"; or "Diminutive Mexican Arrested for Purse Snatching." This is not to say that Hispanics were not subjected to overtly racist reporting in the past—*they were.* (And oftentimes it was harsher than what other groups experienced.) However, today, political correctness has largely prevented blatant racism from surfacing in the press. Thus, "pc" behavior is not without its merits.

Today, many Americans are outraged that hundreds of thousands of illegal immigrants are streaming into the United States each year (mainly via Mexico). These "patriots" are quick to say that the illegals are breaking their country's laws, yet they forget how many of their own ancestors—deemed the "refuse of Europe" by bigots of old—had to come here illegally in order to feed their families. Such people would have us think that illegal immigration is a phenomenon started by (and unique to) Hispanics—of course this is not so.

Now while I must admit that it frustrates me at times to know that such a large group of immigrants are breaking my *country's laws* in order to get here (and are thus making it more difficult for those who want to come here legally), I also understand that they are not breaking any of my own *moral laws* to get here. (As a Christian I am forced to remember Numbers 15:15, "Before the Lord you and the alien are alike.") What I am most concerned with is *why* such yearly exoduses are occurring and why these migrants need to flee their homelands in the first place. I wish more native-born Americans would try to look at the problem from the migrants' perspective; then perhaps more will see that they are dealing with fellow *humans,* not aliens.

Although Hispanics have been pushed aside and victimized by "WASP America" probably for as long as there has been one, it must not be overlooked that today this group enjoys an ever-growing rate of success and has the special advantage of immigrating in a politically-correct, post-Civil Rights era—an advantage that previous immigrating generations did not have. The great bulk of Italian immigrants, for example, came at a time when they were forced to assimilate "or else." For all its problems, modern society truly does welcome diversity (e.g. affirmative action programs in the job market, college admissions, etc.). Another benefit that Hispanic Americans enjoy is the close proximity of their ancestral homelands to the U.S. They can thus contribute a steady flow of newcomers (prospective citizens), strengthen the already powerful Hispanic lobby, and ensure that the Spanish language will increasingly be on an equal footing with English.

The two main issues affecting Hispanics today are immigration and language rights (such as bilingualism in school). Like the anti-Hispanic violence that continues to harass their community, these two concerns are not going to "go away" any time soon.

D. Irish-Americans

Another group that endured many hate inspired attacks was the Irish. They were victimized excessively during the first hundred years of U.S. history. This is because the Irish were the first *real* minority immigrant population to live within the boundaries of the United States. They were neither

Anglo-Saxon by ethnicity, nor Protestant by faith. This presented a great problem for Irish-Americans socially and made them easy targets of hatred.

On account of their teeming numbers and "foreign" religion (Catholicism), the Irish were considered a threat, and so it was difficult at first for them to find work. "No Irish Need Apply" signs began springing up all over the "Land of Opportunity." Many Irish thus found themselves to be in the same predicament in America as in Ireland—abject poverty (Murphy and Driscoll, 1974: 11-13).

Mid-nineteenth century America was in all actuality a tough place to "make it" for non-WASPs. Rallies against Irish immigration were held every week in some parts of the country. Such anti-Irish feeling enabled the Know-Nothing Party to rise to power in various cities and states at the time. Also during this period "nativists" instigated anti-Catholic riots in which the Irish newcomers were physically harmed and their churches razed. The only way the Irish could fight back in most cases was by starting riots of their own. This did not help their cause for equality, however, nor did it improve their overall image in the minds of most WASPs (Murphy and Driscoll, 1974: 16).

By the time of the American Civil War, the feeling of Irish powerlessness hit an all-time high. Although it was said that the Union was championing a noble cause based on the principles of freedom and equality, many Irish-Americans disagreed. Many felt that outsiders did not care about their daily plight, and that while blacks would eventually win their freedom, nothing would change for the sons and daughters of Erin. Frustration, rife among Irish-Americans in the northeast, swiftly turned into rancor. They resented the sympathy southern blacks received from northern abolitionists (often *anti-Catholic* abolitionists) while the Irish themselves were still largely poor and uneducated in northern cities. They also resented the draft law, which allowed rich men to pay their way out of serving in the Union Army. All this Irish resentment led to the bloodiest riots New York City has ever seen, and quite possibly to the most tragic time in Irish-American history—the "Draft Riots" of 1863. During this crisis, the "Colored Orphans Asylum" was set ablaze and several blacks were lynched. In the process of restoring peace, the state militia killed hundreds of rioters. It is important to note that not all the rioters were of Irish extraction and that over 150,000 Irish-Americans served loyally in Lincoln's army (Murphy and Driscoll, 1974: 29-30).

Another bit of misfortune struck the Irish-American community in the 1870s, when twenty were hanged for their alleged membership in a secret society called the "Molly Maguires." The "Mollies" were a group of disgruntled Irish miners who, through violence, tried to attain better working conditions in the coalfields of Pennsylvania. Their plans were destroyed, however, when an informer named James McKenna was recruited into their ranks. His testimony was solely responsible for the hanging of twenty (Murphy and Driscoll, 1974: 39).

Toward the end of the 19th Century, as southern and eastern European emigrants began their long journeys across the Atlantic, Irish-Americans were finally starting to ascend the social ladder. In so doing, they achieved positions of power that had previously been reserved for WASPs. They became politicians, businessmen, lawyers, chiefs of police, etc. (The old stereotype of rowdy Irishmen being carried off in "paddy wagons" soon gave way to the stereotype of the stern Irish cop.) In many ways, through their new occupations, the formerly oppressed Irish became "oppressors" themselves—this is only natural in a society, which favors older groups that have had more time to assimilate. And so, Irish-Americans became the objects of fear and resentment for powerless southern and eastern European immigrants who were just starting to arrive. There was certainly no love loss between these newcomers and the well-established Irish population. In fact, old prejudices have been so hard to kill—and memories of conflict so hard to forget—that even today many second, third, and fourth generation Italian-Americans refer to the Irish as agents of oppression, regardless of how many Irish-American friends or family members they now have.

Irish-Americans, like the other ethnic groups mentioned in this chapter, have a history rooted in oppression and have been defined by their ability to endure and overcome that oppression. And while one can see in retrospect how much the Irish-American community had to struggle for acceptance, one can see today just how accepted and integral a part of society they have become.

E. Jewish-Americans

Probably the most persecuted people in world history (and undoubtedly the most resilient) are the Jews. Since biblical times they have been enslaved, driven from their land, and slaughtered many times over. Still they overcame such adversity and prospered.

From a historical perspective, when one explores the malady of anti-Semitism in its ideological form, one will find that it has plagued the Jewish diaspora in both the Old *and* New Worlds. However, when one looks for evidence of physical violence and truculency inflicted upon Jews, it is found almost exclusively in the Old World. As John Higham said in *Strangers in the Land* (1973), "No pogrom has ever stained American soil." He goes on to add, "nor did any single anti-Jewish incident in the 1920s match the violence of the anti-Italian riot in southern Illinois" (i.e. the riot in West Frankfurt, Illinois, which will be described in detail later on) (278). In *Taking Root: Jewish Immigrants in America* (1976), author Milton Meltzer verified that, "Catholics as a whole were the target of an organized opposition which the anti-Semites never developed to the same degree. And Italians were the victims of far more violence" (55). As for any reasons for this it could be that the Jews had more skilled laborers among them and a higher degree of literacy when they came here, and their numbers were not as threatening as the Italians. Simply put, the latter were in greater competition with native-born Americans for working-class jobs.

Let the reader not get the wrong impression however. Jewish-Americans were physically attacked a number of times during the "Nativist Nineties." In 1891, (perhaps the worst year of "nativism") 500 employees in a New Jersey glass works factory went on a destructive spree when fourteen Russian Jews were hired. The tumult lasted three days and forced most of the Jewish people in that area to flee. In 1893, "night-riders" burned down dozens of Jewish-owned farmhouses in Southern Mississippi. That same year anti-Semitic threats and scare tactics compelled many Jewish businessmen to leave Louisiana (Higham, 1973: 92-93).

Late 19th Century Louisiana was a notorious hotspot for "nativist" (or native-born) aggression against immigrants. Though Italians were typically the ones targeted, Jews and other non-WASPs were singled out as well. As far back as the 1880s, Louisiana Jews were threatened with bodily harm (Higham, 1973: 92). To the American nativist, all that was believed to be "foreign" (and not White Anglo-Saxon Protestant) was also believed to be inimical to the United States and its citizenry. In this warped state of mind, Jews, Italians, and other newcomers were considered a threat (as were the Irish and Germans before them).

Up north, "Jew-baiting"—in the form of verbal taunts and intermittent stonings—was becoming more frequent as the turn of the century approached. However, as Higham attests, "the Jews came off a little better than the other minorities; apparently no lives were lost in any of these episodes." He continues: "In nineteenth century America...the menace of world Jewry was undoubtedly less important than related fears of Italians and Catholics" (Higham, 1973: 92-94).

Probably the most famous case of anti-Semitism in American history was the trial and lynching of Leo Frank. This occurred over the course of 1914-15—a period of time in which 3 Italians were lynched in the mining country of Illinois, and (judging by the victims' names) at least 9 Italian men, women, and children were slaughtered in the "Ludlow Massacre" in Colorado's mining country (Higham, 1973: 184-185; "Inscription on the Ludlow Massacre Memorial"). An American Jew, and the son of an affluent New York merchant, Leo Frank operated a pencil factory in Atlanta, Georgia, which hired females at low wages. Young Mary Phagan was one of the "factory girls" employed there. When her slain body was found one day on factory grounds popular suspicion fell on Frank, though there was little or no evidence supporting his guilt (Higham, 1973: 184-185).

The girl's death kindled great animus among Atlanta's working class. For many, the tragedy became a symbol of southern oppression at the hands of northern "carpetbaggers" (i.e. Northerners seeking private gain in the South). Frank, himself, became a symbol of capitalist immorality that was exploiting and trying to corrupt virtuous southern womanhood. It is no wonder that unfounded accusations spread about Frank being a sexual deviant (Higham, 1973: 185).

In this hostile and unjust climate, Leo Frank was found guilty of murder. As time went on, evidence amassed to prove that the case against Frank was extremely weak. Some wealthy northern Jews demanded a new trial and even financed a legal battle to obtain one, but many more unrelenting Georgians demanded that the death penalty be carried out, and swiftly. Hence, the interests of these two groups were conflicting; both wanted justice, yet both had opposing visions of what that justice was. The hatred Leo Frank was subjected to—originally the hatred of a Northerner who just happened to be Jewish—soon turned into full-fledged anti-Semitism (and those that were already anti-Catholic had no trouble at all becoming anti-Semitic) (Higham, 1973: 185).

Playing off the fears of the working classes, a number of demagogues vociferated their incendiary declamations all across Georgia. Statements were made like the following: "The Jews have said that no Jew has ever been hanged and that none ever will be." This particular statement seemed to be true when the governor commuted Frank's death sentence to life in prison. News of this was all that was needed to plunge the state into unrest. Throughout Georgia, anti-Jewish boycotts began and public meetings were held which called for retribution. There was even one group that assembled at the murdered girl's grave and vowed to avenge her. They aptly named themselves the "Knights of Mary Phagan" (Higham, 1973: 185-186).

With tensions rising, it was almost inevitable that something bad was going to happen to Leo Frank—and it did. An angry mob stormed the state prison and dragged Frank 175 miles across Georgia to be killed in their locale. This is how the "Leo Frank Affair" ended (Higham, 1973: 186). Unfortunately, anti-Semitism did not die out afterwards; it gained strength.

Today, American anti-Semitism is expressed physically through the desecration of synagogues and the spray-painting of swastikas on Jewish establishments. The Leo Frank story was so exceptional a case of brutality against Jews in America that it has been immortalized on Broadway, as well as in the minds of all who wish never to forget this unjust incident.

9: Street Musicians from the Mezzogiorno.

**10: A "Little Mother" on the streets of an impover-
ished town in Southern Italy.**

11: An Italian immigrant woman standing outside her Chicago tenement.

12: Man in black ready to be hanged.

13: Lower Manhattan's Little Italy bustling with the arrival of new contract laborers for the coal mines.

14: Distributing food to a group of defrauded Italian immigrants.

15: Italian men gambling away the little money they possessed.

16: British cartoon of "Britannia," Queen of the Britons, extending a consoling hand to "Italia" who mourns the loss of King Umberto.

17: Men working on the rails.

18: Left homeless by the great Southern Italian earthquake of 1908.

19: Five members of the Croton Lake gang that were executed in 1912. From left to right: Filippo DeMarco and Vincenzo Cona,

Bottom: Angelo Guista, Lorenzo Cali, and Santo Zanza.

20: U.S. Attorney General A. Mitchell Palmer.

21: Closing the door on the "undesirables"

22: Reputed mobster Frank Costello, testifying before the Kefauver Committee.

23: Italian-American family eating dinner in their Corona, Queens home.

24: 9/11 was a day that sent shock waves across the world; a full 25 percent of the victims were Italian-Americans.

Chapter Two

*To this very hour, we go hungry and thirsty, we are
in rags, we are brutally treated; we are homeless.
We work hard with our own hands. When we are
cursed, we bless; when we are persecuted, we endure it; when we are slandered, we answer kindly.
Up to this moment, we have become the scum of
the earth, the refuse of the world.*

Corinthians 4: 11-13

Italian-Americans are a historically oppressed people. That they have
endured a greater number of persecutions than most other American
groups should come as no surprise to those cognizant of Italian-
American history. (That they have not let these persecutions impede
their overall success is, perhaps, a better reason to be surprised.) Unfortunately, too many Americans are totally ignorant of ethnic history (and even
general American history). Jaws drop and eyeballs bulge when a lone
transmitter of knowledge sends forth the following signal: "Italians had it
rough in this country."

In addition to personal ignorance, concepts of identity (which will be ex-
plored in the next chapter) are to blame for the sheer disbelief people ex-
hibit when hearing a statement like the one above. Since Italian-Americans,
today, are considered "white," many assume they were always considered
white and thus always benefited from "white privilege." In reality, nothing
could be further from the truth; due to the large degree of intolerance and
violence their forbears encountered, it has often been said that Italian-
Americans are "historically black."

Also to blame for society's ignorance are modern school textbooks. Increasingly, watered-down so as not to offend any of the minority and special interest groups they depict, modern textbooks do nothing but solidify the reader's ignorance. When describing the "New Immigration" period of the late 19th and early 20th centuries, they tend to lump all the Southern and Eastern Europeans together (as racists had done a hundred years before), totally passing over the social backgrounds of individual groups and the various forms of oppression they faced. The only groups recognized as historically oppressed people are African-Americans, "Native Americans," Asian Americans, Hispanic Americans, and sometimes Irish- and Jewish-Americans. It makes me wonder why the sufferings of Italians, Slavs, Greeks, Hungarians, Gypsies, and Syrians are not also mentioned; all of these groups immigrated in considerable numbers during the period of "New Immigration." When Italian immigrants are actually mentioned in depth, some textbooks have been known to only list their contributions to organized crime (Lagumina, 1999: 304-305).

Certainly there could be an agenda behind it all. But I believe it has more to do with our society's conception of the past. All too often people fall into the trap of using their own prejudiced modern-day experiences (and what they see on television) to judge the past; there is a strong tendency to think that the present minority status of blacks, Asians, Indians, and Latinos, has been a fixed constant and that persecution has only applied to this select group. There is also the belief that even if "white" groups experienced hardships, their plight was not on the same scale as the aforementioned minorities. Such reasoning does not take into account the fact that the so-called "white" groups were not considered white by mainstream society at the time of their persecution. They were ambiguous "others," just as Latinos are today.

Those who do actually claim to know something about Italian-American persecution usually refer to ethnic stereotyping and the way Italian-Americans are portrayed on-screen; one need not be a worldly person to know that Italian-Americans are constantly depicted as criminals, buffoons, ignoramuses, etc. That Italian-American activists have been complaining about media defamation for over a century is no big secret. Yet how many people know that the same anti-Italian images that can be seen on television today spurred white nativists to lynch Italians for a period of decades while the latter group was at the bottom of American society? How many people know that over the course of these decades the number of Italians lynched and executed was second only to blacks? How many people know of the excruciating daily abuses that Italian-Americans endured (both physical and verbal); that an indeterminately large number of Italian immigrants were en-slaved by their employers; and that during World War II 600,000 people of Italian background had their rights besieged by the U.S. government? From my own experience, I can say without hesitation that not too many people (including Italian-Americans) are aware of these historical facts, let alone the dangerous connection between anti-Italian defamation and the often-fatal abuse Italian-Americans suffered. Therefore, while in the process of showing that Italian-Americans may very well be the third most persecuted minority in U.S. history, this chapter will show how anti-Italian beliefs and bigotry led to anti-Italian violence. A timeline will be used to explore these and all other aspects of Italian-American persecution through the years. But first, it is imperative to understand the socio-historical backgrounds of Ital-ian immigrants and their offspring, as well as the origins of modern Italian stereotypes.

A. Backgrounds of a Marginalized Group

The great majority of Italian immigrants to the United States came from Southern Italy, also referred to as the *Mezzogiorno*; the following provinces can be found in this distinct geographic and cultural region: Sicily, Calabria, Puglia, Campania (including the city of Naples), Basilicata, Molise, and Abruzzi. Determined to escape poverty, disease, famine, and oppressive Roman governments, Southern Italians began leaving their homes in record numbers during the 1880s (only a decade after Italian unification). During this time, immigration from northwestern Europe was tapering off and na-tive-born Americans, enjoying a new level of success and prosperity, in-creasingly rejected menial labor jobs (Pisani, 1957: 48). By the 1890s, Ital-ians were the largest group immigrating to the U.S., and it would remain that way until the 1920s (when the Immigration Act of 1924 took effect).

The United States had become the most popular destination for Italian emigrants because it had the most work waiting for them—it was the best prospective place to earn a living. And America, needing immigrant workers to replace her recently emancipated slave class, sent immigration agents abroad (the new "slave hunters" so to speak) to lure the immigrants to her. Sometimes these agents worked for private companies; sometimes they worked for entire states. Thousands of them roamed through the Italian countryside at any given time, promising the peasants they encountered a land much more welcoming—and a future much more rosy—than it actu-ally was. "Agents abounded who promised adequate quarters aboard ship, in return for outrageous terms of repayment, and who actually provided passage in cramped holds with skimpy meals, or who even sold tickets for accommodations that were not available" (Pisani, 1957: 50). When reports of deaths at sea and unsanitary conditions surfaced, the Italian government, always concerned about its citizens abroad, required that each ship must have a doctor who makes sure the emigrants are nourished adequately and treated humanely (Pisani, 1957: 51).

The scam that many immigration agents pulled to bring the Italian to America foreshadowed even greater scams once he arrived. "Real-estate agents would try to sell him worthless land, mining companies advertising in Italian papers would try to defraud him, and unlicensed employment agencies would misrepresent the jobs to which they would send him. Private bankers would embezzle his funds, and patent medicine makers would sell him harmful drugs. Porters would represent themselves as agents of the railroad and charge fantastic fees for carrying baggage. Ignorance of American law might innocently embroil him with the police" (many of whom proved to be dishonest themselves) (Pisani, 1957: 59). Soon, from the firsthand testimony of returning paesani, those back in Italy learned that America was not at all a "gold-paved paradise." As Jerre Mangione and Ben Morreale state in La Storia (1993), "For many, the impression of [America] was that of a violent country with a police force that had no love for them" (117).

Given all this, it is not hard to see why the immigrating Italians kept to themselves and formed a countless number of mutual aid societies—their long history, rooted in oppression at the hands of "non-paesans," forced them to regard foreigners with suspicion and mistrust. The fact that they settled in America (whether in cities or the countryside) in groups according to what village they hailed from proves that, for years, the Italian immigrants did not even trust one another.

Unfortunately, the newly arrived immigrant could not fully trust his own villagers either. Some paesani waited to take advantage of his naivete and powerlessness—especially the *padrone*. Usually an Italian who understood life in both the Italian and American realms could function as a padrone. This was a tyrannical person who hired out his own countrymen, under false business arrangements, to American labor contractors; a man who preyed upon his own people, charging them exorbitant amounts for room and board; someone who indulged in cruelty and avarice and the enslavement of children. To some, the padrone was more evil than the common American crook. The immigrants—segregated as they were—could avoid the latter with relative ease. To others, the following philosophy prevailed: "Better to be cheated by a paesano than by an American" (La Sorte, 1985: 57).

The "padrone system," as it came to be called, plagued the Italian community for decades both in the United States and abroad. By the turn of the twentieth century, "slave children," who were working for *padroni*, could be found in all large American cities. The exploited little Italian children often played musical instruments on street corners and begged for money (Mangione and Morreale, 1993: 158). There can be no doubt that this sinister reality helped sully the reputation of Italian immigrants for years. But it also exposes, for us today, the fact that "Italian on Italian" crimes added to the general suffering of the Italian population. "Evil WASPs," oppressing Italians at all turns is too simplistic a belief. Many diverse groups, at one time or another, helped in oppressing the Italian newcomers; they included Anglos, Irish, blacks, Germans, and yes, Italians, just to name a few.[1] Their oppression at the hands of *paesani* and *non paesani*, alike, reinforced the age-old belief that *la famiglia* was the only safe and trustworthy institution on earth—the family was to be venerated above all things. In time, social workers and others who were in close contact with the Italian community spoke out against the exploitation of Italian men, women, and children under the padrone system. Still other Americans (especially employers and bigots) maintained that, "a strong padrone was necessary to guide and herd the Italian workers, who could not care for themselves because they had the instincts of animals" (La Sorte, 1985: 72).

Truly, the places to which Italian workers were sent to were not even suitable for animals. Although urban life was horrendous,[2] and a good number of social scientists wanted to see Italians adapt to rural life, the "clean" countryside actually offered the worst conditions. Rural work camps (for mining, railroad work, lumbering, etc.) were more like concentration camps in which armed American bosses (frequently of Irish descent) held the power of life and death over their emaciated Italian laborers—beatings, threats, and an occasional death were the norm. Disease, inadequate living conditions, malnutrition, and no pay (caused by an artificial yet never ending debt) added to the immigrants' unfathomable misery. The Italian government protested such conditions as early as the 1880s. Over the years tens of thousands were shipped to the camps almost immediately upon landing in American ports—they truly became America's new slave class (unofficially, of course) (La Sorte, 1985: 78-82). Whole families were also brought by the padroni to rural areas of the American South; there they were herded and divided up "like the former black slaves and cattle." If they attempted to escape their newfound fate in the "Land of Liberty" (and many had tried), they would be "arrested and instantly convicted of debt evasion" (*Italian Tribune*, Aug. 1, 2002). When others ventured peacefully into a nearby town or village they were almost always verbally taunted, physically attacked, or jailed and fined for an unsubstantiated reason (*Italian Tribune, 02-06-03*). The Italian immigrants' lives were cheaply valued. The unskilled jobs they took exposed them to countless injuries and deaths. Furthermore, they lived at a time when there was practically no compensation for the victims of accidents, unless the workers themselves took a collection. The following account sums it up best: When a man visiting a New Jersey work site asked if anyone was killed on the job, a young man answered, "There wasn't any one killed except wops." When the visitor expressed confusion over the term "wops," the young man said, "Wops. Don't you know what wops are? Dagos, niggers, and Hungarians—they were the fellows that did the work. They don't know anything, and they don't count" (La Sorte, 1985: 90). It is estimated that one-fifth of all Italians who labored in the mines, on roads, and in construction, had accidents befall them. It is also estimated that as much as one-quarter of all industrial accidents befell people of Italian background (La Sorte, 1985: 91-92). On the crestfallen acceptance of their fate, one prominent Italian-American, Dr. Antonio Stella, stated in protest: "The Italian immigrant may be maimed and killed in his industrial occupation without a cry and without indemnity. He may die from the bends working in the caissons under the river without protest; he can be slowly asphyxiated in crowded tenements, smothered in dangerous trades and occupations (which only the ignorant immigrant pursues—not the native American); he can contract tuberculosis in unsanitary factories and sweatshops without a murmur, and then do this country an additional favor when, disabled and weak, he goes back to his mother country to die, thus giving the American city the credit for having a low death rate" (La Sorte, 1985: 92).

As far as hard labor was concerned, no group in history worked harder than the Italians. One immigrant recalled seeing a fellow compatriot in Louisiana "harnessed to a plough like a mule, working for 85 cents a day." He spoke of those early days in this country as "the slaving times" (Mangione and Morreale, 1993: 271).[3]

Needless to say, the immigrants' hard labor did not pay off immediately. Unjust social conditions kept Italians in a subservient position to most other groups for approximately half a century (from the 1880s to the 1930s). In addition to social discrimination, the two main setbacks to Italian empowerment were: (1) the immigrants' fatalistic attitude (brought over from the old country) toward wrongs committed against them, and (2) they were both ignorant and fearful of the law in this new land, so they did not attempt to inquire about legal options open to them to improve their situation. Common laborers of native white background were also maltreated, as they were frequently denied such things as workers' compensation; yet, the immigrants were obviously an easy target. "There was collusion among coroners, lawyers, undertakers, and the police to cover up an accident and to profit from work-related tragedies" (La Sorte, 1985: 92). One lawyer, of a more honest sort, openly admitted to the parents of an Italian boy who lost his hand in a factory accident, "For the Italians, there is no justice!" (La Sorte, 1985: 93). Professor Michael La Sorte expounded on the issue of inequities: "Acutely aware of their second-class status, the immigrants learned to distinguish between equity at the abstract level and equity as practiced in everyday life. The law is equal for all, the immigrants would say, but justice is something else. The Italians would take what they could and be satisfied with it. They saw no other alternative. Even when indemnities were paid to injured parties, the Italians were not at all surprised to receive less than others. They knew that they were at the bottom of the pecking order. One instance, among many, of unequal compensation occurred in Black Diamond, California, in the early 1900s. A number of men had been killed or injured in an explosion. The non-Italian workers were awarded $1,200 each in compensation, the Italians only $150" (La Sorte, 1985: 94).

The writer Louis Adamic, himself a Slovene immigrant, had this to say about his Italian counterparts: "I felt, successively, sorry for and disgusted with them. The bosses had them cowed. Their wages were low, but they would have worked for even less. At the end of the day they trudged home, silent, uninspired, a heavy smell of hopelessness about them. They did not belong in America. They knew nothing of the country, nor had the ability or the desire to learn about it. They lived from day to day, from hand to mouth, driven by narrow selfishness" (La Sorte, 1985: 145). Though Adamic probably did not realize it, his eyes undoubtedly looked upon many learned Italians who had the ability to do greater things. For even Italian barons and counts, and skilled members of the immigrant tide such as journalists and artists, were the victims of heavy discrimination and were forced into performing hard labor. When many of them tried making a comfortable living outside the "Italian Colonies" (or ghettos), they were bluntly discouraged and/or prevented from plying their trades, and were instead given picks and shovels by American employers (La Sorte, 1985: 92; Mangione and Morreale, 1993: 273). Such immigrants soon discovered that America could be the complete antithesis of the land of opportunity, and many wanted to be repatriated as soon as possible (Foerster, 1969: 330).

It would be convenient to think that the injustices and inequalities ended when both Italians and natives spoke out and acted as one (as African-Americans and liberal WASPs had done during the Civil Rights era), however it did not happen that way. Things did not change until second and third generation Italian-Americans pulled themselves out of the gutter, through work and education, and finally achieved their own middle-class "American dream" around the time of World War II.

Italian immigration a century ago was a lot like Hispanic immigration today. It started out, largely, as an immigration of adult males. Typically they were impoverished seasonal migrants, coming and going wherever there was more money to be made; travel to and from Italy was frequent, and money was sent home periodically to family members.[4]

After establishing themselves in the New World, the immigrants eventually sent for their wives and children to join them. And though they had all left Italy behind them, they were still fierce Italian patriots (Foerster, 1969: 42-43, 364, 377, 427, 505; Pisani, 1957: 58). This is evident in the fact that the Italian immigrant looked to return home some day—he did not originally plan on staying in a foreign land. As one writer put it, the strangeness of foreign life was tolerated "only for the promise of the return to Italy" (Foerster, 1969: 428). Subsequently, more than half of the 4.5 million Italians who immigrated to the U.S., from 1880 to 1924, returned home (Mangione and Morreale, 1993: 159). The ambiguous loyalty of this immigrant population naturally came under suspicion, and the question of whether or not they made good American citizens hounded the Italian-American community until the end of the Second World War.

As was mentioned earlier, most Italian immigrants came from the Mezzogiorno (or Southern Italy). Northern Italian immigrants who ventured to the U.S. were never as overflowingly abundant as their Southern brethren, yet far from negligible, their numbers contributed significantly to the general Italian-American population. Their immigration was older than that of the Southerners, and included a greater percentage of skilled workers and educated professionals. When native-born Americans saw that Southern Italians were generally unskilled, uneducated, incredibly impoverished, and different in appearance, distinctions were made supporting centuries of prejudice that had its origins in Northern Italy: Northern Italians were more prosperous, more "European," and thus more assimilable to American society; Southern Italians, however, were nothing more than "African savages." Anti-Italianism was therefore not a black and white issue—Northern Italians were favored to an extent by Anglos, and the hatred and stereotypes that led to anti-Italian violence in the United States was inherited to an extent from the much older contempt Northern Italians had for Southern Italians. Yet while there has been a historical difference in identity between Northerners and Southerners, anti-Italian violence affected them both, as the

"Timeline of Tears" will show in section B of this chapter. Thus I am not discussing at length the differences between both groups of Italians; in most regards Italians were Italians to the majority of Americans, and especially to Italophobes. As far as this latter group was concerned, neither Northern nor Southern Italians were genuine "white folks." To them, all Italians were dirty, stupid, criminally prone, and lacking a certain level of whiteness that would make them suitable American citizens.

Almost as soon as they began arriving in America, sweeping assumptions were made that Italians were innately stupid and inferior in all ways to Anglo-Americans and other peoples of European ancestry. It was said that Italian immigrants could not adapt to Western societies—that they were too different, too backward (Foerster, 1969: 420). This belief might seem laughable today, but it must be remembered that one hundred years ago Italy (especially Southern Italy) might as well have been 15,000 miles from the industrialized nations of Western Europe; likewise, the Italian immigrants were all products of the underdeveloped Italy from whence they came. That said, their unskilled job status did not help them in the fight against bigotry. At the height of their immigration the proportion of skilled Southern Italians was less than the proportion for all other nationalities combined.

Of a thousand Italians in Richmond, Virginia, in 1909, it was reported that not one of them was a professional person. Illiteracy also worked against the Italian immigrants—it was rampant. Not only were they ignorant of English, they were also ignorant of how to read and write in their own Italian dialects. When the first Italian newspaper was started in New York, in 1882, there was not one Italian reporter to be found (Foerster, 1969: 330-332). These realities forced the Italian newcomers into the lowliest lines of work—in the countryside, they were common laborers (as previously described), and in the city they took jobs as street-sweepers, rag pickers, street musicians (invariably the organ grinder and his monkey come to mind), bootblacks,[5] and more. Many Americans scorned these types of occupations, and believed that only inferior beings should perform them. Thus was born the stereotype that Italians are dumb.

Anti-Italian beliefs also took on a racial tone. This greatly inhibited the group's social betterment in a nation stratified along racial and ethnic lines. Racial distinctions were made when Americans discovered that Southern Italians, in particular, had darker skin. The Mezzogiorno had long been associated with Africa due to the region's close proximity to that continent; greatly exaggerated stories of miscegenation between Southern Italians and Africans had circulated in Northern Italy for centuries.[6] When the stories reached America by the late 19th Century, they were swiftly used as racist propaganda against the Italian newcomers. The alleged inferiority of the "Italian Race" was reverberated many times around the country by politicians and writers, as if it was common knowledge or scientific fact. Italian physical attributes (essentially their Mediterranean looks) were accepted to be inferior to Anglo-American (Nordic) features, and thus it was accepted that Italians were inferior in every way (Foerster, 1969: 361-362). Italians shared this strike against them with racial minorities.[7] The early twentieth century expert on Italian immigration, Robert Foerster, wrote, "In a country where yet the distinction between white man and black is intended as a distinction in value as well as in ethnography it is no compliment to the Italian to deny him whiteness, yet that actually happens with considerable frequency" (Foerster, 1969: 408-409).[8] It was believed that the Italians were even more loathed than the Irish and Chinese who preceded them (Foerster, 1969: 326). Nativists spread the belief that Italians were almost another species in order to end their immigration. These immigrant bashers (or "nativists") inherited their views from the older Know Nothing Party of the mid-nineteenth century. The "Know Nothings" played on popular fears, highlighting the differences between the native-born and the foreign-born. Drawing attention to the poverty and foreign ways of the immigrants, they convinced many Americans that the newcomers were here for one reason only: "to steal American jobs." This same phrase is still used to galvanize anti-immigrant support, even though immigrants have historically taken the jobs that Americans refuse.

Criminality was another issue used by nativists to bash immigrants.[9] Racist cartoons surfaced in major newspapers, depicting boatloads of Italian "desperadoes" eagerly awaiting entry into the United States so they could begin their dirty work. Frequently, newspaper columns depicted the same thing, only in words. Mass deportations of entire ethnicities were often called for when one ethnic criminal was found. "Beware of the devious foreigner!" the cry went.[10] Not surprisingly, rumors of secret criminal organizations among the immigrants were fully exploited by the press in order to sell papers. New exotic terms like "the Mafia" and "Black Hand" made headlines. The fact that Italian criminal organizations existed cannot be disputed (all groups have their own "rotten apples"); however, media sensationalism has historically blown Italian criminality out of proportion and has found a popular scapegoat in Italians. The average American a hundred years ago, having little or no contact with actual Italian immigrants, had no choice but to believe the defamatory stories and come to the conclusion that all crime stemmed from the Italian community. The popular acceptance of phony Mafia myths was thus responsible for the lynching of eleven Italians in New Orleans in 1891 (and countless other persecutions). Today, the "Mafia mystique"—continuing its legacy of prejudice and persecution—makes big money for "Tinsel Town." What too many Americans have forgotten, however, and what Herbert Asbury's book (and now Scorsese's film) *The Gangs of New York* confirms, is that organized crime had existed in America's urban centers long before the first *contadino* (*Southern Italian peasant*) stepped off the boat. The criminal employment of political protection, hired hitmen, and the intricate organization of various vices, such as gambling and prostitution, seem to have been founded by Irish-American gangsters (Mangione and Morreale, 1993: 243-247). Similar to the Irish experience, the criminality that flourished a century ago in Southern Italy reflected the long-time destitution of an oppressed and impoverished region. The American media never seemed to understand this. Up until the latter half of the nineteenth century, the Italian people (both Northerners and Southerners) had been dominated for 1,500 years by ruthless *straniere*.[11] It is only natural that native Italians would, in self-defense, form secret societies that tried to match the ruthlessness of their foreign overlords. Southern Italians had had the cruelest and widest variety of oppressors through the centuries, so organized criminal activity was the strongest among them.[12] Even so, the vast majority of Italian immigrants was law abiding and had no connections to organized crime whatsoever.

The ineffable poverty and destitution that characterized Italian immigration cannot—and must not—be denied. We need only to read Jacob Riis' *How the Other Half Lives* or *Out of Mulberry Street* to understand that Italians endured horrific living conditions—undoubtedly the worst in American cities. Things like electricity, running water, and bathtubs—common necessities to modern ghetto dwellers—were nowhere to be found in the crowded tenements. The sons and daughters of "sunny Italy" were even denied sunlight, living in the windowless recesses of stuffy brick buildings as though they were subterraneans instead of Mediterraneans. The unhealthy urban living conditions led to high mortality rates, especially among Italian children (Foerster, 1969: 382-388). Tuberculosis was so widespread that sanitariums were built in Italy with the express purpose of caring for returning émigrés (Mangione and Morreale, 1993: 144). Hardly relegated to just an urban plight, substandard habitation and disease awaited Italians in rural America as well. Life was particularly hard in the Italian communities of the American South, where one-room shanties (often former "slave shacks") were the norm and malaria was rampant. Like the Irish before them, Italians were for many years the largest immigrating population and the most impoverished. Both friends and foes of the Italian people were concerned about the lingering poverty this group experienced decade after decade. While a considerable number of social workers, philanthropists, and others wanted desperately to help, classifying themselves as "friends," they were all too often patronizing and insensitive toward the immigrants and their backgrounds. The "foes" of the Italians (of which there were many from all walks of life) obviously did not look to help the newcomers; rather they sought to marginalize them further and put an end to their immigration. To achieve their goals Italophobes drew attention to the staggering rates of Italian poverty and concluded that Italians were naturally filthy. Newspapers constantly printed and disseminated these views from one end of the country to the other, thus strengthening anti-Italian sentiment. In reality, while Italians did bring their poverty with them across the Atlantic, disease and unhealthy living conditions, as we have seen, were already waiting for them when they landed.[13]

Since Italian immigration was motivated, generally speaking, by economics, the belief that Italians were genetically predisposed to poverty and filth, criminally prone, racially inferior, and hopelessly ignorant,[14] were great reasons in the nativist's opinion to restrict their immigration and fanatically support native labor. These stereotypes and playing off the workingman's fears went hand in hand. For nativists knew that labor was always a "hot-button" issue and that orating about losing one's job was guaranteed to get the crowd's attention—and from there the crowd could quickly turn into a mob. Historically, when native job security was threatened, immigrants suffered. When Italians began their trans-Atlantic migration in the late nineteenth century, labor unions were unheard of; job security for the common man was non-existent. Add to this the fear that Italians were bringing with them radical political ideas, and one can picture the truly explosive climate the immigrants were entering into.

In late nineteenth century, America's anti-immigrant violence was always close at hand. Lynching, in particular, was a big problem for the early Italian immigrants, especially in the South; it continued, unfortunately, well into the twentieth century. Between 1870 and 1940 Italians were the second most lynched minority group in the United States (the first, of course, were blacks) (Gambino, 1998: 135). Though non-Italian groups representing the "New Immigration" definitely experienced less fatal forms of violence, hardly any of them had one or more of their people lynched during this period—Italians seemed to be systematically targeted, however, as scores were killed in a 70 year time frame. That Italians were the largest immigrant group, the most "visible" European population in the country, and that the most negative attention surrounded them, cannot be denied as factors contributing to their higher rate of victimization.

Violence against the Italian immigrant started even before the vessel carrying her landed in an American port. Every now and then, the sailors on steerage ships molested Italian women who were sent for by their husbands. Upon hearing that the women were violated, Italian male passengers often avenged them by roughing up and sometimes killing the offending sailors. Of course when the ships landed the American newspapers sensationalized the stories (not taking the time to interview the Italians), thus leaving out important facts. And so, further "evidence" was amassed to prove that the innate Italian criminal did not belong in the United States.[15] Sometimes the Italian passengers would be blamed for crimes that the sailors committed against each other (Gambino, 1974: 105-106).[16]

When disembarking in New York, many Italians congregated at the Battery and were greeted by their friends and family members. It was a congested scene with lots of joyous gesticulation for sure. Unfortunately, such images prompted the New York newspapers to falsely report that Italian "riots" infected the docks (Mangione and Morreale, 1993: 117). Most likely, if there was trouble, it was started by non-Italian dockworkers. They either had insulted or physically accosted the immigrants.[17]

In addition to violence, some combination of involuntary segregation, discrimination (in its many forms), and overtly racist laws affected most immigrant groups at one point or another; but, again, not all groups were victimized to the same degree—Italians from at least the 1890s to the 1920s were the most persecuted of immigrants in all respects. Segregation was in no small way a part of the Italian-American experience for years. (Let the reader not be fooled into thinking that segregatory practices were only implemented against African-Americans.) In the South, rules were established preventing Italian children from attending certain "white" schools, and in the North, Italian laborers sometimes had to form their own labor unions because they were not allowed to join "American" ones. Also, in many parts of the country, churches and movie houses required that Italians sit separate from the general public. The segregation that existed in American churches was especially widespread. "Some churches sat the Italians with the blacks in rear pews. Others told worshippers bluntly that they were not wanted and even denounced them as 'Dagoes.'" Still other congregations forced Italians to worship in the dark, dank church basements. Even a reprimand from the Pope in the form of an edict did not end this anti-Italian (and thoroughly anti-Christian) practice (Mangione and Morreale, 1993: 328-329).[18]

Patterns of ethnic settlement also reflected segregation. Granted, Italians *preferred* settling in their own enclaves like most other immigrant groups, but make no mistake, it was a choice they made out of necessity, out of not yet being able to function as fully assimilated Americans, and out of experiencing oppression first hand. In addition, there was very little tolerance for those who wished to settle in "American" (or even mixed) neighborhoods. Opposition to Italian settlement occurred in localities scattered all over the nation, especially where nativism was strongest. Ku Klux Klan activity against them, typically in the form of cross-burning intimidation, was not rare in the more rural sections. In South Carolina, there was such strong anti-Italian feeling that "in 1904 its state legislature restricted immigration to 'white citizens of the United States, and citizens of Ireland, Scotland, Switzerland and France together with all other foreigners of Saxon origin.' Alabama and North Carolina followed suit with similar legislation" (Mangione and Morreale, 1993: 213). These laws, spearheaded by nativists and racists, eventually led to the National Origins Act of 1924, which effectively cut off Italian immigration for good.

The overall discrimination Italians were subjected to was incredible. During the thirty years their immigration was strongest (1890s to 1920s) it seemed that no Italian could advance in society and that the entire group was doomed to remain an inferior caste. As the upcoming timeline will show in section B, qualified Italians were not allowed to teach at leading universities, nor were they permitted access to prestigious social circles. Police brutality at this time was rampant, and consequently Italian deaths were all too frequent. Once again, Italian lives were cheaply valued. It was said, "An Italian was not an Italian. He was a wop, dago, duke, gin, tally, ghini, *macaroni, spaghetti* or *spaghetti*-bender. He was also Hey Boy or Hey Youse, or he was given a generic name: Joe, Pete, Tony, Carlo, Dino, Gumba" (La Sorte, 1985: 138). (Today the derogatory generic name is "Guido.") In 1909 the editor of *La Tribuna* concluded, "The Italians are viewed by the Americans as so much meat to be consumed. Italians are maltreated, mocked, scorned, disdained, and abused in every way. The inferiority of the Italians is believed to be almost equal to that of the Asiatics" (La Sorte, 1985: 139, 213). Like other racial minorities, Italians were ostracized in ways we today would not often think. For instance, if an Italian was walking on the sidewalk in an "American" neighborhood some 80-plus years ago, there was a good chance a "white man" passing by would push him off and make a disparaging remark.[19]

Of the Italian immigration of Robert Foerster's time (i.e. the early twentieth century) he wrote, "The Greater Italy is an empire—but a proletariat empire. It bestrides the world like a Colossus—but a Colossus arrayed in rags." He went on, "In nearly every country which they enter, the mass of the Italians, at least for a period of years, are at the social bottom". In truth [the immigrant] is neither an Italian nor an American, but a denizen of some Third World.... The Italian abroad does not want to be absorbed, he wants some day to return home....[20] To press naturalization upon such persons, as is sometimes done in the United States, is a one-sided idealism, and may be the reverse of kindness. The Third World dilemma has yet to be solved." (Foerster, 1969: 504-505).

The preceding was one American's very honest assessment of Italian immigration as he saw it around him. And truly, the "Third World dilemma" of which he spoke still has yet to be solved in our nation. No matter the time period, immigrants have always been torn between two cultures, the one they were born into and the one they adopted. This clash of cultures presents many problems for the newcomers, especially if they are a group that is poor, highly visible, ignorant of their adopted country's official language, and large in number. Historically, conservatives have argued that immigrants fitting this description were hopelessly unassimilable. Today, right-wingers attack Hispanics just as their forbears attacked Italians; and although the goal of immigration restriction is still the same, it must be remembered that society was much less "accommodating" when the majority of Italians immigrated (for this was a time when civil rights activism was totally lacking, political correctness was not in style, gross intolerance— exhibited by bigots and politicians alike—was all the rage, and as a rule, ethnic pride was practiced solely in "the closet").

In our modern era, even the most impoverished of immigrants would hardly believe the wretched conditions that Italians survived. Also hard to fathom, yet indisputable, is the degree to which the Italian "character" was blamed for the group's social problems. As a class, Italians were believed to be dirty, stupid, animalistic, and criminal (among other things). Some of these stigmas continue to harass Italian-Americans today. And, herein lies the problem of modern stereotyping. The media constantly portrays the Italian-Americans as Mafiosi (and other forms of cartoonish degenerates) thus keeping alive the racist beliefs of another era—a crueler, harsher era that could still be repeated if we forget our history.

B. Timeline of Tears:

A Chronological Listing of Lynchings, Executions, Mass Expulsions, Cases of Slave Labor, Defamation, Negative Statistics, and Other Hardships Italian-Americans Have Endured Through the Years. (This timeline does not attempt to be a finite project, nor does it claim to document all of the numerous injustices, which people of Italian descent have had to face in America on a daily basis. Ideally, this timeline is a list of the most notable wrongs inflicted on Italian-Americans.)

Era of Physical Attacks— Late 19th Century to 1920s

June 1869: Probably the first recorded Irish-Italian gang fight took place at Karl's Germania Park in New York; it occurred on a Sunday evening, following an Italian festival. Irish hoodlums looking for trouble were seen patrolling the outskirts of the Italian gathering all day. When the number of Italians decreased to a mere dozen around 10pm, the Irish attacked; they threw stones, swung clubs, flashed knives, and reportedly shouted "Down with Garibaldi! Long live the Pope!" The unprovoked aggression did not end until one Sicilian lay dead and another was seriously wounded (La Sorte, 1985: 150-151). Thus began the "special hatred," as one writer put it, which defined the Irish-Italian relationship for a century to come.

As can be seen from what the hoodlums allegedly shouted, the Irish had a great disdain for the strange and seemingly irreverent ways of Italian Catholics. In addition to religious hostilities, labor tensions also widened the Irish-Italian rift. Until the Italians arrived, the Irish held a near monopoly on menial labor jobs; soon, however, even Irish bosses were replacing their countrymen with Italian laborers. The result was that Italians were constantly victimized. It is unfortunate that both groups, being at the bottom of the social ladder, were put in a position where they would almost inevitably have to fight like cocks in order to survive. The Irish were fortunate enough, however, to start moving up the ladder as the Italians began immigrating in large numbers. The Irish also delighted in the fact that the Italians were even more hated than they were. (For, although Americans of Celtic descent were still considered "strangers" by many, the populace tends to fear "newer strangers" more.) As a Protestant minister declared at the time, "An Irish Catholic is preferable to an Italian Catholic, an Irish shillelagh to an Italian knife." And so, upon arrival, many of the hostile encounters Italians faced were not merely American instigated, but of Irish-American provocation (La Sorte, 1985: 148-152; Gambino, 1974: 236-237).

1870-1940: During this seventy-year period, Italians were the second most lynched ethnicity in the United States; their rate of victimization was second only to African-Americans (Gambino, 1998: 135).

1872: In New Orleans, there was a Mardi Gras float of "Pope Pius IX blessing two brigands, who were kneeling before him with knives between their teeth" (La Sorte, 1985: 142). Here one can see that anti-Italian/anti-Catholic defamation was already underway a full decade and a half before the great exodus of Italian immigrants started coming to America.

1873-1899: Twenty-two Italians were legally executed in the United States during this latter period of the 19th Century (this does not include lynchings); most were hanged. These are the numbers of Italians executed in each state (and federal district): New York—5; Pennsylvania—5; Connecticut—4; Illinois—3; Maine—2; New Jersey—2; Washington D.C.—1 ("Before the Needles").[21]

As early as the 1870s Italians started making headlines as criminals in the U.S. In truth, some did turn to crime in order to better their lot, but the vast majority of the newcomers were honest—their only crime was being poor and foreign-born. With a great amount of prejudice in America at this time, it is very possible that some of the 22 Italians executed were innocent, or at least the recipients of unfair or biased trials.

June 1874: After replacing striking Irish laborers, thirteen Italian workers were injured in a fight with union men in New York. Due to police intervention the next day, a major riot was avoided (*The Pennsylvania Magazine of History and Biography*).

September 1874: When Italian workers arrived in the mining country around Pittsburgh, Pennsylvania, three initial disturbances were observed: "nine frame houses at the Fort Pitt mines burned to the ground, and three nights later six more buildings were set on fire. Another night, four shots were fired into the home of Charles McDonald, superintendent of the National Coal Company..." The day of their arrival, "the old miners taunted the Italians, and that night stray shots were fired." For their own protection, the Italian workers were armed with guns (*The Pennsylvania Magazine of History and Biography*).

This is the unfortunate situation many immigrant strike-breakers were put in. In many ways, the employers who hired the immigrants (and the cheap labor they provided) were no better than the ruffians who resorted to violence. For the employers exploited the poverty of both the immigrants and the natives and deliberately placed them in these confrontational environments; in this way, they helped provoke the violence.

October-November 1874: Tensions flared between the Italians and the striking miners in Buena Vista, Pennsylvania (a small mining town outside Pittsburgh). Daily exchanges of gunfire were commonplace (with the Italians, more often than not, on the receiving end) (*The Pennsylvania Magazine of History and Biography*).

To the people of Buena Vista, the Italians were not only objects of hate, but objects of fear as well; this is because the Italians were well-armed foreigners in their midst. Even so, the weapons were for purposes of self-defense, and the native population and its officials—through acts of aggression and paranoia—were the ones most at fault for souring relations (*The Pennsylvania Magazine of History and Biography*).

November 28, 1874: An Italian miner was wounded when shooting broke out between the two sides (*The Pennsylvania Magazine of History and Biography*).

November 29, 1874: A group of Italians went into Buena Vista and five residents fired shots at them, driving them away. This act caused a battle to erupt. For hours, the Italians traded fire with hundreds of Buena Vista citizens (the American flag was even used to rally the natives). In the end, however, the Italians surrendered—but not before three of them had died. The names of the dead were: Ambrozia Fuccei, Rancigio La Vechi, and Giuseppe Raimondo. Eight others were wounded (*The Pennsylvania Magazine of History and Biography*).[22]

1878-1919: Lynching expert Professor Michael J. Pfeifer established that "at least 140 blacks, 14 whites, 13 Italians, and 1 Latino" were lynched in the state of Louisiana during this period ("Lynching and Criminal Justice").

1880s: As swarthy Italian peasants began their mass migration to American cities, race-conscious WASPs took notice and sounded the same xenophobic alarm that was used against the Irish, blacks, Jews, and Asians. Countless newspapers and periodicals warned that the white race was in danger. Since New Orleans had been taking in more Italian immigrants than any other U.S. city (due to its warm climate and need of labor), there were many in that town who wanted to see the contadini deported back to Italy. Their racist views were championed in papers like *The Mascot* and *Picayune*. "In *The Mascot*, the Italian immigrant was drawn as a dirty, bearded, hook-nosed man carrying a battered basket filled with bananas. Italian fruit peddlers were pictured with broad thick mouths and hooked noses, cluttering up the walks with their fruit stands. They slept ten to a room in the midst of filth and were seen killing one another with knives. The best way of disposing of them, the next series of drawings suggested, was to drown them in batches, or at least beat them and jail them" (Mangione and Morreale, 1993: 201).[23] One might expect to find similar depictions of Jews in Tsarist papers of the time. (Pogroms in Eastern Europe and lynchings in the United States were naturally the results of such depictions.)

Since Sicilians were the largest Italian group in New Orleans, they were singled out as the most dangerous class in the city. The police blamed them for practically all the murders that took place, and the press reinforced the propaganda with lies—by Italianizing the names of the actual non-Italian killers. So when Pedro Echave was found murdered at the hands of Jose Bilboa in 1883, the *Picayune* deliberately changed the names to "Pedro Escaro" and "Joseph Bilboa." Similarly, in 1885, when John Martin (a German-born man) was found slain, the *Picayune* reported that "Juan Martini" had been the victim of a "Mafia killing." And when two French nationals, Jean and Dominique Trebique, were killed, the paper changed the names to "Jean Tamora" and "Domenica Tribega" (Mangione and Morreale, 1993: 203; Nelli, 1976: 32-34).[24] Soon the press in other cities followed New Orleans' lead; the widespread defamation of the Italian newcomers apparently sold newspapers. And so, the linking of Italians with crime firmly took root.

March 28, 1886: In Vicksburg, Mississippi, a group of masked men forced an Italian named Fred Villarosa out of his jail cell and hanged him to a tree in front of the jail. Prior to this incident no one had been lynched in Vicksburg for 50 years, (since well before the Civil War) (Iorizzo and Mondello, 1980: 290; *The Vicksburg Evening Post,* Mar.29, 1886).

December 28, 1886: John Elia was lynched in Bienville, Louisiana[25]

1888: American archbishops showed concern at a conference they held that Italians were becoming "slaves to wage-masters." The Society of St. Raphael was set up, as a result, to aid incoming Italian immigrants and provide them with food and temporary shelter (Pisani, 1957: 170).[26]

March 4, 1888: Police in Buffalo, New York, unlawfully searched 325 Italians for concealed weapons. "All the saloons and boarding houses in Peacock, Evans, Fly, State, Water, Commercial, Scott and Washington streets and Burwell Place were raided"; 250 of the Italians were taken to the police station. In the end, only two knives were found. The Italians were repeatedly described by the city's paper as "dagos" and "swarthy" of skin (*Buffalo Daily Courier*; Mar. 5, 1888).

June 24, 1889: Tony Cravasso and his brother were lynched in Cumberland Gap, Kentucky (Katz, 1969: 65).[27]

1890-1900: During the last decade of the 19th Century, according to the Commissioner of Labor, "one-third of all Italians in the four largest cities in the country were living in deplorable poverty" (Pisani, 1957: 96). This "deplorable poverty" was described in detail by many urban writers of the period (usually from viewpoints reflecting their own anti-Italian biases) and mirrored living conditions only in the absolute poorest nations of our own times. (Truly, the "Italian Quarters" of the late 19th Century make our modern ghettos look like veritable paradises of running water and electricity.) And as is the case in modern third-world nations, the children of the impoverished districts were often the ones who suffered most. Even the popular social commentator Jacob Riis (a man with his own prejudices against Italians) admitted in his 1892 book, *Children of the Poor*, that charitable programs were discriminatory, and often looked to avoid helping Italian children (Gambino, 1974: 256).

October 15, 1890: Unknown assailants gunned down David C. Hennessy, New Orleans Chief of Police. He died the next day. Allegedly, a close friend had heard Hennessy say, on his deathbed, that "dagoes" were responsible for the shooting. When the people of New Orleans heard this, it was further rumored that a secret society of criminals known as the "Mafia" had conspired to kill him (Gambino, 1998: 1-9).[28] Thus, at the moment of Chief Hennessy's death on the sixteenth of October, "some fifty Italians had already been arrested [in New Orleans], and between one and two hundred more were to be taken during the next twenty-four hours" (Gambino, 1998: 8). Outside the police station, the wives of the arrested Italians (along with other female kin) were brutalized and driven away by an angry crowd (Gambino, 1998: 16-17). The mass arrests of Italians (in addition to beatings and searches of homes) were common in New Orleans following Hennessy's death. In one instance, police burst into an Italian establishment and arrested thirty men simply because they could not speak English. Little Italian boys were also arrested (Gambino, 1998: 12-13). Eventually nineteen Italian men were held in connection with the murder of Hennessy.

All throughout October of 1890, the New Orleans' *Mascot* ran a series of cartoons titled "The Italian Population." In one scene a bunch of caged Italians are being plunged into the river—"The Way to Dispose of Them" is what the caption says (Mangione and Morreale, 1993: 201). Conveniently published the same month Hennessy died, this cartoon clearly calls for genocide; indubitably, it helped make the upcoming lynching of eleven Italians a reality.

Two months later, in December of 1890, an article appeared in Popular Science Monthly titled "What Shall We Do With the Dago?" The article was a typical one at the time, full of anti-Italian prejudice and bigotry. It reinforced white America's fears by portraying Italians as knife-wielding criminals who eat and kill with the same "stiletto" (Gambino, 1974: 279).[29]

March 14, 1891: Eleven of the nineteen Italians wrongly indicted for the murder of Chief Hennessy were lynched by a mob of 10,000. The victims' names are as follows: Pietro Monasterio, Joseph P. Macheca, Antonio Marchesi, Antonio Scaffidi, Emmanuele Polizzi, Antonio Bagnetto, James Caruso, Rocco Geraci, Frank Romero, Loretto Comitz, and Charles Traina. In all cases, the eleven lynched were either not found guilty, not tried, or no verdict was reached (the charges against the eight remaining men were dropped, and they were set free) (Mangione and Morreale, 1993: 208; Gambino, 1998: 150). This tragedy is often referred to as "the largest lynching in American history"; for sure, it was the deadliest act of nativism to occur during the 1890s (Gambino, 1998: ix).

In the wake of the lynching, thousands of Italians were abused and beaten in the streets of U.S. cities. A great number were also "fired from their jobs or denied employment." Thus, the lynching led to a long lasting wave of nativism and anti-immigration hysteria (Gambino, 1998: 111, 137-138).[30] Many newspapers across the country defended the lynching in New Orleans and even encouraged the masses to perform future ones. Senator Henry Cabot Lodge, an ardent nativist, railed against Italians and the "New Immigration" in racist terminology (this, from a man who spearheaded a drive for black suffrage in 1890) (Mangione and Morreale, 1993: 211; Higham, 1973: 141).

The accomplished Italian-American author Richard Gambino shows in his book, *Blood of My Blood*, how the Mafia stereotype was greatly responsible for both the New Orleans lynching and future lynchings to come: "While some Americans and newspapers condemned the lynching and other assaults against Italian-Americans in New Orleans, many condoned it, including Theodore Roosevelt.[31] The tone of those who approved illustrates the first major manifestation of the Mafia image and the problems it presents to Italian-Americans. Ignorant rumors of an Italian secret society of criminals circulated, and all Italian-Americans were accused either directly or by implication of being somehow responsible. For example, the New York Times editorials of March 16 and 17, 1891, justified the New Orleans lynchings. 'These sneaking and cowardly Sicilians,' said the first editorial, 'the descendants of bandits and assassins, who have transported to this country the lawless passions, the cut-throat practices, and the oath-bound societies of their native country, are to us a pest without mitigation.' On the following day the paper said, 'Lynch law was the only course open to the people of New Orleans to stay the issue of a new license to the Mafia to continue its bloody practices..." (Gambino, 1974: 280-281). Here one can see the birth of the American Mafia image, how it took shape, and how the American press was ten times more responsible than actual organized crime for creating it. We are also forced to realize that the New Orleans lynching was as much the result of popular hysteria over the newly created Mafia image as it was blind revenge for Hennessy's death.

Other factors contributed to the New Orleans lynching as well. Economic jealousy, on the part of the city's non-Italians, probably played a significant part in both the development of the Mafia mystique and in the lynching. As Humbert S. Nelli stated in The Business of Crime: "The obviously increasing economic success of [New Orleans] Italians stirred hatred, envy, and fear among the other citizens." (Nelli, 1976: 61). The next step of course was violence. European Jews have known this cycle all too well through the centuries; they also know that conspiracy theories (like Mafia myths, and the Zionist agendas for world domination) are often fabricated in an attempt to prove that certain groups cannot prosper legitimately. The South American fruit trade made a lot of money for two rival groups of Italian businessmen, the Matrangas and Provenzanos; thus it is no coincidence that both were at the center of the Hennessy trial. They were unfairly labeled "Mafiosi" because they were successful and Italian. If these New Orleans businessmen were of Irish or French or Spanish descent (i.e. if they belonged to older, more assimilated city stock), they would not have been defamed in such a manner. Also disconcerting to many New Orleans natives was that the city's Italian population was rapidly increasing; this meant Italian votes could disrupt the city's delicate political balance (Nelli, 1976: 61). And so, the lynching could be used as an excuse to keep the Italians in line politically as well (African-Americans understand this form of intimidation better than any other group).

Whichever way one wishes to analyze the tragic lynching that occurred on March 14, 1891, one thing is clear: it was one of the saddest days in Italian-American history.

March 22, 1891: In Troy, New York, the police broke up a peaceful meeting of Italian-Americans who were protesting the lynching at New Orleans. "The cops fired upon the protesters, claiming they were 'armed with knives and guns.' At least one of the crowd was shot" (Gambino, 1998: 111; Lagumina, 1999: 87).

For about a year after the lynching, there was a tremendous fear on the part of Americans that Italy would send its massive navy and army across the Atlantic to demand retribution. Thousands of people from all over the country (and even some from Britain and Ireland) were eager to go and fight the "dagoes" and their "Mafia" army. For the first time in America since the Civil War, Northerners and Southerners were volunteering themselves in astonishing numbers to fight the foreign "enemy." Both Union and Confederate veterans were sending Washington many letters demonstrating their willingness to fight the Italians. This heightened state of paranoia helped mobilize the United States for an eventual war against Spain in 1898, and thus prepared the nation to enter the 20th Century with the expansionist mindset it has had ever since (Gambino, 1998: 116-122).

Also in 1891, "a wild rumor that drunken Italian laborers had cut the throats of a whole American family in West Virginia set off further rumors of a pitched battle between a sheriff's posse and the assassins" (Higham, 1973: 90).

April 2, 1891: It was reported that a group of miners went on strike in Wheeling, West Virginia, "because their employer refused to discharge two Italians" (Higham, 1973: 91, 350; Mangione and Morreale, 1993:211).

May 11, 1891: A vicious mob attacked a group of Italian-American workers in Wheeling, West Virginia, "killing three of them and injuring an unknown number" (Gambino, 1998:111).

May 13, 1891: In Pennsylvania, "authorities had to assign forty deputy sheriffs to protect two hundred Italian immigrants who were on their way from Pittsburgh to work in the H.C. Frick Company coal mines in Fayette County" (Gambino, 1998:111).

November 1891-April 1892: Italian workers from New York were deceived and forced into conditions of slave labor in South Carolina. Initially told they would be working in Connecticut, they were taken south instead—to the "Tom Tom" sulphate mines. There, they worked all day, slept in miserable shanties, were malnourished, and were constantly watched by armed guards. (Many Italian laborers were treated like this during the early years of their immigration.)[32] Eventually, on April 1, 1892, the Italians were let go due to exhaustion (Cordasco, 1974: 393-394; *Forum*, Apr.1893).

December 1891: In Crested Butte, Colorado, "a strike involved a walk-out of 130 Austrians, 70 Italians and 30 English speaking mine workers. As was often the case, the company blamed the Italians for the walkout and afterwards rehired everyone—but the Italians." Such treatment was quite common. The United Mine Workers journal at this time referred to Italians as "Dagoes," and reinforced the prejudices of American society by stating: "Every day thousands of Italians are landing on our shores steeped to the lips in ignorance and superstition, unscrupulous, treacherous, revengeful, bound by secret oaths to their societies, brigands at home, prepared to resume their infamy in their new country" (*Italian Tribune*, Feb. 6, 2003).

July 1892: In Kings Bridge, New York, a contractor employed approximately 200 Italians without paying them for a period of three months. Out of all the Italians wronged, only two dared to go on strike (Cordasco, 1974: 393).[33] Around this time, near Deal Lake, New Jersey, a group of Italians, "failing to receive their wages, captured the contractor [responsible] and shut him up in [their] shanty, where he remained a prisoner until the county sheriff came with a posse to his rescue" (Cordasco, 1974: 393).

1893: A group of Italian Protestants from Northern Italy, known as the "Waldensians" (or Valdese), was swindled into buying 11,000 acres of unfarmable land in North Carolina. Land agents purposely misrepresented the tract as being highly fertile and suitable for growing almost anything; yet, what the Waldensian settlers found was eleven thousand acres of "barren scrub brush, overgrown with pine." Instead of complaining to the point of bringing a lawsuit against the land agents, however, the Waldensians acted as their Italian peers from other regions had acted, and as subsequent generations of Italian-Americans have acted—they made the best of a bad situation. The Waldensians sold off seven thousand acres of the land and retained the rest to pursue viticulture, milling, and lumbering. The colony of "Valdese," North Carolina, flourished well into the twentieth century (Pisani, 1957: 74-75).

April 1893: In *Forum* magazine, Italian-American activist S. Merlino wrote of the many labor abuses his people faced over the past months. One recent case in Cleveland, Ohio, involved a contractor who ran off with his workers' money; "neither the press nor an attorney—succeeded in compelling the company which employed him to pay the workmen." This was a common occurrence, and Merlino states that contractors were never caught (Cordasco, 1974: 393).

Merlino also reported a tragedy that had just occurred in Logansport, Indiana: a "shanty where the Chicago National Gas-Pipe Company huddled its Italian workmen...was blown down by a wind-storm and several men were killed. Neither the number nor the names of the dead were known, as Italian laborers are designated only by figures" (Cordasco, 1974: 392). Apparently, little concern was shown for the Italian victims.[34]

July 26, 1893: In Denver, Colorado, a vengeful mob numbering 10,000 strong (the size of a veritable army) ripped Dan Arata out of jail, hanged him, and riddled his body with bullets. His corpse was then dragged naked through the streets of Denver and strung up again. Arata was accused of murdering a beloved local veteran by the name of Benjamin C. Lightfoot (*Rocky Mountain News,* Jul.27, 1893).[35]

1893-1894: Great masses of unemployed native-born American men (so numerous they were described as "armies") marched on Washington demanding relief. This was at a time when nativism was at its peak and 72,000 Italian immigrants were arriving on these volatile shores. Fear of anti-immigrant purges might explain why the number of incoming Italians fell to 35,000 in 1895 (Mangione and Morreale, 1993: 270).

1894: Though it was said he had a real sympathy for "disadvantaged groups," Nathan Shaler (the Harvard geologist) helped spread the belief that it was "impossible to Americanize immigrants from southern and eastern Europe since they were non-Aryans" (Higham, 1973: 140-141; Mangione and Morreale, 1993: 217).

February/March? 1894: A riot occurred in New York City when police officers broke up a game of "craps" that some young Italian boys were playing on First Avenue. The trouble started when the boys were arrested and Italian adults tried coming to their aid (Lagumina, 1999: 114-115).

March 20, 1894: A hostile contingent of 300 men and boys attacked 75 Italian laborers who were hard at work in Altoona, Pennsylvania. The mob used sticks, stones and pistols to drive the Italians out of the city. One laborer was severely wounded by gun shots; another was critically beaten, and several more were seriously injured. The angry mob then notified the residents of the Italian quarter that they must leave immediately. One angry nativist was even said to have made "a speech in which he advised killing all the Italians." The next day (March 21), two hundred Italians were driven from Altoona (*The Pittsburgh Post*; Mar.21, 1894).

July 10, 1894: The following is an account of an anti-Italian incident perpetrated by a group of Irishmen in Somerville, Massachusetts: "An Irish work gang was digging a sewer ditch. The men had been drinking the night before and continued drinking on the job. Their employer, frustrated in his attempts to get any work out of the drunken and rowdy crew, fired one man as a lesson to the others and hired two Italians who happened by. The Irish workers grabbed the Italians, pushed them into the ditch and beat them senseless." To show how common an occurrence this was, the writer went on: "And there were more serious incidents. One occurred at a work site in the village of Mamaroneck, New York, where a small Italian colony had been established. Some Italian workers were receiving their monthly pay when 200 Irishmen, who were also working in the vicinity, fell on the outnumbered Italians, injuring several and forcing them and their families to abandon their homes and flee south to Morrisania in the Bronx, where they were placed under the protection of civil authorities" (La Sorte, 1985: 151; Gambino, 1974: 236-239).

July 17, 1894: Louis Laferdetta was lynched in Boone, Kentucky.[36]

1895: As the Croton Reservoir was being built in Westchester, New York, a labor recruitment notice appeared in newspapers—it showed three groups the daily wages they could expect: "Common labor, white $1.30 to $1.50"; "Common labor, colored $1.25 to $1.40"; "Common labor, Italian $1.15 to $1.25." Italian laborers in the South were also generally being paid less than blacks at this time. Thus, they had already started replacing black labor on the old plantations and farms (Gambino, 1974: 77-78, 99-100).

March 12-13, 1895: Almost four years, to the day, after the lynching of the eleven Italians in New Orleans, five Italian miners in Huerfano County, Colorado, were attacked by several masked men, while in police custody, on two separate occasions.[37] The Italians were being held by the police as suspects in the murder of saloon- keeper Abner J. Hixon. They were hastily rounded up and implicated in his death the same day his body was found— March 11 (Moore, 1906: 841-842; Woodall, 1987: 1-7).

Stanislao Vittone, Francesco Ronchietto, Pietro Giacobino, Antonio Cobetto, and Lorenzo Andinino were the names of the five victims. Though three of them (Vittone, Ronchietto, and Andinino) were successfully lynched, two (Giacobino and Cobetto) managed to escape. Two of the unlucky ones, Andinino and Ronchietto, happened to share a jail cell with a German immigrant convicted of rape; when the masked men stormed in to kill the Italians, the German was left untouched (Moore, 1906: 841-842; Woodall, 1987: 1-7, 15-16). Clearly, this was a racially motivated act of brutality, and was something that we today would call a "hate crime."[38]

While it is true that Southern Italians bore the brunt of anti-Italian sentiment in American society, Northerners were also mistreated. All five of the victims in this particular incident were natives of the Piedmont region in Italy's extreme north (Woodall, 1987: 15). Quite simply, when an American mob smelled blood, Italian regional distinctions went unnoticed.

This episode of injustice is commonly referred to as the "Italian Massacre" (Woodall, 1987: 2, 9).

August 3, 1895: In the mining town of Spring Valley, Illinois, an Italian immigrant, Barney Rollo, was mugged by a gang of men who were allegedly black. This incident sparked outrage from the town's immigrant mining community (a polyglot assortment of European nationalities). Anti-black violence ensued the next day when black men, women, and children were dragged from their homes and beaten with blunt objects in the streets. Though there were over a dozen casualties, fortunately no one was killed (Guglielmo and Salerno, 2003: 87-89).

This precursor to the 1951 riots in Cicero, Illinois, was significant in that the perpetrators of the violence (on both occasions) were not White Anglo-Saxon Protestants, but ethnics whose racial identities were often in question. In a town like Spring Valley, where the differences were sharp between foreign-born and native-born, black and white, worker and scab, victimizing blacks (those lowest on the societal totem) was the path these immigrants took (a number of Italians among them) toward greater assimilation. Ironically, this act of lawlessness did nothing to consolidate the immigrants' "whiteness"; it actually had the opposite effect. Native whites condemned the attack, viewing it more as a foreign-native conflict, as opposed to a racial one. The black press saw the conflict the same way and "singled out Italians for the brunt of [its] criticism" (just as it would over 50 years later during the Cicero Riots). Spring Valley Italians were called everything from "misguided foreigners" to "a band of lousy, dirty, despicable, low bred, treacherous dago miners" (Guglielmo and Salerno, 2003: 90-94). It is quite clear that both blacks and whites believed the ethnics—and Italians in particular—overstepped their racial boundaries.

1896: In Tontitown, Arkansas, the Italian Catholic church was burned down twice (*Italian Tribune*, Aug. 1, 2002).[39]

August 9, 1896: Three Italian prisoners (Salvatore Arena, Lorenzo Salardino, and Giuseppe Venturella) were lynched in Hahnville, Louisiana, when angry citizens stormed into the local jail. The Italians "were accused of murdering white natives, despite lack of evidence to support the charge" (Mangione and Morreale, 1993: 212; Moore, 1906: 843-845). This act of fury was unmistakably similar to what had occurred in Colorado a year before.

1897: An article in Arena magazine helped spread another popular anti-Italian stereotype: that Italians were "especially licentious and passionate" (Gambino, 1974: 282). African-Americans had also been tagged with this stereotype for years.

September 10, 1897: Italian immigrants (as well as Austrians, Hungarians, and Germans) were brought in as strikebreakers for a coal strike in Pennsylvania. When they decided to join forces with those striking, the local sheriff and his deputies opened fire on them, shooting most in the back. A total of 19 ethnics were killed and 50 wounded. The incident, occurring near the Latimer mine, became known as the "Latimer Massacre" (Brinton, "Chapter IV"; Zinn, "Massacres of History").

1898: A new Louisiana state constitution was adopted which denied a large number of Italian-Americans the right to vote (Gambino, 1998: 132-133).

Also in 1898, just a little further north, approximately fifty Italian families left the failed agricultural colony of Sunnyside, Arkansas, and headed for Knobview, Missouri. A number of deaths caused by malaria and labor abuse forced them to leave Sunnyside. The "foremen" there (who were really former slave overseers) committed unspeakable atrocities against them. The Italians soon learned, however, that life in Knobview would be just as tough. While there were no foremen working against them at this new settlement, the soil did happen to be poor and the immigrant settlers were on the verge of starvation. With no other options, the settlers put together makeshift dwellings and the men hired themselves out as railroad laborers. In time the agricultural colony at Knobview became a success and was renamed the more Italian-sounding "Montebello" (Pisani, 1957: 75-76).

1899: Severe anti-Italian bigotry reared its head in the settlement of Tontitown, Arkansas, when racist locals committed numerous raids and acts of vandalism against the foreign community. The violence peaked with the razing of an Italian schoolhouse. Tired of living in fear, the Italians finally decided to fight back; twenty-four hour patrols were established to protect their property. The next time the marauders attacked, armed Italians were ready and put them to flight. Though tensions with neighboring Anglo-American communities remained, Tontitown was undisturbed thereafter (Gambino, 1974: 103-104; Pisani, 1957: 77-78).

June 26, 1899: In Wampum, Pennsylvania, an Italian by the name of "James Wilson" narrowly escaped being lynched by a mob consisting of 300 coal miners and their wives. He was accused of drugging and taking advantage of a fifteen-year-old girl named Lizzie Hubbard. (She was said to have been the prettiest girl in her community.) The rope was literally around the Italian's neck when he was saved by police officers and put into protective custody (*Pittsburgh Daily Dispatch*, June 27, 1899).

The alleged rape or molestation of white women has certainly been a popular excuse, through the years, for Americans to indulge in the barbarous act of lynching. The above case also demonstrates that, in America, Anglicizing one's name does not exempt an ethnic individual from racism.

July 21, 1899: Five Italian storekeepers were lynched in Tallulah, Louisiana. The victims' names were: Giovanni Cirano, Rosario Fiducia, and Francesco, Carlo, and Giuseppe Difatta. A fight between Carlo Difatta and a "Dr. Hodge" (over a goat that was in the possession of the Difattas) was said to have caused the violence. However, the fact that all five Italians treated blacks and whites equally in their store was probably the underlying reason for why local whites lynched them (Moore, 1906: 845; Mangione and Morreale, 1993: 212; Higham, 1973: 169; Gambino, 1974: 118-119).

1900-1910: Just as anti-Asian sentiment ("Yellow Peril" demagoguery) had plagued the West Coast for the last twenty years of the nineteenth century, a burgeoning anti-Italianism (or what one can aptly call an "Olive Peril") gained momentum during the first decade of the twentieth, as Italian workers came into contact with the native-born. "Cheap labor" became synonymous with "Italian labor," and fear spread of lowering wages. Union leaders in the Pacific Northwest were the most ardent Italophobes, moving to bar Italians from certain fields of employment (and menial labor employment at that!). The Anglo community in that region, both children and adults, viewed the Italians as "Dark People" (or inferior, criminally-prone beings not belonging to the white race). This was an ethnocentric perception that could be found in virtually all Anglo communities scattered across the nation during the early 1900s. The only difference was that the West Coast variety of anti-Italianism was less deadly than that practiced in other regions (Mangione and Morreale, 1993: 191-193).[40]

1900-1920: Over the course of the first two decades of the 20th century, the United States legally put to death 178 Italians by hanging or electrocution (and in one case, by firing squad). Broken down by state and federal district, the numbers executed are as follows:

New York—66;	*Pennsylvania—48;*	*New Jersey—20;*
Connecticut—17;	*Ohio—7;*	*Louisiana—4;*
Illinois—3;	*Massachusetts—3;*	*California—2*
Colorado—1;	*Indiana—1;*	*Maryland—1;*
Montana—1;	*Oregon—1;*	*Utah—1;*
Washington—1;	*Washington D.C. —1.*[41]	

From the data, one can see that the state of New York has led the other states considerably in putting Italians to death (much as the southwestern states have led all others in executing Hispanics). One can truly say that New York has been the world capital of "Italocide." That states like New York, Pennsylvania, New Jersey, and Connecticut have executed so many should not come as a shock since these northeastern regions have historically taken in the great bulk of Italian immigrants. (After all, where a particular population is most concentrated is where its criminal element can be found in the greatest numbers.) It should be known, however, that if one looks at the data, only a handful of the Italians executed were classified as "gangsters" (or professional criminals) —most of the executed were apparently hardworking paupers. (Thus, the myth that all Italian criminals were/are somehow "connected" is dashed to pieces.) Furthermore, since this executed population was at the "bottom of the barrel" socially, and since an unknown number probably did not receive fair trials, some were in all likelihood innocent of the crimes with which they were charged.

1900: Four thousand Italians, in the process of constructing New York City's Lexington Avenue Subway, formed their own union and went on strike. Salvatore Ninfo, a 21-year-old Italian immigrant, led them, and its outcome was "mostly successful" (Mangione and Morreale, 1993:139; Gambino, 1974:116). Such large-scale labor organization was new to the historically marginalized and unconfrontational Italian population. As the early years of the twentieth century passed, more and more Italian workers joined unions in order to avoid being used as cheap, replaceable pawns by big business.

Also, in 1900, Italian construction workers in Montclair, New Jersey, were so destitute that they were forced to live on the streets while they dug trenches for the water system. At night, they made bonfires and sung hymns of worship around them. These workers founded the Italian Mission of Montclair ("Italian/American Timeline," Seton Hall). This kind of severe poverty, yet great willingness to work, defined the Italian immigrant population for decades.

Early 1900: The Italian language newspaper *Cronica d'America* reported that "thirty Italians had been arrested and fined $10.00 each for rag-picking; that police killed two Italians who were having an argument; [and] that thirty Italian workers in West Troy [New York] were burned as strikebreakers" (Cordasco, 1975: 206). These incidents, randomly selected, were reported in an era in which anti-Italian violence was a daily reality.[42]

Summer 1900: The Italian miners of Retsof, New York, went on strike to earn just as much money for their work as non-Italians. The strike, however, did nothing but increase tensions between Italians and non-Italians in that community; eventually the former were intimidated into going back to work (Krase and De Sena, 1994: 177-178).

For decades, a less equitable rate of pay was the norm for Italian-Americans in many parts of the nation. Italians were truly considered "somewhat less than second-class citizens" (Krase and De Sena, 1994: 178). This same treatment was prevalent north of the border as well. In Ontario, Canada, from 1906 to 1912, there were violent clashes between the authorities and hundreds of Italians who demanded higher wages. In these "pitched battles" that their employers provoked, Italian laborers were shot and injured; Italian households were even ransacked by soldiers and police in an effort to find weapons—yet none were ever found. Like their countrymen in the U.S., Italians in Canada were often victimized by vicious employers, prejudiced natives, and by a hostile and demeaning press (Vecoli, 1987: 139-147).

July 29, 1900: Angelo Bresci, an Italian anarchist from Paterson, New Jersey, assassinated King Umberto I of Italy. This act helped stereotype all pro-labor Italians (who just wanted to be treated like human beings) as anarchists and radicals. Many defamatory accusations were hurled at the Italian population in the United States ("Italian/American Timeline," Seton Hall; Mangione and Morreale, 1993: 248). The assassination of King Umberto thus reinforced the belief that the Italian worker was the enemy of mainstream Americans (i.e. the "white man").[43]

July 3, 1901: Striking miners rioted in Telluride, Colorado. It was reported that a number of Italians were involved ("Mine Workers Strike in Telluride," RMPBN). During this time period (the early twentieth century), Italian miners were frequently not permitted to lodge with whites or blacks in the work camps (*Italian Tribune*, Aug. 1, 2002).

July 11, 1901: Three Italians were attacked by an armed mob in Erwin, Mississippi. Two of them, Giovanni and Vincenzo Serio, were killed; the third, Salvatore Liberto, was wounded. This particular lynching (or "hate-crime") seems to have been committed in order to keep the Italian population subordinated (Moore, 1906: 848-849; Katz, 1969: 77, 82; *Italian Tribune*, Aug. 1, 2002).[44]

It should be known that Italian children were being barred from attending white schools in parts of the South at this time—in places like Sumrall, Mississippi (Higham, 1973: 169; Mangione and Morreale, 1993: 212; *Italian Tribune*, Aug. 1, 2002).

November 18, 1901: Four Italians were driven from Marksville, Louisiana (Iorizzo and Mondello, 1980: 290).

1903: Contrary to the popular belief that Italian workers were anti-union and eager to serve as strikebreakers (or "scabs"), the United States Immigration Commission "found that Italians were black listed out of the [mining industry] for their strong pro-Union leanings more often than any other group. It also found that only Chinese, Japanese and American Blacks appeared to be discriminated against more openly than Italians" (*Italian Tribune*, Feb. 6, 2003). Since Italians still took the most undesirable jobs in society, and were a highly visible minority (having Mediterranean features), it is not surprising that popular prejudice continued to view them as racially ambiguous wage depressors, despite the facts the Immigration Commission put forth.

Also, during 1903, an immigration law was passed "forbidding the admission and authorizing the deportation of foreign proponents of anarchism." This was the first time since the Alien and Sedition Act of 1798 that the law penalized immigrants for their political views or opinions (Higham, 1973: 112). A nation-wide fear of "foreign radicals," steadily rising since the Nativist Nineties, was chiefly responsible for getting the law passed.

March 1903: Twenty-three Italian laborers were sent from New York to Beckley, West Virginia, to work on a railroad that was being constructed in the Piney Creek district. Once they arrived, they were driven four miles from town to a secluded place called "Harmon's Camp," where conditions of slave labor and the presence of armed guards awaited them (*Outlook*, Jun. 13, 1903).

When their situation grew too severe, the 23 Italian laborers left the work camp. They were then arrested for non-payment of board under West Virginia's "Boarding-House Law" (even though the Italians were deprived the right to earn money for their labor), and were locked up over night in the County Court House. The next morning the contractor came to retrieve his "property," binding six of the Italians with ropes, tying them to a mule, and parading them through the streets of Beckley. All of them were then taken back to the camp to "work off" their boarding and transportation fees (*Outlook*, Jun. 13, 1903).

In June of 1903, Gino C. Speranza and the Society for the Protection of Italian Immigrants exposed the injustice above and testified that there was frequent labor abuse. In one case, Speranza cited the testimony of a Piedmontese immigrant named "Girardi"; he worked for Boxley & Co. near Kayford, West Virginia. The immigrant was ordered to lift a heavy stone. When he asked a black co-laborer for help, the foreman "called him a vile name and thrust a revolver in his face. Thereupon Girardi lifted the stone, at the cost of a very bad rupture." For that injury, he received no compensation from his employer. In other cases, Italian laborers told of how they were severely beaten with blunt objects and terrorized by camp guards (*Outlook*, Jun. 13, 1903).

Thus, Speranza and the Society for the Protection of Italian Immigrants investigated four West Virginian counties (Kanawha, Raleigh, Clay, and Wirt) in response to the many complaints of labor abuse coming from the region. A number of camps were visited and much evidence was obtained (*Charities*, 1903: 26-28).[45]

1903-1904: Foreign miners (mainly Italians and Mexicans) went on strike when they were denied an eight-hour work day by their employer—Colorado Fuel and Iron (a company that essentially ran Colorado and would be responsible for the "Ludlow Massacre" of 1914). The immigrant miners were treated worse than their American-born co-workers, and their employers often accentuated the differences between both groups in order to keep them divided and powerless. Colorado Fuel and various "citizens' alliances" (i.e. local nativist groups) managed to convince the English-speaking miners that these "foreigners" were their enemies. Thus, this strike of 1903 - 1904 pitted foreign-born against native-born, and impoverished workers against big business. The latter eventually won the struggle when it employed the state militia to round up the immigrant miners and drive them from their living quarters at Cripple Creek (some were even driven all the way out of Colorado). In the middle of the night, the miners were dragged from their tents and forced to march 18 miles over mountain roads; rounded up in their sleep, they were not properly clothed for such a hike, nor were they given any food or water. Before the brutality ended, the militia had shot several miners, and others were forced to work in chain gangs. The workers' rights were violated in every way. Even their wives and children were roughed up and herded into cells like quarantined cattle. Of all the immigrant miners driven from Cripple Creek, eighty were Italians.[46] A similar exodus of Italian laborers occurred a few years earlier in another part of Colorado (Mangione and Morreale, 1993: 186-187; "The Autobiography of Mother Jones").

1904: Five thousand Italian workers who were building the Bronx Aqueduct unionized and went on strike. They were successful (for the most part), proving that unity can overcome hardship (Higham, 1973: 116).[47]

1905: A book by James Cutler, *Lynch Law: An Investigation into the History of Lynching in the United States*, exposed the on-going problem of lynching in American society and broke down the number of those lynched on the basis of race, ethnicity, and sex. Cutler found that aside from blacks, American Indians and Italians were lynched most often. Between 1882 and 1903, forty-five American Indians and twenty-eight Italians were lynched.[48] Also, during this period it was discovered that 20 Mexicans, 12 Chinese, and 1 Japanese were lynched (Cutler, 1905: 172).

From Cutler's data, one can see that Italians (like Mexicans) were considered neither white nor black. The lynched Italians were more often placed in the "Others" category. In fact, all nineteen victims in Louisiana's "Others" category were Italian. Cutler also found that while only 5 percent of those lynched in the Western States were black, almost 12 percent were "Others"—meaning Indians, Italians, Chinese, and Mexicans (Cutler, 1905: 179, 181).

Also, in 1905, Adolfo Rossi of the Italian Emigration Office investigated and exposed a scheme that "left one hundred [Italian] men, women, and children stranded in Alabama." Apparently the victims were lured to a settlement called "New Palermo" and were promised all kinds of work, in addition to plenty of land and houses. Upon arrival, however, the immigrants saw that only a handful of houses were built, and if they were going to stay, they first needed to clear many acres of land. Furious, they decided to leave. The man responsible for misrepresenting the advertisements of New Palermo was neither an anti-Italian bigot, nor a "native American"— he was an Italian-born swindler named Salvatore Pampinella. Like other con artists, who preyed on helpless immigrants, this man was untouchable to both the American and Italian authorities; if anything, the law protected such an individual and faulted the victims for not conducting a background check on him. The type of scam Pampinella pulled off was common at this point in Italian-American history—it occurred again and again, so it is not surprising that he got away with it. What is surprising is that this time he did not get away with it for long. Soon after the settlers found out they were bamboozled, one caught up with Pampinella and shot him to death (Mangione and Morreale, 1993: 184).

1906: Several Italians were killed, and several more were maimed, by a mob in West Virginia (Gambino,1974: 119).

May 14, 1906: In North Carolina, a deputy sheriff and his posse attacked 1500 semi-enslaved Italian laborers, killing two Italians and severely wounding five (Mangione and Morreale, 1993: 272; Iorizzo and Mondello, 1980: 290). The tragedy was the product of a grave misunderstanding—the kind that led to anti-Italian violence time and time again. It was believed that the laborers were criminals, as nine of them were jailed for threatening to kill the South & Western Railroad Company's superintendent of labor (their employer). Prior to their arrest, the nine Italians formed a committee and met with the superintendent, asking him if the workers could "be paid back wages in order to feed themselves properly." Unable to speak English, "the committee spokesman resorted to sign language to spell out his message. First, he pointed a finger to his mouth, then to his stomach; finally, with his foot he scratched out the form of a box on the ground, meaning that unless the workers were paid so that they could purchase food, they would wind up being buried. The superintendent misinterpreted the signs to mean that unless the Italians were paid, the superintendent would be buried." This misinterpretation led to the jailing of the nine men, the raising of a posse, and the deaths of two Italians caught in the middle of the cultural divide. Thus another tragedy had occurred simply because some folks insist on believing the worst about Italians. "In August 1906, due largely to Italian diplomatic pressures, the railroad company settled out of court for $7,500 in damages to the families of the murdered men" (Mangione and Morreale, 1993: 272). Even though a mere $7,500 could not replace the lives of the men, it was better than nothing, which was exactly what most Italian victims' families received at the time.[49]

1907: Due to labor tensions, an Italian social leader was severely beaten by a mob in Mississippi. Poor, native whites resented the productivity of Italian farm laborers and the fact that they worked for cheaper pay. Anti-Italian sentiment spread through Mississippi as a result, and one candidate for governor even used the ill feeling as a main issue of his campaign (Pisani, 1957: 68, 187-188).

The year 1907 saw other anti-Italian abuses further south. In his book *La Merica*, Michael La Sorte describes one nefarious incident that occurred in Florida: "the East Coast Florida Railroad Company hired a large number of Italians to build the 153-mile line from Miami to Key West. Once the workers reached the camps on the coral islands, they realized that they had been trapped into a system of involuntary servitude. Some managed to escape to the mainland and make their way back to New York, but others who tried to leave were apprehended, by order of the company, for vagabondage and were transported back to the camps" (La Sorte, 1985: 82).

Also in 1907, federal investigators and the Society for the Protection of Italian Immigrants found that, throughout the country, "immigrants traveling by train got the poorest cars in the service; that the cars were overcrowded (some to the point where there were no seats available on long journeys); that immigrants were denied the use of dining and sleeping cars; and that no porters or brakemen were provided to assist women with their children and baggage…. Even after agencies were created to protect the immigrants, railroads still engaged in the cruelest practice of all: separating families by placing members on different trains arriving at different times. The purpose was to allot each of the railroads in the consortium its share of the immigrant patronage. At imes, this meant sending family members to their destinations by the most roundabout and expensive routes." (Mangione and Morreale, 1993: 122-123). Though they were greatly mistreated, immigrant passengers still had to pay, like anyone else, the same price for a train ticket; they received no "discount" for the abuses they experienced. In looking back on this unjust chapter of American history, it is hard for one not to notice the appalling irony of the train situation: the immigrants were denied the right to travel freely and unmolested on railroads that they themselves built.[50]

1908: More than 100 Italians were accidentally killed while working on the railways of Pennsylvania. Similarly, in Pennsylvanian mines, it was discovered that "the deaths of Italians exceeded 100 per year" during the early part of the twentieth century. Since employers identified their workers by number (instead of by name), in many cases, the positive identification of victims was nearly impossible. Friends and family were frequently uninformed when fatal accidents occurred (Foerster, 1969: 389).

Also in 1908, the Italian journalist Giuseppe Prezioso found that his countrymen were treated like slaves in the American South, and while working there were paid the lowest wages in the nation. Prezioso took an honest look at his people's plight and came to the conclusion that, while Americans were wrong to exploit them, the Italian padroni were chiefly to blame (Mangione and Morreale, 1993: 183). After all, the padroni were the ones who sent entire families to live and labor in the unhealthy pigsties of rural America; they made deals with American employers and sold out their people in the process.

This same year, in New York City, "270 Italian families [were] charged with violation of the Compulsory Education Law compared to 66— Russian, 56—German, 55—Irish, and 7—English families" ("Italian/American Timeline," Seton Hall). Unfortunately, Italian children growing up in this era needed to work in order to help their families from going hungry.

February 1908: "When a recession in the lumber industry brought a drop in work and wages in the Tangipahoa [Louisiana] town of Kentwood, fifty to sixty white men 'decreed that the Italians would have to leave Kentwood under pain of death.' They sent a committee of twelve to the Italian section to convey the message and to threaten to blow up the homes of Italians who did not leave town. About twenty families left for New Orleans." (Guglielmo and Salerno, 2003: 73, 283).

February 24, 1908: On this date an Italian anarchist killed a Catholic priest in Denver, Colorado; paranoia then spread throughout the country that the "Black Hand" was responsible and was gaining strength. Although the paranoia proved to be just that (as an anarchist would not typically associate with a capitalist criminal organization), the priest's murder gave anti-Italian bigots another excuse to indulge in their hateful and defamatory acts (Gambino, 1974: 282-283; "Italian/American Timeline," Seton Hall).

November 1908: In Rochester, New York, a group of Sicilian-Americans produced a religious play defending themselves against unfair accusations that they were members of the "Black Hand" (Gambino, 1974: 282; "Italian/American Timeline," Seton Hall). For years, life was tough for the Italians of Rochester—"the townspeople did everything possible to encourage Italians to leave. Storekeepers refused to serve them; landlords would not rent to them. When the weather was mild, these early immigrants lived in boxes and make-shift tents, subsisting largely on dandelion greens." (Mangione and Morreale, 1993: 162).

December 28, 1908: The great Messina-Reggio earthquake hit Southern Italy, killing nearly 100,000 people; it is known as the deadliest earthquake in European history. Thousands of Italians in America were suddenly cut off from relatives in Calabria and Sicily. Though a massive international relief program was started, the region remained broken physically and economically for decades to come (Gambino, 1974: 65; "The Messina-Reggio Earthquake," Frank Ardvini).

1909: Over the past three years, thirty-eight Italians were killed in mining accidents in Minnesota's "Iron Range." *Unaccidentally,* labor and racial strife long affected this area of northern Minnesota. In 1916, labor leader Carlo Tresca was arrested here for a couple of murders he did not commit; and, as in the majority of places in America at this time, Italians on the Iron Range were not considered "white" in either the social or racial sense. There was a particularly strong effort made by whites in this region (i.e. people of Northern European background) to keep the "black races" of Southern Europe segregated and away from themselves.[51] (As one might expect, there was a good deal of Ku Klux Klan activity here.) This high level of ostracism had been maintained on the Iron Range—as well as in other parts of the country—until the World War II era, when Italian-Americans began climbing the social ladder (Vecoli, 1987: 182-186).

March 12, 1909: Giuseppe Petrosino, the first NYPD detective of Italian background and the founder of the "Italian Branch" of undercover officers, was killed in Palermo, Sicily, while gathering information on alleged organized crime members (Mangione and Morreale, 1993: 248-249; Gambino, 1974: 275; "Italian/American Timeline," Seton Hall). Detective Petrosino went to Palermo mainly "to assuage a public hysteria about Italian crime that was as irrational as it was widespread…. The hysteria had been simmering ever since Southern Italians began to come to the United States in significant numbers after 1875." While the paranoia (and subsequently the *bigotry*) stemmed from an American fear of the foreigners' poverty, ignorance, customs, religion, ethnic features, etcetera, the belief that Italians were innately criminal (or that they had a higher crime rate than other groups) was not at all supported by any facts. Statistics from this period usually show that Italians had a much lower crime rate than other groups (Gambino, 1974: 277-278). This led Detective Petrosino to believe that "there was no organized crime syndicate in New York" (at least during the early years of the twentieth century). Furthermore, "His findings told him that the criminals in the Italian immigrant culture were petty hoodlums who victimized their own people and that the thugs acted as common criminals either alone or with a few accomplices and not as members of an organized and disciplined illegal society" (Gambino, 1974: 276). Research shows that Petrosino was correct; however, the press (and of course the *New York Times*) did not concern itself with the facts—it only concerned itself with sensationalism and selling more papers. It was largely on account of this sensationalism that Detective Petrosino was forced to go to Sicily and ultimately lose his life. His murder was even immediately sensationalized to have been the work of the Sicilian Mafia. No one had entertained the possibility that anarchists or crooked Italian officials were responsible. The overall bigotry and defamation that resulted from Detective Petrosino's death was immense. Whenever unsolved murders surfaced in major U.S. cities, rumors of the mysterious Black Hand circulated, newspaper sales were boosted, and Italians were scapegoated (Gambino, 1974: 275-277, 282-283, 286-287).

Just two days after Detective Petrosino's death, the *New York Times* called for an end to all immigration from Italy and Sicily. As Richard Gambino wrote in *Blood of My Blood*, "the effects of the news of the [Petrosino] murder were calamitous for Italian-Americans. Petrosino's death brought a plague of vilification and persecution upon them. The edition of the *New York Times* that reported the murder…ran column upon column speculating about Italian crime and a list of alleged Black Hand crimes committed that year in New York City. Most were bombings, but the list also included one body found dead of 'stiletto wounds.' The killers were unknown, but evidently, the *Times* could distinguish between wounds caused by Italian knives and those caused by other knives. Another case involved twelve Italians who attacked three revenue officers on a street corner who were taking two of their countrymen to a post office to be arraigned. A third case, [the] murder of a butcher, was linked to the criminal society because 'the cartridge that held the bullet that killed him came from Italy'" (Gambino, 1974: 283, 286).[52] Such blatant defamation, operating on the assumption that *all Italians are guilty until proven innocent*, led to mass police raids in Italian communities all over the United States. In one typical raid, the police charged into Chicago's Little Italy and arrested 194 Italian-Americans. When they were unable to link any of the prisoners to crimes committed, they eventually released them. These tactics, clearly designed to keep a minority population "in line," contributed to the mutual mistrust and hostility that existed between Italian-Americans and the authorities; such acts guaranteed that Italian victims would never go to the police for help. Police officers were not only viewed as oppressors, but they were *straniere* as well (Gambino, 1974: 278, 286).

March 16, 1909: A contingent of 600 Italian laborers went on strike complaining that the West Point military academy did not permit them to use its "main entrance and roads" while working on academy grounds. For a period of weeks leading up to the strike, violence rocked the Italian camp; a series of Italian-on-Italian crimes illuminated the feelings that only a severely marginalized and oppressed group experiences.

May 1909: When police entered the Italian section of Hoboken, New Jersey, in response to rumors of Italian-American "criminal activity," a riot broke out. It was reported that, "Italian residents exchanged gunshots with police from tenement windows during the disorder" (Gambino, 1974: 286-287; "Italian/American Timeline," Seton Hall).

November 13, 1909: Of the 259 killed in a mining disaster at Cherry, Illinois, seventy-three were of Italian extraction ("Cherry Mine Disaster"; Mangione and Morreale, 1993: 280-281).[53]

1910: The U.S. Immigration Commission found that people of Italian background had a lower income than both whites and blacks: "of males eighteen years or older, the national average for whites was $666. For blacks, it was $445. For American-born Italian-Americans the figure was $408 and for the Italian-born it was $396." It would not be until 1970 that Italian-Americans caught up to the white average and surpassed the black one (Gambino, 1974: 339). Of the millions of Italians that came to the U.S. by 1910, only 94 attended colleges in the nation. Furthermore, the teaching of the Italian language and culture was out of the question at this time (French and German were upheld as the languages of success). Only toward the end of the 20th century were Italian courses finally accepted by the U.S. educational system. Also, by 1910, there were only 14 elementary school teachers, nationwide, who were second generation Italian-Americans (of Southern Italian descent) (Gambino, 1974: 254-256). As for those few Italian-Americans who sought employment as professors in American universities, they were "met with curious glances, a stormy reception, deliberate animosity, and discouragement." In addition, Italians were prevented altogether from teaching English (La Sorte, 1985: 143).

September 14, 1910: John F. Easterling, a bookkeeper at a cigar factory in West Tampa, was shot and wounded when he was about to enter his place of employment. While he did not see who shot him, Easterling claimed that a crowd of striking cigar workers (predominantly Hispanic and Italian ethnics) was responsible. Tampa's decidedly anti-immigrant/ antilabor press took the opportunity to incite further hatred and vigilantism against the ethnic strikers. (Many bogus articles about the violent tendencies of the cigar workers had already been printed in an effort to sway public opinion in favor of a nativist agenda.) The *Tampa Tribune* was full of incendiary lines like the following: "If the authorities prove incapable of handling the situation, citizens should organize and insure peace and order"; "the first American to be attacked"; etcetera. What the press totally ignored was Easterling's own violent past—just a couple of months before he was shot, Easterling pulled out a gun and fired on a member of a union organizing committee. Fortunately, for both the disgruntled book-keeper and his intended target, he missed (Ingalls, 1988: 95; *Tampa Tribune*, Nov. 22, 1992).

Six days after Easterling was shot, on September 20, two Italian immigrants, Angelo Albano and Castenge Ficarrotta, were arrested and charged with his attempted murder; they were briefly held in the West Tampa jail, for a period of about three hours. Then, while a sheriff's deputy was transporting them in a horse-drawn carriage to a different jail, an armed mob of 20 to 30 individuals surrounded them, grabbed the hand cuffed prisoners, and sped off in automobiles. (One can see that this incident bore a striking resemblance to what had occurred in Walsenburg, Colorado, fifteen years earlier.) Soon thereafter, the police found the corpses of the two Italians hanging to a giant oak tree near the spot where they were abducted. There was a note attached to Albano's clothes, which read: "BEWARE! OTHERS TAKE NOTICE OR GO THE SAME WAY. WE KNOW SEVEN MORE. WE ARE WATCHING YOU. IF ANY MORE CITIZENS ARE MOLESTED, LOOK OUT." It was signed, "JUSTICE." No one involved in the lynching of Angelo Albano and Castenge Ficarrotta was ever identified (Ingalls, 1988: 96; *Tampa Tribune*, Nov. 22, 1992).

After the two Italians were lynched, the *Tampa Tribune* continued speaking ill of the dead, calling Ficarrotta "a professional murderer" and Albano his "assistant." As might be expected, the paper also assigned the term "Black Hand" to the Italians, and praised the lynch mob for helping to rid Tampa of "crime" (i.e. hardworking, yet undesirable immigrants). In time, a great amount of evidence surfaced proving that neither Ficarrotta nor Albano shot Easterling, and that they were both *entirely* innocent. A variety of sources agree that the lynching was pre-planned to intimidate the striking cigar workers. Ultimately, the only offense Albano and Ficarrotta committed was being Italian—the Cigar Makers' Union even vehemently denied the two were either cigar workers or strikers. (Albano himself was an insurance salesman.) There was also evidence of police involvement in the lynching (Ingalls, 1988: 97-99; *Tampa Tribune*, Nov. 22, 1992).

On **September 25**[th] (five days after the two Italians were lynched), John Easterling died of his wound. Months later, the cigar workers' strike was eventually crushed. Tragically, the workers gained nothing for their efforts. The brutal lynching of Angelo Albano and Castenge Ficarrotta, the shooting and eventual death of John Easterling, and the starvation and great suffering of the cigar workers' families were the grave human costs of the strike of 1910 (*Tampa Tribune*, Nov. 22, 1992).[54]

1910s-1920s: A new form of segregation against Italians could be found in the city of Philadelphia—movie house segregation (Mangione and Morreale, 1993: 153).

1911: Due to long standing claims that Southern Italians have a considerable amount of "Negroid" blood, "the U.S. House Committee on Immigration openly debated and seriously questioned whether one should regard 'the south Italian as a full-blooded Caucasian'; many representatives did not seem to think so. From the docks of New York to railroads in the West, some native-born American workers carefully drew distinctions between themselves 'white men' and 'new immigrant' foreigners like Italians" (Guglielmo and Salerno, 2003: 36). Already, for quite some years, employers in many sections of the country had classified Italian laborers as non-whites. In Arizona, for example, "some copper companies categorized their workers into three main groups—whites, Mexicans, and Italians/Spaniards" (Guglielmo and Salerno, 2003: 38).

March 25, 1911: A fire at the Triangle Shirtwaist Company in Lower Manhattan claimed the lives of 145 female workers, "seventy-five of whom were young Italian women" (Mangione and Morreale, 1993: 292). The tragedy forced the government to pass legislation that improved working conditions ("The Story of the Triangle Fire," Cornell University).

1912: In California, 600 work-related accidents befell Italians, "including 26 deaths and 35 cases of permanent incapacity to work" (Foerster, 1969: 389).

January 12, 1912: In Lawrence, Massachusetts, a strike began in which more than 200,000 immigrant textile workers would stand in solidarity against their oppressive employers. The largest group of workers, and thus strikers, were Italians; 45% of the workers were females; and 12% were children under the age of eighteen. Their bleak existence was described as follows: "the workers lived in filthy, overcrowded slums, where the infant mortality rate was one of the highest in the nation. Tuberculosis was rampant. The [textile] mills were highly mechanized and industrial accidents were common. More than 33 percent of all mill workers died before they reached the age of 26. The workers were treated as slaves. They had to pay for drinking water, they were docked an hour's pay for arriving minutes late—and the women were often forced to sleep with the foremen to keep their jobs" ("The Lawrence Strike of 1912 and the IWW," Loyola University). Child workers were also forced into buying phony birth certificates if they were not yet old enough to work (14 years being the legal age), and all who worked overtime were not paid for it (Mangione and Morreale, 1993: 288). From their own native countries, these downtrodden foreigners escaped similar "third world" conditions. Little did they know, before voyaging across the ocean, that their lives were going to be the same (or *even worse*) in the land of liberty. In addition to the barbaric working conditions they endured daily, the immigrants did not possess an adequate knowledge of the English language, they were extremely impoverished, and were frequent targets of nativist hatred—all this took its toll. (Today, many of the descendants of these immigrants do not realize that whenever they recite the Pledge of Allegiance, whenever they buy a new house in a "nice" neighborhood, or whenever they bite into a hotdog at a baseball game, an expensive price has already been paid for all the benefits of Americanization.)

And so, by January 12, 1912, "the long-suffering Italian workers" had had enough. They were the ones who organized and led the strike after finding out that they were not going to get the pay raise they were expecting, and after finding that two hours worth of pay had actually been deducted from their salaries (i.e. 32 cents worth—this could have purchased ten loaves of bread, by the way). The Italian strikers went from mill to mill destroying the machines they toiled on, slashing machine belts and cloth. The state militia was then called in, and joined "the police and firemen in turning hoses on the mob" of workers ("The Lawrence Strike…" Loyola University).

The next day (**January 13th**), two experienced strike organizers, Arturo Giovannitti and Joe Ettor (both Italian-Americans), arrived in Lawrence to lead the masses in their struggle (Mangione and Morreale, 1993: 284-285; "The Lawrence Strike…" Loyola University).

On January 16, policemen with their clubs wounded scores of strikers, and several were injured when the state militia conducted a bayonet charge against them. "A Sicilian boy," Dominic Raprasa, was bayoneted to death (Mangione and Morreale, 1993: 286).

On January 20th dynamite was found in several locations, and the strikers were immediately suspected of planting it. It was later discovered, however, that the dynamite had been "planted by operatives of the American Woolen Company, under the direction of its president, William Wood." He was never prosecuted ("The Lawrence Strike…" Loyola University).

On the 29th of January, a policeman shot to death an immigrant worker named Anna Lo Pizzo, when a scuffle broke out between them and the strikers. "Although no strikers had been armed, they were blamed for the death." A few days later, "Ettor and Giovannitti were charged as accomplices of Giuseppe Caruso, the worker accused of the murder. All three were arrested. The trumped-up charge was designed to break the will of the strikers. All three men were denied bail and remained in jail until their trials, almost a year later" ("The Lawrence Strike," Loyola University; Mangione and Morreale, 1993: 287). Three-hundred others were also arrested indiscriminately alongside Ettor, Giovannitti, and Caruso (Gambino, 1974: 116).[55]

The strikers of Italian background "recommended sending [all] the children" to other cities for care "in order to remove the children from the violent atmosphere and harsh winter and to lessen the strain on relief programs." The mill owners, however, still trying to break the strikers' resolve, "convinced the marshal to forbid the removal of children from the city." Nevertheless, on February 24, approximately 200 children and their mothers arrived at the Lawrence train station to say their goodbyes. That was when the unthinkable happened: "In a vicious and brutal display of force," the police and militia "beat mothers senseless and clubbed children as well as the women who had come to take them away." Many women and children were tossed into the backs of military trucks "like so much meat." Due to the planting of dynamite, the false arrests, and now the beating of women and children, popular opinion turned in favor of the strikers; the mill owners and police were increasingly viewed as villains in the conflict ("The Lawrence Strike..." Loyola University; Mangione and Morreale, 1993: 288).

On March 12th (exactly two months after the strike began) a settlement was reached which met the strikers' demands—they would receive a 15% wage increase and double pay for overtime, the 54-hour work week would be recognized, the premium and bonus system would be done away with, and there would be no retaliation against those who struck. On the 24th the strike was officially called off and the militia moved out. Ettor and Giovannitti, however, would remain in police custody until November 26—when they were finally acquitted of the bogus charge thrown at them. Ironically, Ettor, Giovannitti, and Caruso were tried in Salem. In his defense, Giovannitti could not help but make mention of the "town where they used to burn the witches at the stake..." All three Italians were, of course, found not guilty ("The Lawrence Strike..." Loyola University; Mangione and Morreale, 1993: 292-293).

Because of the Lawrence Strike of 1912, wages in the textile industry were raised throughout New England, it was finally proven that foreign workers could organize successfully, and mainstream Americans attained a better understanding of the incredible hardships that unskilled immigrant workers faced ("The Lawrence Strike," Loyola University).

August 12, 1912: Five Italian immigrants were executed at Sing Sing Prison for a murder they neither committed nor planned. The previous November (of 1911), Filippo DeMarco, Vincenzo Cona, Angelo Guista, Lorenzo Liborio Cali, and Salvatore DeMarco were in the process of robbing an upscale farmhouse in the Croton Lake area (just north of New York City) when their partner, Santo Zanza, took it upon himself to kill a female boarder in an upstairs room. Except for Guista, who was ransacking dresser drawers in the victim's room, the others did not even know a murder was committed until they were caught by police. Santo Zanza, the actual murderer, was executed on July 12, 1912—exactly one month before the others ("The Croton Lake Murder," Crimelibrary.com).

That all six men were criminals cannot be disputed. However, the sound judgment and morality of their condemners most certainly can be disputed. The "Croton Lake Murder" still remains the only crime in New York State history that sent six men to the electric chair for a single murder; and it is surely the only case in which five men were executed, one after the other, for a crime they did not commit. What could also be called into question were the ultra-fast trials and sentencing of the Italians. From jury selection to sentencing, a mere 17 hours was the total time required for the first four trials. The *New York Times* reported that Westchester County "had established a new record for the quick disposal of murder cases in this state." And in only one day's time, Salvatore DeMarco was tried, convicted, and sentenced to die. The only probable reason for this swift brand of justice was that the defendants were *Italian*—members of a loathed and powerless immigrant class. Anti-Italian sentiment was as thriving in the Croton Lake area of Westchester, New York, as it was in the rest of America at this time. There were many Italian day laborers working on the Croton Aqueduct project (including Lorenzo Cali and Santo Zanza), and they were of course at the bottom of the social ladder. Native-born Americans believed the Italians were genetically predisposed to criminality and in all ways inferior. It was these severely prejudiced people who acted as judge, jury, and executioner, as not even one juror was of Italian descent. In many places (such as Croton), Italians were not even allowed to use the front door when entering affluent homes; one of the key witnesses to the robbery first noticed something was wrong when she saw the Italians entering the farmhouse through the front door. Extensive ethnic profiling (i.e. the random searching of Italians for weapons) also occurred during the trials. Fearing a militant gang of Italians storming into the courtroom, the Italophobic *New York Times* declared, "No Italian who could not prove that his presence in the courtroom was necessary should be admitted to the Court House" ("The Croton Lake Murder," Crimelibrary.com).

Two other Sing Sing prisoners were executed the same day as the five Italians (August 12, 1912), for unrelated crimes—one was a black man and the other was Italian ("The Croton Lake Murder," Crimelibrary.com).

1913: In a period stretching from January to July, sixty Italians were murdered in New York City. Also, during these seven months, over ninety explosions rocked the Italian sections of the five boroughs (Foerster, 1969: 405; Lagumina, 1999: 103). Although the murders were sensationalized by the press as the work of the "Mafia," "Camorra," or "Black Hand," most were probably committed by petty criminals who turned to crime in order to escape the sub-human living conditions (which many had been living in for decades) in the Italian ghettos.[56]

February 25, 1913: Thousands of Italian-American silk workers went on strike in Paterson, New Jersey. They were forced back to work a few months later ("Italian/American Timeline," Seton Hall).[57]

October 22, 1913: Two hundred and sixty-three miners were killed in a mine explosion in Dawson, New Mexico—a hundred or more were of Italian extraction ("Dawson—New Mexico Ghost Town," Ghosttowns.com; Foerster, 1969: 389).

1914: In a classic example of xenophobic nativism, the White Farmers Association of Ponchatoula, Louisiana, "specifically forbade membership to Italians, Sicilians, Japanese, Chinese, Mongolians, Asiatics, Africans, or descendants of African farmers" (Guglielmo and Salerno, 2003: 73).

Anti-Italian bigotry was so ingrained in American society by this year that even the "progressive" E.A. Ross declared the following in an article he wrote in *Century* magazine: "That the Mediterranean peoples are morally below the races of northern Europe is as certain as any social fact. Nothing less than venomous is the readiness of the southern Europeans to prey upon their fellows..." (Gambino, 1974: 287; Lagumina, 1999: 135-137). Ross also had this to say in an additional article: "Steerage passengers from a Naples boat show a distressing frequency of low foreheads, open mouths, weak chins, poor features, skew faces, small or knobby crania, and backless heads. Such people lack the power to take rational care of themselves; hence their death-rate in New York is twice the general death-rate and thrice that of the Germans" (Lagumina, 1999: 138, 141). A Nazi propagandist could not have made a more unflattering assessment of undesirables.

April 20, 1914: Striking coal miners and their wives and children were slaughtered in the infamous "Ludlow Massacre" in Colorado—eighteen were killed (mostly women and children). Their names were: Louis Tikas, James Fyler, John Bartolotti, Charlie Costa, Fedelina Costa, Onafrio Costa (6 years old), Lucy Costa (4 years old), Frank Rubino, Patria Valdez, Eulala Valdez (8 years old), Mary Valdez (7 years old), Elvira Valdez (3 months old), Joe Petrucci (4 1/2 years old), Lucy Petrucci (2 1/2 years old), Frank Petrucci (6 months old), William Snyder (11 years old), Rodgerlo Pedregone (6 years old), and Cloriva Pedregone (4 years old).[58] As one can see, about half of those slaughtered were of Italian origin.[59] The other victims came from diverse ethnic backgrounds. Italians, Greeks, Slavs, Mexicans, Austrians, and even British-born immigrants represented the vast bulk of those on strike. The reason they went on strike was because they were treated like animals (or perhaps worse). Armed guards constantly watched the miners, and they were denied basic freedoms such as living and shopping where they wanted. As Italian-American commentator Floyd Vivino put it, "They were denied the rights of civilized people" (Mangione and Morreale, 1993: 268-269; "Ludlow Massacre," Holt Labor Library; *Italian Tribune*, Feb. 6, 2003).

Upon striking in September of 1913, the miners and their families were evicted from the company owned dwellings they inhabited. With little options, and facing the elements, they swiftly set up a tent colony on public property near the Ludlow coal mines. About a thousand men, women, and children lived there for a period of several months, through the long, hard Colorado winter. All the while, their employer, John D. Rockefeller's Colorado Fuel and Iron Company, strove to break their resolve and make their lives even more of a living hell. The Colorado state militia—CFI company guards, strikebreakers, and hired thugs were all used in order to terrorize the impoverished immigrant miners. For months, these forces physically beat the miners, arrested hundreds of them, trampled their wives on horseback, and more—still the strike was not subdued. The most stringent measure taken by Rockefeller and his company occurred on April 20, 1914, when the Baldwin Felts Detective Agency was called in. Members of this agency patrolled the Ludlow tent camp in an armored car that had a machine gun mounted on it; they then sprayed the camp with bullets and set the miners' tents ablaze. These dastardly acts claimed 18 lives that day ("The Ludlow Massacre," UMWA website; Mangione and Morreale, 1993: 268; "The following was..." Spunk.org).

When news of the massacre spread, Ivy Lee, one of Rockefeller's public relations men, stated that the two women and eleven children died as a result of an overturned stove—not because CFI purposely slaughtered them. As if the many machine gun bullets were not enough to disprove Lee's shameful statement, it was later found through investigation that kerosene had been poured on the tents deliberately. Nonetheless, Ivy Lee's whitewashing of the Ludlow Massacre so impressed Hitler, years later, that the Third Reich hired him to paint a favorable picture of the "New Germany" within the U.S. ("The Ludlow Massacre and the Birth of Company Unions," Hartford-hwp.com; "The Ludlow Massacre," UMWA website). Surely, such a man could have sold the American people on the great benefits of putting undesirables in concentration camps. Fortunately, we are not *that* gullible.

Thus ended the Ludlow Massacre; however, the strike itself continued until the end of 1914. In fourteen months' time, nothing had been gained but 66 deaths and hundreds of casualties. Yet while the strike ended in temporary failure, the legacy of the Ludlow Massacre (much like the Triangle Shirtwaist tragedy) gained popular sympathy and helped stimulate progressive reforms. (It should be known that no one was ever punished for the massacre that took place on April 20, 1914) ("Colorado Coal Field War," ColoradoDigital.Coalliance.org; "The Ludlow Massacre," UMWA website).

August 28, 1914: The second worst mining disaster in West Virginian history occurred at the No. 5 mine in Eccles, claiming over 180 lives. Approximately thirty of the men killed (or 1/6) were of Italian origin.[60]

October 12, 1914: Albert Piazza (a subject of Italy) was lynched outside the small mining town of Willisville, Illinois, by a mob of 30 to 40 people.[61] The day before (October 11), Piazza and his brother got into a fight with two "Americans" on the streets of Willisville—both Americans were mortally injured (one dying of his wounds on Oct. 12, the other on the 13th) and Piazza's brother was killed instantly.

Willisville's population was divided rather evenly at this time between native-born Americans and foreign-born Italians, with each group staying in their own respective parts of town. In addition to both sides mistrusting each other, the native-born harbored a particularly acute hatred for the Italians, and scuffles between the "races" were frequent. So when the native citizenry found out that two Americans had been harmed (and eventually died) as a result of an altercation they had with an Italian alien, their fury was kindled. On October 12, the streets were filled with hundreds of outraged citizens, and a crowd gathered around the jail that held Piazza. It was then decided by the authorities to move the prisoner to the county jail—but before the carriage holding him arrived at its destination (in a scene reminiscent of past lynchings), a group of approximately three dozen vigilantes surrounded it and shot Albert Piazza repeatedly in cold blood. There were at least a hundred bullets fired into his body; and it appeared as if Willisville's mayor had even played a role in the lynching. In the end, however, only one man was punished for the lynching of Albert Piazza—he served 90 days in the county jail (*Yale Law Journal*, May 1916: 561-566; Iorizzo and Mondello, 1980: 290; *Marion Evening Post*, Oct. 13-14, 1914). No matter how outrageous this light sentence seems to us today, it was actually an improvement from the days when no one would so much as be reprimanded for lynching a "dago."

In the immediate aftermath of Piazza's lynching, the press made it seem as if a race war between the Americans and the Italians was inevitable. It never came (*Marion Evening Post*, Oct. 13-14, 1914).[62]

1914-1915: Met Life gathered information on the heights and weights of 10,000 child workers in New York City (about 1/5 of whom were Italian) and found the Italian children to be shorter and lighter than all the others (Foerster, 1969: 387).

1915: *The Italian*, a silent film starring George Beban was released. It was probably the first movie to stereotype Italians as a vengeful, slum-dwelling people.[63]

June 10, 1915: Joe Speranza was lynched in Johnston City, Illinois (not too far from where Albert Piazza was killed).[64] The circumstances surrounding this lynching were quite similar to those in the Piazza case a year before. Johnston City, like Willisville, was a mining town that had a divided population, half native and half foreign, and great antipathy existed between the two sides. As was the case in so many other places, anti-Italian racism pervaded many facets of daily life in Johnston City and naturally affected both sides of the town. And so, on June 9, when a mine superintendent's father-in-law was found murdered in his home, immediate suspicion fell on the Italians and an alleged Black Hand (or Mafia) society. (While it is likely that the former Willisville case triggered, to some extent, the anti-Italian sentiment in Johnston City, the Mafia stereotype was also to blame.) It was therefore decreed that all Italians suspected of *anything* be rounded up for questioning. The search party, looking for defenseless Italians to sacrifice, came across Joe Speranza the following morning. Although there was no proof, *whatsoever,* that he had done anything wrong, Speranza was taken into custody. That day, some one thousand angry citizens banded together and marched on to the village jail. While the chief of police conveniently went home for lunch, members of the mob broke into the jail, pulled Speranza from his cell, and hanged him a block away, near the railroad station (*Marion Daily Republican*, Jun. 11, 1915; *Yale Law Journal*, May 1916: 566-567; Iorizzo and Mondello, 1980: 290). Thus, an American mob, sacrificed its latest Italian victim. Once again Americans proved that nativism was not driven by justice, but by an "eye for an eye" mentality, which, more often than not, killed the innocent. Such ruthless acts of "mob justice" also proved that White Anglo-Saxon Protestants could be as "hot-blooded" (to use a phrase commonly hurled at Italians) as any other group when it comes to committing crimes.

Joe Speranza was the first person to be publicly lynched in Williamson County, Illinois; however, it would not be the last time that Italians were victimized by racist mobs here. (In only a few short years, anti-Italian riots erupted giving the county a new reputation; from then on, it would be referred to as "Bloody Williamson.") On the very same day that Joe Speranza was lynched, an Italian storekeeper and his family narrowly escaped death when anti-Italian racists bombed them. Interestingly, just a few days later John Garavalgia, a man described as a "north Italian" (as opposed to the "Sicilian" Joe Speranza),was put on trial in nearby Herrin, Illinois, for killing a policeman. The trial was described as the "most sensational" in Herrin's history—so many attended that there was not enough room in the courthouse, forcing large crowds to gather outside. This was at a time when the press identified a person of Italian background by his "race" first (either "Italian" or "Sicilian") and the details of his alleged crime second. Anyhow, John Garavalgia maintained he acted in self-defense (*Marion Daily Republican*, Jun 11 & Jun. 14, 1915; Gambino, 1974: 119-120; Higham, 1973: 264-265).

October 1915: Former President Theodore Roosevelt *again* went out of his way to insult Italian-Americans and *all* the children of immigrants when he stated the following in a speech to the Knights of Columbus in New York's Carnegie Hall: "There is no room in this country for hyphenated Americans.... There is no such thing as a hyphenated American who is a good American." That same year the current president, Woodrow Wilson, made his own anti-ethnic declamation: "hyphenated Americans...have poured the poison of disloyalty into the very arteries of our national life...such creatures of passion, disloyalty and anarchy must be crushed out" (Gambino, 1974: 118; Lagumina, 1999: 231-232). The persecution of people for ethnic and political reasons, occurring on a grand scale during the World War I period, should come as no surprise—America's premiere leaders were the ones fanning the flames of fear and xenophobia.

1916: A book by racial theorist Madison Grant was published titled *The Passing of the Great Race.* Widely acclaimed at the time, the book was indicative of mainstream America's contempt for foreigners and ethnics, especially Mediterraneans. Richard Gambino gave it an accurate review: "The great race was the WASP ethnic group, or, as Grant called it, 'the Nordics.' The thesis of the book was as simple as it was vicious. The immigrants of Eastern and Southern Europe were 'storming the Nordic ramparts of the United States and mongrelizing the good old American stock,' and threatening to destroy American institutions. Grant singled out Italians as inferiors. In his crackpot explanation, Italians are the inferior descendants of the slaves who survived when ancient Rome died." Grant also believed that if and when the United States entered the Great War, it would be Anglo-Americans and "Nordic" Europeans who perished to near extinction. Little did he know that Italian-Americans (only 4 percent of the U.S. population) comprised a full 10 percent of all U.S. casualties (Gambino, 1974: 123, 318).

December 14, 1916: NAACP records show that a non-black named "Paulo Boleta" (probably *Paolo Boletta*) was lynched on this date in Greenwich, New York, for allegedly committing a "murderous assault" (Katz, 1969: 83).

February 5, 1917: Congress passed a literacy law, which was specifically designed to bar many Italians from entering the U.S. This restrictive law excluded immigrants who could not read a particular passage in a particular language (not necessarily English). Although such a policy had been pushed for since the 1890s, when Italians started immigrating in alarming numbers, it gained official acceptance now because America was on the brink of entering World War I and was going through a period of anti-foreign/anti-radical paranoia. Ethnic and racial diversity was deemed inimical to America at this time (Gambino, 1998: 138; Higham, 1973: 202-205).

September 1917: In the Italian section of Milwaukee, immigrant and Methodist minister August Giuliani led a patriotic march in support of American troops overseas. When local anti-war sentiment broke out, however, two Italians believed to be "anarchists" were killed while resisting police, and several others were wounded ("Milwaukee's Italian Flavor Runs Deep," OnMilwaukee.com; Foerster, 1969: 399).

Two months later, a cleaning woman at Giuliani's Third Ward church found a suspicious package and notified the police, but they never came. So, a young male parishioner took the package to the police station himself. When it was opened it exploded, killing 10 (including a civilian woman). This incident, though accidental on the part of the young man, was responsible for the greatest loss of law enforcement prior to the tragedy of September 11, 2001. Following the explosion, there were roundups of Milwaukee Italians and anti-Italian sentiment ran high ("Milwaukee's Italian Flavor," OnMilwaukee.com).

1918: A small book, *Italian Prisoner's of War and the Enemy's Barbarity*, was published in English. It exposed the many war crimes that the Austrian army perpetrated against thousands of Italian POWs. (A sizeable portion of the victims could have been Italian Americans, who had returned from America to enlist in the Italian army—that was common during World War I.) The reader sees, on page after page, photographs of the extremely gaunt and emaciated Italians. The images are identical to the familiar scenes of the Holocaust. Upon reading testimony of the atrocities committed, it is undeniably clear that the Austrians cared little (if at all) for the lives of the Italians and regarded them as racially inferior (Unione Tipografico-Editrice Torinese, 1918: 1-19). Although these were the absolute worst conditions any group of human beings could be subjected to, this was nothing new to the long-suffering Italian people. Italians had been subjected to the genocidal acts of European conquerors (including Austrians) for many centuries.

1919: Italian parishioners at Our Lady of Mount Carmel, in East Harlem, were finally allowed to worship in the main part of the church. Before this, for a period of 35 years, they were forced to worship in the basement, even though they constituted the overwhelming majority of church members (Orsi, 1985: 54; Cordasco, 1974: 237-238).[65]

1919 was also the year in which Robert Foerster's *The Italian Emigration of Our Times* was originally published. The book is an invaluable source of information on Italian emigrants to all parts of the world, spanning the period of the *Risorgimento* to the First World War. It opens ones eyes to the fact that Italian migrants in other countries endured living and labor conditions that were the same as in America, and oftentimes worse.[66]

March 1919: A. Mitchell Palmer took office as the new Attorney General (Higham, 1973: 229). "During his three-year tenure of office, he raised a red scare to mammoth proportions by prosecuting aliens, including Italians, as suspicious and dangerous radicals. His most infamous tactic was the Palmer raid. Agents of the Department of Justice would descend upon an immigrant family, or sometimes a whole neighborhood, in the middle of the night, arresting people indiscriminately. In violation of every decent legal ethic and the due process of law itself, non citizens were kept incommunicado by Palmer's witch hunters, and many were summarily deported. Years later, inquiries failed to find any links between those deported and subversion. It was cold consolation to those sent back to the Old World misery they had labored so hard to escape. This insane persecution, equating foreign birth with subversiveness, created panic among all immigrant groups. Among Italians, it strengthened their insularity from the larger society--an old inclination traceable to the maxim of the Mezzogiorno that 'the law works against the people'." (Gambino, 1974: 117-118).

May 6, 1919: Labor leader and radical Nino Capraro was abducted by "a gang of hired thugs" and driven to a remote location "where they beat him senseless and threatened to lynch him" (Mangione and Morreale, 1993: 303). A mill workers' strike was taking place in Lawrence, Massachusetts, at the time. Capraro had been championing a 48-hour-work week with 54-hour pay. Obviously, this cause was considered by some to be too "radical," but the strikers stood firm in their demands. Later that month the strike ended in success; the workers were granted "a 15 percent increase [in pay] and a promise of no discrimination against the strikers" (Mangione and Morreale, 1993: 301-303).

Era of Americanization and Political Persecution— (1920s to 1950s)

April 15, 1920: A group of five men robbed a shoe factory in Braintree, Massachusetts, killing a paymaster and guard, and then fleeing in a car with $15,000. Witnesses claimed that the holdup men looked Italian. Thus, "When two Italians, Nicola Sacco, a factory worker from Puglia in South Italy, and Bartolomeo Vanzetti, a mustached fish peddler from the Northern Italian province of Piedmont, came to claim a car that police had linked with the crime, they were arrested" (Gambino, 1974: 120; Mangione and Morreale, 1993: 299).

On May 3, 1920—two days before Sacco and Vanzetti were arrested at gunpoint while trying to hide their *anarchistic literature* (not weapons or money)—fellow anarchist Andrea Salsedo (a Brooklyn painter) "either jumped or was pushed to his death from the fourteenth-floor window of the Justice Department's offices." He was one of the many victims of the "Palmer Raid," as he was arrested in the middle of the night without due process. It was also revealed that Salsedo had been tortured by the Department of Justice. Bartolomeo Vanzetti, prior to his arrest, went to New York to investigate Salsedo's disappearance (Mangione and Morreale, 1993: 297-298). Right then and there, he probably got in over his head.

"Anti-Italian fever was virulent" when Sacco and Vanzetti were arrested, and "when it was discovered that they were under surveillance by Palmer's

Department of Justice as political anarchists and that they carried firearms, a cry for their heads was raised all over the land." Nonetheless, "Circumstances linking them to the crime were questionable," and furthermore the men "were tried under conditions that were a mockery of the judicial process and found guilty. The prosecuting attorney appealed to the worst biases of the jury, treating Italian-American witnesses in an outrageously insulting manner. The testimony of eighteen Italian-born witnesses was dismissed out of hand by the court as unreliable....After the trial, the judge who had presided is alleged to have commented to a Dartmouth professor: 'Did you see what I did to those anarchistic bastards the other day? I guess that will hold them for a while.' The same judge, Webster Thayer, an old immigrant-hating pillar of Back Bay Society, one year before had presided over another trial in which Vanzetti had been accused of a holdup in Plymouth. At the time, the judge had instructed the jury that, 'this man, although he may not actually have committed the crime attributed to him, is nevertheless morally culpable, because he is the enemy of our existing institutions.... The defendant's ideals are cognate with crime.' Despite the testimony of thirty witnesses, that Vanzetti was elsewhere at the time of the crime, Vanzetti was convicted of the Plymouth holdup." (Gambino, 1974: 120).

During the trial of Sacco and Vanzetti, "nine witnesses, including the clerk of the Italian Consulate, swore that Sacco was in Boston at the time of the Braintree robbery. Six witnesses placed Vanzetti in Plymouth making his door-to-door rounds as a peddler during the time of the crime. The two Italians were found guilty, and after seven years of protests and appeals they were executed" (Gambino, 1974: 120-121). Only after it was too late did it surface that some of the key witnesses for the prosecution were vehement Italophobes. Apparently much of the case rested on the belief that since the perpetrators "looked Italian" (i.e. were of dark complexions), they *had to be* the two Italians on trial (Lagumina, 1999: 240-241). The jury could have easily been persuaded by the racist beliefs of the time.

Harvard University's president headed a commission that found nothing wrong with Sacco and Vanzetti's trial. This prompted a reporter for the New York *World* to sarcastically write the following: "What more can the immigrants from Italy expect? It is not every person who has a president of Harvard University throw the switch for him. If this is a lynching, at least the fish-peddler and his friend, the factory hand, may take unction to their souls that they will die at the hands of men in denim jackets or academic gowns" (Gambino, 1974: 121).

An innumerable amount of Italian-Americans contributed to Sacco and Vanzetti's defense fund, the vast majority believing that the two had been railroaded simply because they were Italian—a simple yet very plausible belief. As Jerre Mangione and Ben Morreale put it, "The trial pitted two immigrant workers against all those of power and authority" who were threatened by immigration and those with different political views—such people felt threatened by the very principles of democracy. "That these two foreigners were as intellectually and socially aware as the most educated American was another source of fear and resentment" (Mangione and Morreale, 1993: 299).

Before he was sentenced, Nicola Sacco stated in court: "I know the sentence will be between two class, the oppressed class and the rich class, there will be always collision between one and the other. We fraternize the people with books, with the literature. You persecute the people, tyrannize over them, and kill them. We try the education of people always. You try to put a path between us and some other nationality that hates each other. This is why I am here today on this bench, for having been the oppressed class. Well, you are the oppressor" (Mangione and Morreale, 1993: 299).

Denying his own guilt before sentencing as well, Vanzetti stated: "I would not wish to a dog or to a snake, to the most low and misfortunate creature of the earth—I would not wish to any of them what I have had to suffer for things that I am not guilty of. But my conviction is that I have suffered for things that I am guilty of. I am suffering because I am a radical and indeed I am a radical; I have suffered because I was an Italian, and indeed I am an Italian" (Mangione and Morreale, 1993: 299-300).

Richard Gambino summed up the aftermath of the Sacco and Vanzetti case perfectly: "The outcome of the affair was simply another confirmation of the ancient belief of the Italian immigrants that justice, a very important part of their value system, had little to do with the laws and institutions of the state. The poison of the Sacco-Vanzetti affair was not to be purged from relations between Italian-Americans and the United States until years later when Italian-Americans faced a new crisis of nationality in World War II [this time, not being denounced as radicals but as *fascists*, on the opposite end of the political spectrum], and resolved it with resounding loyalty to the United States. The unequivocal loyalty of Italian-Americans to their country is astonishing when one considers much of their ill treatment at the hands of America" (Gambino, 1974: 122).[67]

August 1920: Anti-Italian mobs invaded the Italian section of West Frankfort, Illinois, "dragging people of all ages and both sexes from homes, beating them with weapons and burning whole rows of their homes." The Italians tried to fight back as best as they could, turning that part of southern Illinois (long a hostile and bloody region for Italians) into a veritable battleground. The violence lasted three days and required 500 state troopers to re-establish the peace. When it was all over, hundreds of Italian-Americans were homeless and a few had even died of their injuries (Gambino, 1974: 119-120; Higham, 1973: 264; *Illinois History*, Dec. 1999; "The Life of an Italian Immigrant," Cecilia P.).[68]

This outbreak of nativism was sparked by a "series of bank robberies, popularly attributed to a Black Hand Society," and by the discovery of the bodies of two "native" boys (i.e. white, non-Italian boys) who had recently been kidnapped (Higham, 1973: 264-265; "The Life of an Italian Immigrant," Cecilia P.).[69] (Once again it is perfectly clear how the Mafia image—or in this case, the "Black Hand" image—is as dangerous to the safety of Italian-Americans as it is to their emotional stability.) What also played a probable role in this particular outbreak of nativism was the fact that thousands of coal miners (natives as well as Italians) were "restless" and not working due to a strike (Higham, 1973: 264). It is easy to see how tensions could have mounted during such a time, but it does not excuse the atrocities and acts of hate that ensued.

What occurred in West Frankfort, Illinois, in August of 1920 was only the beginning of more anti-Italian acts to come. The KKK (recently reborn) and Protestant fundamentalist groups were chiefly to blame. They loathed the Italians on account of their non-Nordic, Mediterranean features, their Catholic religion, their foreign ways and poverty, job competition, the fact that they continued making wine during Prohibition, and on account of the belief that all Italians were corrupt and vicious. Around the same time as the riot in West Frankfort, the KKK conducted nighttime cross burnings on Italian property in other rural parts of the U.S., like Mechanicville, New York—by no means was the North exempt from such racial scare tactics ("The Life of an Italian," Cecilia P.; "Contadini in the New World Paese," Mechanicville.com).

December 10, 1920: Charles Valento was lynched in Santa Rosa, California.[70]

1921: A new immigration law went into effect, greatly limiting immigration from southern and eastern Europe. The new law was passed to ensure the continued dominance of "old stock" Americans (i.e. people who could trace their ancestry to the countries of northwestern Europe) and so that "in a generation the foreign-born would cease to be a major factor in American history." The anti-immigrant, pro-Nordic ranting of leading writers and politicians was obviously very popular and influential at this time (Higham, 1973: 311, 300-316).

In the February 1921 edition of *Good Housekeeping*, President Calvin Coolidge asserted his pro-Nordic stance, stating (like the countless other racial theorists of his day) that the "Nordic Race" deteriorates and degenerates when mixed with other "darker races" (Higham, 1973: 318).[71] Hence, the theory of, "mongrelization."

Anti-Catholic/anti-Italian feeling was summed up in these words which appeared on a 1922 coin minted by the KKK: "I would rather be a Klansman, in a robe of snowy white, than a Catholic Priest, in a robe as black as night, for a Klansman is an American and America is his home, but the Priest owes his allegiance to a dago Pope in Rome."

November 1921: After enduring "twelve months of hunger," Italian women working in Tampa's cigar factories walked out; they were then promptly arrested by the authorities. After that, "the leaders [of the strike] were walked to a spot where strikers had been lynched in 1908 and shown a rope. The strike collapsed; none of the Italians returned to the factories." Fear and intimidation had won the day (Mangione and Morreale, 1993: 278).

1921-1941: During this twenty-year period a total of 202 Italians were legally put to death in the United States (thus averaging 10 deaths per year). The numbers executed by each state are as follows: New York—71 (still the Italian execution capital of the world, up 5 executions from the last twenty year period); Pennsylvania—33; New Jersey—25; Ohio—16; Louisiana—12; California—10; Illinois—10; Massachusetts—5; West Virginia—5; Missouri—4; Colorado—2; Connecticut—2; Florida—2; Delaware—1; Indiana—1; Montana—1; Virginia—1; Washington D.C—1.[72]

1922: One Italian was lynched in Louisiana (Gambino, 1998: 135).

April 28, 1924: Exactly 10 years (*to the day*) after the mining disaster that claimed over 180 lives in Eccles, West Virginia, another occurred in Benwood killing 117. Approximately 30 Italians were killed in this disaster as well ("1924 Coal Mine Disaster," Rootsweb.com).

May 9, 1924: After experiencing police brutality and an unfair trial, six Italians were hanged for a botched robbery in Amite, Louisiana (Baiamonte, 1986: 30, 92, 226-238).

May 26, 1924: The infamous Immigration Act of 1924 (also known as the "National Origins Act" and the "Emergency Quota Law") was passed, restricting immigration from southern and eastern Europe even further (until it was virtually non-existent). Since the "immigration problem" was synonymous with a particular "race problem" of undesirable Italians, Jews, Greeks, and Slavs flocking to America, both problems, in the minds of the racist elite, would be solved with the passing of this new law (Higham, 1973: 316-324; Gambino, 1974: 124).

One of the sponsors of the Immigration Act, Senator Reed (R-PA), stated the following reasons for the new law: "There has come about a general realization of the fact that the races of men who have been coming to us in recent years are wholly dissimilar to the native-born Americans; that they are untrained in self-government—a faculty that it has taken the Northwestern Europeans many centuries to acquire. America was beginning also to smart under the irritation of her 'foreign colonies'—those groups of aliens, either in city slums or in country districts, who speak a foreign language and live a foreign life, and who want neither to learn our common speech nor to share our common life. From all this has grown the conviction that it was best for America that our incoming immigrants should hereafter be of the same races as those of us who are already here, so that each year's immigration should so far as possible be a miniature America, resembling in national origins the persons who are already settled in our country. It is true that 75 per cent of our immigration will hereafter come from Northwestern Europe; but it is fair that it should do so, because 75 per cent of us who are now here owe our origin to immigrants from those same countries" (*Literary Digest*, May 10, 1924: 12-13). Though more eloquent than his KKK supporters, Senator Reed nonetheless shared their concerns. That year (1924) the Ku Klux Klan had great influence on local, state, and national elections; and many of their own were elected to positions of power throughout the nation. Strong Klan sentiment also prevented the 1924 nomination of Al Smith as the Democratic candidate for President—Smith was both Catholic and of Italian descent (Higham, 1973: 321, 328; "People & Events," PBS.org).

Although the Immigration Act of 1924 was hard on Italians and other ethnic minorities at the time, American immigration laws were to become even more anti-Italian as the years went by. Latin Americans and Canadians benefited, however, since the 1924 law did not restrict immigrants from countries of the Western Hemisphere (Gambino, 1974: 122).[73]

Around the time of the 1924 immigration law, a war was raging between Italian-Americans and the Ku Klux Klan in Herrin, Illinois (not too far from West Frankfort). A lack of strict law enforcement allowed saloons to operate visibly during this era of Prohibition, to the chagrin of many native whites, who had supported a *different* kind of "tolerance" movement (i.e. an anti-alcoholic movement). Mobilizing on popular outrage, the Klan decided to go after Herrin's most visible and oppressed immigrant community—the Italian Catholics. Mass raids on Italian homes and pitched battles between the two sides carried on for 2 years. The Klan even "seized the city government by force" at one point (Higham, 1973: 295; Angle, 1992: 134-205). In addition to the obvious ethno-religious hatred, Klansmen and other nativists disdained the historical affinity Italians had for wine. Nonetheless, the fact that Italians were neither Anglo-Saxon nor Protestant was the main reason they were attacked repeatedly during the 1920s. The Klan's platform against Catholics and "foreigners" even took precedence over the hatred of blacks for a time (Higham, 1973: 290-295).

In some rare instances, the Klan actually fell prey to the hyphenated Americans' wrath. There was a series of anti-Klan outbreaks in 1923. One case occurred in Perth Amboy, New Jersey, when a mob of 6,000 (jointly led by Catholics and Jews) "closed in on a Klan meeting place, overwhelmed the entire police and fire departments, and fell upon some five hundred Ku Kluxers, kicking, stoning, and beating them as they fled" (Higham, 1973: 298-299).[74]

Memorial Day 1927: Two Italians were killed when a brawl broke out between pro-Fascists and anti-Fascists in an Italian section of New York City. While it is true that many Italian-Americans looked up to Mussolini during the 20s and 30s (not so much on account of his ideology, but because he was a symbol of Italian strength and because he played on the feelings of inferiority that Italians seemed to have experienced everywhere they lived in the diaspora), it is also true that most anti-Fascist activity in the United States was first carried out by Italian-American groups. The labor leader Carlo Tresca organized a great deal of anti-Fascist resistance within Italian-American communities, and the impending confrontations were often violent. On one occasion, more than a dozen lives were lost. When two "Black Shirts" (i.e. Italian Fascists) were killed on Memorial Day in 1927, New York City police raided Tresca's newspaper offices, destroying property and beating workers—yet no evidence was found linking Tresca or his newspaper to the killings (Mangione and Morreale, 1993: 318-320).

August 22, 1927: After seven years of international and domestic protest demanding the release of Sacco and Vanzetti, the two Italians were executed in Massachusetts. It is maintained by many that the execution of Sacco and Vanzetti "was just as much a lynching as that of the more than thirty Italians lynched elsewhere in the nation" (Mangione and Morreale, 1993: 301).[75]

1928: An anti-Catholic campaign spearheaded by the KKK "flared up violently" when New York Governor—and long time champion of the poor—Al Smith ran for president. Smith was viewed as "the Pope incarnate" (Higham, 1973: 329). Though he was thought to be of strictly Irish heritage at the time (and certainly no Italian-Americans identified with him ethnically), Al Smith's "biggest secret" was recently revealed—that his father was of Italian background (Publishers Weekly online). Given the times, it is understandable why Smith wanted to keep that side of him hidden; after all, he had enough trouble just being Catholic! America was nowhere near ready to elect an Italian-American/Catholic president. In many ways, it is still not ready. One can imagine the kind of severe scrutiny and hostility he would have been subjected to if he "came out of the closet," so to speak, about his Italian background.

May 18, 1929: An "altercation" occurred that resulted in the lynching of E.R. Romeo in Columbia, Florida.[76]

1930s: This decade saw a marked decrease in nativism and race consciousness in America, mainly because: 1) southern and eastern Europeans were no longer coming in considerable numbers (due to the Immigration Act of 1924), 2) the Ku Klux Klan lost the powerful grip it had on the nation, and 3) the Great Depression forced people to worry less about each others' backgrounds and to focus more on day to day survival. In addition, the paranoia Americans had of foreign radicals diminished greatly. Many now had pro-leftist sympathies because they were out of work and experienced poverty for the first time (Higham, 1973: 324-328). A new *class* consciousness took root in the U.S., gaining the most ground among mainstream Americans.

This is not to say that anti-Italian racism was nowhere to be found in 1930s America—it only took a more subtle form, as in the cinematic stereotyping of Italian-Americans. Instead of coming straight out and saying how dangerous and degenerate Italians were (as the newspapers had done for years) the cinema would get its message across by constantly portraying Italians as criminals and buffoons under the guise of "entertainment" or "art." Movies like *Little Caesar* (1931) and *Scarface* (1932) set the standard for a countless number of subsequent films defaming Italian-Americans.[77]

1932: John Picco, who served as the Italian Consul in Springfield, Illinois, was murdered in an apparent hate crime. At the time of his death, Picco was investigating the anti-Italian riots that had occurred in southern Illinois a decade earlier. Picco's home was also "twice the target of bombs." Obviously, John Picco was getting too close to finding out who was responsible for the violence. His assassins were never brought to justice (*Italian History*, Dec. 1999).

1934: Henry Luce's *Fortune* magazine praised Italy's Fascist Party and Mussolini while at the same time degraded the Italian people. Through fascism, the magazine declared, "Wops are unwopping themselves" (Gambino, 1974: 319). Many other prominent Americans, including Cole Porter and even President Roosevelt, made no attempt at hiding their support of Italy's Fascists during the early 1930s (up until Italy invaded Ethiopia)—this, at a time when Italian-Americans were being persecuted for their own support of Mussolini.

October 1935: When Italy invaded Ethiopia, rioting broke out between Italians and blacks in Harlem. The violence was sparked when a contingent of African-Americans disturbed the businesses of Italian vendors on 118th Street, carrying a sign, which read "Let's get Italians out of Harlem." Fistfights were the main acts of violence during the riot, yet 10 percent of New York City's entire police force was mobilized into action. In Brooklyn, fights broke out between black and Italian youths. Police had to respond to anti-Italian disturbances in other cities as well (Ashyk, 1999: 124-125; Lagumina, 1999: 251).[78]

Animosity between Italians and blacks in Harlem had been building up for months due to a growing international situation between Italy and Ethiopia. The Great Depression was also a cause of tension (though to a lesser degree) since both groups were competing for jobs at the bottom of the social ladder, and since Italians were expanding into black neighborhoods in Harlem, renting apartments, and displacing the inhabitants. (Conversely, in South Philadelphia, blacks had begun moving toward Italian areas.) Despite the current conflict of interests, the blacks of Harlem and the Italians of East Harlem (for many years the nation's largest "Little Italy") had gotten along peacefully and rather amicably. Both groups recognized the fact that they were oppressed people. This commonality is the reason that tensions did not last long after the October 1935 riot. Though the press tried to exploit the situation and create hostility between the two groups over and over again, the Italians and blacks of Harlem did not let them succeed (Ashyk, 1999: 122-123, 128-129, 131-132, 135).

Memorial Day 1937: In Chicago, police became extremely belligerent when striking steel workers formed a picket line near the plant that had employed them. When the non-violent strikers declared that they had a legal right to picket, the cops exclaimed, "You got no rights. You Red bastards, you got no rights." At that point, tear gas was fired into the line of strikers (which included their wives and children). Adrenaline-filled cops then started shooting their revolvers into the breaking line. When one woman fell to the ground, "four cops gathered above her, smashing in her flesh and bones and face." (This was at a time when many of our "finest" thought nothing of beating up on prostitutes and street peddlers in cities all over the nation—especially in Chicago, crooked town that it was.) When the acts of unwarranted police aggression finally ended, ten were left dead, and over a hundred were wounded. World War I veterans who were present even went on record stating that they had never witnessed anything as brutal and cowardly as this in Europe. Among those killed were two strikers of Italian background: Anthony Tagliori and Leo Francisco. This infamous incident in American labor history (occurring exactly ten years after 2 Italians were killed for political reasons) became known as the "Memorial Day Massacre" (Trussel.com).

December 1940: Due to excessive ridicule by his non-Italian peers, an Italian-American schoolboy (whose name was never disclosed) attempted suicide in a major metropolitan area. The boy later told his Italian-American doctor that he was victimized on a daily basis simply for the political and military policies of Italy (to which he felt no attachment). This was not at all a lone incident. Similar culture clashes between Anglo- and Italian-Americans occurred to such an extent that Italians in the United States had triple the suicide rate of Italians in Italy (Lagumina, 1999: 254-255; Mangione and Morreale, 1993: 219).

1941-1945: The World War II period was an extremely trying time for Italian-Americans, as a great paradox occurred during these years: At the same time hundreds of thousands of Italian-Americans were fighting for their country abroad, many tens of thousands more had their civil liberties violated at home (by the same government they were fighting for). Fortunately, in the end, there would be no doubt as to where their loyalty and patriotism stood—for just as the Civil War acted as the conflict in which Irish-Americans proved themselves, the World War II period proved beyond a shadow of a doubt that Italian-Americans were indeed loyal and even fiercely patriotic. It must not be forgotten, however, that this eventual acceptance (limited though it was) came at a great cost—and that cost was a campaign of terror waged against law abiding Italian-Americans, resulting in the destruction of their civil liberties and the accelerated abandonment of certain characteristics deemed "un-American" (such as speaking Italian).[79]

For decades, long before the outbreak of the Second World War, the question of Italian-American loyalty to the United States arose a countless number of times publicly, privately, and in the political realm. Such scrutiny was not reserved for Italian-Americans alone, but for minorities of all kinds. However, because the Italians had been the largest immigrant population in the last decades, and because they were culturally, ethnically, and religiously different from the WASP majority—thus being one of the most visible minorities in the U.S., and one of the least assimilable, they were among those groups exposed to a greater scrutiny. This was certainly the case on the eve of World War II. As soon as war broke out in Europe—two years before the U.S. joined the fight—the FBI had already compiled ABC lists of Italian aliens. These were essentially "enemy lists" in which the Director of the FBI, J. Edgar Hoover, indiscriminately listed the elderly and the young, male and female, regardless of any background information on the individuals (other than the fact that they were Italian). Hoover's effort was so shaped by paranoia that Attorney General Francis Biddle admitted, at a later date, the lists could neither logically determine who was a threat to U.S. security, nor justifiably detain the accused. Logic and justice obviously did not matter to Hoover and his FBI, however (*Italian-American Internment*, The History Channel; *Report to the Congress...* U.S. Dept. of Justice: 2-3; "When Speaking Italian Was a Crime," About.com).

On March 30, 1941 (more than 8 months before war was officially declared), President Franklin D. Roosevelt took action against Italian interests, ordering the U.S. Coast Guard to board "enemy" ships on both the East and West Coasts even though the vessels were of a commercial or merchant nature, and not a threat militarily. In all, twenty-eight Italian ships were seized and 1200 Italian crewmen arrested at gunpoint. The 1200 men (plus hundreds more) were sent to Ellis Island where they were incarcerated in cramped, squalid quarters—ironically, in the shadow of the Statue of Liberty. Also arrested were 62 Italian waiters who over-extended their visas. From Ellis Island, the prisoners were then shipped to Fort Missoula in Montana (the most well-known internment camp that held Italians and, later on, Italian-American non-citizens). They began arriving on May 9, 1941 (*Italian-American Internment*, The History Channel).[80]

Only hours after the Japanese attacked Pearl Harbor (**on December 7, 1941**), "the FBI took into custody hundreds of Italian-American aliens previously classified as 'dangerous' and shipped them to camps where they were imprisoned until Italy surrendered in 1943" (Commdocs.house.gov, p. 10).[81] In the days immediately following Pearl Harbor, "scores of persons of Italian descent, most but not all of them aliens," had their homes raided by federal agents and "generally were not told the specific reason for the raid, only that their arrest was 'by order of President Roosevelt.'" Many of the unsuspecting Italians had their homes broken into in the middle of the night, while they were sound asleep, were ordered to get dressed and were whisked away without knowing (and without their families knowing) where or why they were being taken (U.S. DOJ, Part II, Sec. A, p. 5). On December 8, the United States issued Proclamation 2527 against Italy; Italian nationals living in the U.S. were thus officially "rendered 'enemy aliens' and were subject to apprehension, detention, and various restrictions" (U.S. DOJ, Appendix B, p. 2). Eventually hundreds of Italian-Americans and thousands more of Italian ancestry were placed in camps of internment scattered all over the U.S. They remained imprisoned in these camps for many months. The courts never convicted one of these "enemy aliens," however, on charges of sabotage (*Italian-American Internment*, The History Channel).[82]

Fearing another imminent Japanese attack, the West Coast was declared, on December 11, a "Western Theatre of Operations" by the Western Defense Command. That same day, the ultra-aggressive Lieutenant General John L. DeWitt was put in charge of the WDC. Wasting no time, DeWitt called for the removal of *all* Japanese, Italian, and German aliens from the "Pacific Slope" (i.e. the vast region stretching from the Pacific Ocean to the Sierra Nevada mountains). Though this particular plan of his was never fully acted upon, it did explain why Italians and other "enemy alien" nationalities were more persecuted on the West Coast than in the East (U.S. DOJ, Appendix B, p. 3 & Section B, p. 9).

On December 12, the day after DeWitt was appointed to his new post, the U.S. Navy requisitioned 15 fishing boats belonging to "enemy aliens" in San Francisco and Monterey. All of the vessels were the property of hardworking Italian-American citizens and non-citizens. Thus began the restrictions placed on Italian-American fishermen and the destruction of their civil liberties and livelihoods (U.S. DOJ, Part II, Sec. D, pp. 30-37 & Appendices B, G, H, I and J). In addition to individual families being hurt by such policies, as Joe DiMaggio's family was (even though the baseball legend and his brother both enlisted in the army), the loss of so many Italian-American fishermen on the West Coast did not help the wartime economy.

Posters of propaganda soon popped up calling for an increase in "American" fishermen; to boost patriotism and productivity, fish was referred to as a "fighting food" —all this because loyal Italian-Americans, who sent their sons overseas to die in record numbers, were *prevented* from going about their business and doing their part in the war effort. Increasing hostility toward Italians caused them to lose employment in other fields as well (*Italian-American Internment*, The History Channel). California's governor even proposed that all enemy aliens "forfeit their businesses and their professional licenses." Fortunately, this extreme step was never taken. However, even when Italians did not lose their jobs outright, a watchful eye was kept on them in many cases.

In New York, "several labor unions, including the International Longshoremen's Association whose membership contained a high percentage of Italians, placed the Italians in special working gangs"—this, on the less oppressive side of the nation (Pisani, 1957: 205-206). Conversely, in many parts of the nation, Italian-Americans actually benefited to some degree from the general labor shortage that the war produced—for it opened up new employment opportunities to them. Still, as in so many other industries, "Italians often met with discrimination in attempting to find employment in war work. Employment managers were sometimes highly dubious about hiring men in any way connected with an enemy country, no matter how slightly" (Mangione and Morreale, 1993: 341; Pisani, 1957: 206).[83]

On December 30, 1941, FBI agents "were given the authority to search the homes of enemy aliens if there was reason to suspect contraband (i.e., radios, guns, or cameras) on the premises" (U.S. DOJ, Appendix B, p. 3). The following was found after "spot searches were conducted in almost 2,900 Italian homes across the nation": "1,632 individuals had contraband confiscated. Roughly, two-thirds of these searches were conducted in just four states: New York and Pennsylvania on the East Coast, California on the West Coast, and Louisiana along the Gulf of Mexico. In these four states, 1,907 searches of Italian-American homes were conducted, resulting in 1,077 instances of contraband confiscation. The coastal locations of New York Harbor, San Francisco Bay, and New Orleans were apparently determining factors in the concentration of raids. Nationwide, the confiscation rate averaged 56%, although Massachusetts and Louisiana had higher rates. A majority of searches was conducted on the East Coast" (U.S. DOJ, Part II, Sec. C, p. 24). That Massachusetts and Louisiana had the highest rates of confiscation is not surprising when one considers the former state's historic mistrust of Italians (as in the Lowell Strike and the Sacco and Vanzetti case) and the latter's unmatched oppression of them (as in the numerous lynchings). January 5, 1942 was the "deadline for enemy aliens in San Francisco to surrender radio transmitters, shortwave receivers, and precision cameras to the Western Defense Command" (U.S. DOJ, Appendix B, p. 3). Confiscating, or rather *stealing*, the Italians' radios, cameras, and other personal possessions, was as unproductive for the war effort as it was foolish and a waste of time. The act of "confiscation," much like rape, was a demonstration of power more than anything else—government power.

On January 14, 1942, Roosevelt signed Presidential Proclamation 2537 "requiring that enemy aliens register to obtain Certificates of Identification from the Attorney General and carry them at all times" (U.S. DOJ, Appendix B, pp. 3-4).

One month later, on **February 19, 1942,** President Roosevelt signed Executive Order 9066 giving the Secretary of War the authority "to exclude any and all persons from designated [geographical] areas" (U.S. DOJ, Appendix B, p. 4). This act led to the greatest erosion of civil liberties during the war years—it affected people of Italian, Japanese, and German ancestry. As a result of Executive Order 9066, approximately 52,000 Italian-American non-citizens in the state of California "were subjected to a curfew that confined them to their homes between 8 p.m. and 6 a.m. and a travel restriction that prohibited them from traveling further than 5 miles from their homes. These measures made it difficult, if not impossible, for some Italian Americans to travel to their jobs, and thousands were arrested for violations of these and other restrictions" (*Italian-American Internment*, The History Channel).[84]

On February 24, also as a result of Executive Order 9066, enemy aliens were ordered to evacuate scores of "prohibited zones" on the West Coast. Ten thousand Italian-American non-citizens residing in California were forced from coastal and military areas. "Most of those who had to abandon their homes were elderly, some of whom were taken away in wheelchairs and on stretchers." The so-called "enemy aliens" were also restricted from—and ordered to evacuate—"areas surrounding forts, camps, arsenals, airports, electric or power plants, docks, piers, railroad terminals, depots, yards, and other storage facilities" (U.S. DOJ, Appendix B, pp. 4-5; Commdocs.house.gov, p. 11). And so it appears that the U.S. government was ready to wage a war on prospective terror some 60 years before the attack on 9/11. There was only one problem: Unlike the 19 Arabs responsible for bringing down the Twin Towers, Italians had never committed an act of terror designed to bring down the U.S. government—their only crime was being a part of that immigrant tide responsible for "building things up" in America. Furthermore, most of the 600,000 "enemy aliens" of Italian background had lived in the United States for more than 20 years—many even had sons fighting in the war (*Italian-American Internment*, The History Channel).

Depending on the source, between 500,000 and 1.5 million Italian-Americans served in World War II.[85] This made them the single largest ethnic group fighting to defend and uphold American democracy. This also made Italians one of the most killed and wounded American groups in the Second World War. "A full 20 percent of the 'Honor List of Dead and Missing for the State of New York'" were Americans of Italian heritage. On the West Coast, the Italian casualty rate was also way out of proportion to the population (Anthonysworld.com; FieriManhattan.org; ItalianInfo.net, "Knock-Knock"). Truly, the bravery and courage Italian-Americans exhibited in World War II could not have been surpassed by any other group. (It could have only been matched, ironically, by Japanese-Americans—another group that had their civil liberties virtually eradicated on the home front; the

Japanese-Americans who served in the 442nd Regimental Combat Team and the 100th Battalion comprised the most decorated U.S. fighting force in both the war and U.S. military history.)
"Captain Don S. Gentile, perhaps the deadliest man ever to pilot a fighter plane, destroyed 30 Nazi aircraft, becoming the highest scoring fighter pilot in American history. Gentile had eclipsed Captain Eddie Rickenbacker's 26 'kills' of World War I and, in the process, America's 'Ace of Aces' shot down Major Kirk von Meyer, the Nazi's top fighter pilot." In addition, "Marine Gunnery Sergeant John Basilone, [called] 'A one-man army,' by General Douglas MacArthur, 'annihilated an entire Japanese regiment on Guadalcanal'.

"Retired from the Marines--but not content to rest on his laurels, John Basilone [joined] the Navy. 'Manila John' [as he was called] was killed during the landing at Iwo Jima. For his bravery during that fierce battle, Basilone was posthumously awarded the Navy Cross, becoming the only soldier in American history to win the [nation's] two highest military honors, the Congressional Medal of Honor and the Navy Cross" (ItalianInfo.net, "Knock-Knock").

Such men, together with other Italian-Americans (like atomic physicist Enrico Fermi—who became a U.S. citizen in 1944), were invaluable to the American war effort.[86] It is interesting to note that in the same way Japanese-Americans were prevented from fighting in the Pacific theater, Italian-Americans were in many instances prevented from fighting in Europe—bigoted theories on race and loyalty were the main reasons for this (Mangione and Morreale, 1993: 341; Aquila, 1999: 42).

The Italophobia of the U.S. government grew so strong during the war years that even the world renowned opera star Ezio Pinza was arrested and held for a period of months. Pinza was a resident alien under contract to the New York Metropolitan Opera when he was arrested on March 12, 1942.[87] The paranoia peaked when San Francisco's Mayor Angelo Rossi came under suspicion of disloyalty, proving that no Italian was exempt from government scrutiny—for it was rumored that he had given the "Fascist salute" in public. Unlike his downtrodden brethren who were denied fair trials when subjected to Uncle Sam's wrath, Rossi used his political clout to fight back against his attackers denouncing them as racists and forging a transcontinental alliance with New York's Mayor Fiorello LaGuardia. Due to their efforts, the two Italian-American mayors helped eliminate the negative "enemy alien" status affecting people of Italian ancestry. Finally (and symbolically) on October 12, 1942, during a Columbus Day celebration in New York City, Attorney General Francis Biddle gave a speech declaring that the restrictions placed on people of Italian ancestry were no longer necessary and that their "enemy alien" status would be dropped. Biddle also assured the Italian-American community that their wartime efforts on the home front and their sacrifices overseas were recognized and appreciated by the government.[88] Thus, Italian-American loyalty was now officially recognized. However, the actual *liberation* of Italian-American non-citizens from camps of internment would not come until Italy itself was liberated in 1943.[89]

By the time the internment had actually ended, several internees had taken their lives on account of the poor living conditions in the camps and because they felt they had been shamed or disgraced for having their loyalty doubted (*Italian-American Internment*, The History Channel).

And so, at the same time that 100,000 Japanese-Americans were being interned, a total of "600,000 Italian-Americans were deprived of their civil liberties by Government measures that branded them 'enemy aliens'" (Commdocs.house.gov, p.10). This made Italian-Americans the largest group targeted. Stephen Fox, author of *The Unknown Internment* (1990), maintains that the prime reason not all 600,000 were interned was that the group was simply too large—it was not because Italians were favored racially to Asians (183-185). Those who believe otherwise are ignorant of Italian-American history and the racial struggle Italian-Americans fought on a daily basis for decades. If anything, unlike Germany or Japan, Italy posed the least threat militarily to the United States; yet, the Italian-Americans were targeted by the government for more than immediate political reasons. The tragic story of Italian-American internment is often called *Una Storia Segreta* (The Secret Story) because most Italians, wanting to be considered good citizens, willingly brushed all the abuses they suffered under the rug.

Italians were the victims of World War II era persecutions in other English-speaking countries as well—specifically in Britain, Canada, and Australia. The living conditions and discrimination that Italians faced in these non-Latin countries were very similar to the American experience. So, when Italy entered the war in June of 1940, anti-Italian riots naturally broke out in the most "Anglo-Saxon" of all nations—Britain. Italians who had been living there for generations were rounded up and interned as "enemy aliens." The authorities then decided to deport them. This plan backfired on the British government, however, when a German U-boat sank the ship carrying the deportees and 486 Italians lost their lives. Still, the propaganda against *Italianita* was so strong in Britain that even "an inoffensive song called *Papa Nicolini*, which portrayed an old Italian storekeeper in a kindly light, was banned as stirring friendly feelings toward an enemy nation" (Italian-heritage-ancoats.org.uk, "Manchester's Little Italy"; Pisani, 1957: 206).[90] In Canada, hundreds of Italian-Canadians were also interned. After being snatched from their homes or workplaces, weeks had elapsed before the families of the victims found out where they were. Many of the internees spent years without hearing from their families. And, like their Italian-American counterparts, *none* of the Italian-Canadians interned were ever convicted or charged with any acts of treason (Italian.About.com, "When Speaking Italian Was a Crime").[91]

In Australia, when the war began, many Italians who were working on sugar-cane plantations were interned.[92] The broader internment, however, came in February of 1942 when the Australian government believed that some Italians were helping the Japanese war effort through "the use of secret fifth-column radio transmitters." Though the Italians were in Australia for economic reasons, more than 2,000 were interrogated over where they stood politically (the same approximate number were questioned in Canada). By September of 1942, almost 4,000 Italians were interned in Australian camps. These same camps were also used after the war to hold a great number of incoming Southern European refugees (Home.st.net.au, "Italians Interned in Australia..."; Heritage.nsw. gov.au, "Hidden Italian Heritage").[93] As Italians were being stripped of their civil liberties in the diaspora, wartime atrocities were committed by *both* Axis and Allied forces against Italian civilians in the ancestral homeland. Italian prisoners of war were also the victims of atrocities (Members.iinet.net.au, "Massacres and Atrocities of WWII").[94]

After World War II the people of Italy, like the Germans and Japanese, had a lot of rebuilding to do. With U.S. aid, the Italians would eventually restore their country to a level of greatness not seen on the Italian peninsula since the days of the Roman Empire. Conversely, in the United States, the wartime destruction of civil liberties dealt a crushing blow to Italian-Americans and their culture. Though the "enemy alien" status was officially lifted by the war's end, and though a proclamation was issued that did away with the restrictive orders on the West Coast, the hurt remained. Not knowing how to prove their loyalty after sacrificing countless sons to the Allied cause, Italian-Americans began to rapidly abandon many aspects of their culture—the greatest and most obvious part to be abandoned was the Italian language. In an increasingly materialistic and prosperous post-war era, many second and third generation Italian-Americans did not see any benefits in retaining their parents' tongue; some even Anglicized their names to appear more "American"—and so we see the effects of government bias through the use of posters proclaiming "Don't Speak the Enemy's Language! Speak American!" (U.S. DOJ, Appendix B, p. 6; Italian.About.com, "When Speaking Italian Was a Crime"). Indeed the post-war era was a time in which an unprecedented amount of Italian-Americans ascended the social ladder—now it was their turn to be added to the Great American Melting Pot and to finally achieve their American Dreams. The drive to drop any lingering foreignisms was not the only factor that led to their newfound prosperity, however: the curbing of Italian immigration for the past two decades, and new opportunities produced by the booming economy also contributed to their success and assimilation (Pisani, 1957: 209). Italian-Americans were swiftly becoming *American-Italians*. And though it would appear there was a growing acceptance of these Americanized "paesans," the former bigotry remained and would take on a whole new dimension with the advent of television.

1942-1962: During this twenty-year period, 44 people of Italian background were legally executed in the United States. (All were executed by electrocution or gas; none were hanged.) The breakdown by state is as follows: New York—23; Pennsylvania—5; California—3; Connecticut—3; Illinois—3; Massachusetts—2; Nevada—2; Colorado—1; Florida—1; New Jersey—1.[95]

July 1, 1945: A U.S. Senator from Mississippi called a certain female citizen from Brooklyn a "dago" before his colleagues. The woman he insulted (merely because he disagreed with her) had three brothers who served in the war and one of them was killed (Lagumina, 1999: 268-272).

September 27, 1945: When a fight broke out between a group of Italian-American and African-American youths who went to the same East Harlem school, the *New York Times* was quick to label it a "race riot." The paper even went as far as to report anti-black assaults that never occurred in an attempt to make the Italian students look bad (Guglielmo and Salerno, 2003: 161-164). National attention was then focused on Benjamin Franklin High School, up till then a highly praised and rare institution where a multi-ethnic student body was encouraged to embrace its diversity. The school was able to survive the press' scrutiny, and the mounting ethnic tensions that followed, only through the efforts of two men: the school's principal, Leonard Covello (the first Italian-American to hold that position in a New York City high school) and East Harlem's legendary congressman Vito Marcantonio. The duo effectively restored peace to Benjamin Franklin High by illuminating the similarities between the long suffering African- and Italian-Americans and by appealing to the good will in both communities. This was one of the first of many subsequent incidents where the *New York Times* portrayed Italian-Americans as cold-hearted racists. Instead of investigating the reasons that led a historically oppressed group like Italian-Americans to feud with blacks, the *Times* (and other so-called liberal papers) scapegoated them as the embodiment of senseless white rage in America's urban centers. The stereotype of the Italian-American bigot was thus etched in many people's minds.

Era of Sociological Statistics—(1950s to 1970s)

1950-1951: A series of U.S. Senate hearings, led by Senator Estes Kefauver, re-acquainted the American populace with the term "Mafia" and the entire Mafia image (Gambino, 1974: 299).[96]

For the previous 50 years the term "Black Hand" had been used most often when describing Italian organized crime. But something really captivated the American people when they heard the word "Mafia." Perhaps it was because it sounded more Italian than "Black Hand" (and was less difficult to say than *mano nera*). Or maybe the word "Mafia" had been stored in the collective memories of Americans since the 1890s and had been, all along, associated with the "Great Italian Problem" of that decade—most notably the rumored events leading to the lynching of 11 Italians in New Orleans (i.e. the rumors that a Sicilian Mafia was responsible for Chief Hennessy's death). No matter what specifically triggered the nation's psychological fixation on the Mafia, it cannot be denied that as a result of the 1950s hearings, the "m-word" generated a new wave—a popular wave—of the same old problems for Italian-Americans; this time it was not physical lynchings that would make a comeback, but media lynchings—that is, massive stereotyping and defamation. The 1950s television show *The Untouchables* was a product of this new interest in the Mafia, coupled with a blatant and pre-existing anti-Italianism. So many villains had Italian names that the show was referred to by many as "Cops and Wops" (Gambino, 1974: 274).

July 1951: Several days of rioting occurred in Cicero, Illinois, when a black family moved into an apartment building there. The people of Cicero were primarily of southern and eastern European background, and between 4,000 and 8,000 of them participated in the riot; 117 were arrested. This was the worst mob violence to hit southern Illinois in two decades (Ashyk, 1999: 13-14). More than anything else, the ethnic rioting symbolized the post-World War II acceptance of racism as a vital part of the Americanization process. Where blacks and European ethnics once cooperated, even if minimally, in the face of oppression (or at the very least were indifferent toward one another), they now found themselves increasingly at odds, mainly because the "ethnics" wanted more and more to forget their own troubled past and assimilate into white society.[97] Though the Cicero riot was especially traumatic for the black family that wished to move there, it was extremely damaging to the reputation of Italian-Americans all over the country due to the media slander that was unleashed on them. *Life* magazine depicted Italian-Americans as bloodthirsty gang members (with the stereotypical slicked back hair and leather jackets), and even the Baltimore *Afro-American* described the rioters as "8,000 frenzied, blood-thirsty descendants of immigrants from the Mediterranean area of Europe."

As one source truthfully stated, "The national response to the Cicero riots focused largely on the ethnic background of the attackers" rather than on the problems blacks faced when they attempted to move into non-black neighborhoods. The *New York Times*, unsurprisingly, "encouraged African Americans to blame ethnic Ciceroneans rather than challenge the hierarchies maintained along the lines of ethnic, racial, class, and sexual boundaries" (Ashyk, 1999: 14, 17-18). In this way, upper class WASPs (the maintainers of the racial status quo) began shifting some of the guilt they had for 300 years of black persecution on to the newly arrived ethnics. "Race problems" started being portrayed by the media as stemming from the unique intolerance that blue-collar ethnics harbored for encroaching blacks. By playing one group off against another, upper-class whites ensured their dominance at the top of the social ladder (Ashyk, 1999:19-25).

1952: Congress passed an immigration law that was even more anti-southern/eastern European than the quota laws of the 1920s. The new law reduced the Italian quota to one-seventh of what it had been under the 1921 law. Fortunately, President Johnson in 1968 abolished the national origin quotas (Gambino, 1974: 124-125).

Late 1950s-1970s: The government put into motion its massive plan of "urban renewal" in order to provide affordable housing for the poor. America's urban landscape was forever changed in the process: countless rows of buildings were demolished, highways were built through the middle of vibrant inner-city neighborhoods, and the residents of these neighborhoods were uprooted against their will. Many of those who had their lives disrupted by urban renewal were the "new immigrants" and their offspring (i.e. southern and eastern European immigrants of the "New Immigration" period stretching from the 1880s to the 1920s). It is no wonder that Italian-Americans look back at the period of urban renewal with a dual sense of melancholy and ire. For, it was during those years that their tight-knit communities died and the impersonal suburban diaspora swallowed them up. If "road builder supreme" Robert Moses had it his way, he would have leveled

Manhattan's Little Italy and put a super-highway through it. Fortunately the people of the Lower East Side, both Italians and Jews, fought him every step of the way and won![98]

1959: B.C. Rosen found in a study he conducted that "Italian-American schoolboys scored very low on tests designed to measure 'achievement aspirations' and 'achievement-related values'" (Gambino, 1974: 268). They obviously had a lower self-esteem than other students, perhaps due to feelings of cultural, social, and ethnic inferiority.

1960: Lawrence H. Fuchs found that Italian-Americans were underrepresented as "New York City's Democratic assembly district leaders"; out of a massive Italian-American population in New York, they only represented eleven percent of the total (Gambino, 1974: 350).[99]

1965: Italian-American writer Daniela Gioseffi was raped by a sheriff in a Selma, Alabama jail while fighting for civil rights. Her traumatic experience is recounted in the short story "The Bleeding Mimosa" (Ashyk, 1999: viii;Gioseffi.com.).

Also in 1965, in the Corona section of Queens, New York, seventy Italian-American homes were planned to be destroyed in order to make room for a high school that would service young people from other neighborhoods. For seven long and tense years, Corona's residents fought City Hall on the issue and eventually won. Had they lost, the building of the school "would have destroyed a substantial number of homes and moved their families, thereby decimating a community Italian-Americans had spent two generations in building" (Gambino, 1974: 322-323).

1966: New York Congressman Joseph Resnick called for an investigation of state adoption laws when an Italian-American couple, Mr. and Mrs. Michael Liuni, were denied permission to adopt a Nordic-looking girl. The Liunis maintained that they were discriminated against on account of their dark coloring and features (Lagumina: 1999, 303-304).

This same year, Bernard E. Segal, in his book *Racial and Ethnic Relations*, found that out of six U.S. ethnic groups (Italians, "Negroes," Jews, French-Canadians, Greeks, and white Protestants) Italians had the lowest achievement motivation, achievement values, higher educational aspirations, and vocational aspirations. These findings give good insight into the class background of Italian-Americans and highlight the struggle they had to fight well into the Civil Rights Era. In some cases, the struggle was with themselves as many second and third generation Italian-Americans equated their ethnicity with being pre-disposed to failure (Gambino, 1974: 269, 272).

1960s & 1970s: Government programs, while aiding the newly arriving Spanish-speaking people, remained unresponsive to the special needs (mainly economic and educational) of the vast Italian-American lower-middle class (Gambino, 1974: 158). Virtually no effort was made to either understand or help. In this regard, Italian-Americans were in the same predicament as their late 19th century ancestors.

1968: Confirming yet again that Italian-Americans held a disproportionately low amount of political power, Lawrence H. Fuchs found that although they constituted the largest ethnic group in Providence, Rhode Island's Republican Party, Italian-Americans held very few positions of power within it (Gambino, 1974: 350).

This same year, San Francisco Mayor Joe Alioto and Massachusetts Governor John Volpe were dropped as presidential running mates for Hubert Humphrey and Richard Nixon, respectively. They were dropped for no other apparent reason than because they were of Italian descent. Such political voicelessness on the part of Italian-Americans led to the founding of the National Italian American Foundation in Washington D.C. (Ashyk, 1999: 52-53). After Nixon had been elected, the following was picked up on the notorious "tapes"; the president had been talking in a racist and sarcastic manner to his aide, John Ehrlichman, about rewarding the groups that supported him:

Nixon: "The Italians. We mustn't forget the Italians. Must do something for them. The, ah, we forget them. They are not like us. Difference is they smell different, they look different, act different. After all, you can't blame them. Oh no. Can't do that. They've never had the things we've had."

Ehrlichman: "That's right."

Nixon: "Of course, the trouble is...the trouble is, you can't find one that's honest" (Italian-American.com, "The Italian-American Website of New York").[100]

Also, in 1968, five men were imprisoned for "mob hits" they did not commit. Their names were: Joseph Salvati, Peter Limone, Henry Tameleo, Louis Greco, and Ronald Cassesso. Peter Limone and Joe Salvati were released thirty years later when it was discovered that certain FBI informants wrongfully accused all five of the men. Unfortunately, Henry Tameleo, Louis Greco, and Ronald Cassesso died while still in prison. The families of four of the men (Salvati, Limone, Tameleo, and Greco) sued the government for billions of dollars in damages (Crimelibrary.com, "All About the Providence Mob").

1969: When a famous Yale professor heard that an Italian-American was running for the position of New York mayor, he reportedly said: "If Italians aren't actually an inferior race, they do the best imitation of one I've seen." This level of bigotry is far from surprising when one takes a look at the studies which prove that having an Italian surname condemns one to a state of inferiority and even ugliness in our Anglo society (Gambino, 1974: 108; Lagumina, 1999: 307).

In a 1969 study of "the educational achievements of major ethnic groups," the U.S. Census Bureau found the following: "In every category of accomplishment Italian-Americans were the lowest or near lowest of all groups"; the Hispanic newcomers were also shown to have scored low (Gambino, 1974: 245-246).

August 10, 1969: A happily married Italian-American couple, Leo and Rosemary La Bianca were savagely killed by followers of Charles Manson. They were both bound and then stabbed to death; Rosemary was stabbed 41 times and the word "war" was gruesomely carved into Leo La Bianca's stomach. The war these sick individuals were referring to was a racial one in which whites would be exterminated by blacks and Manson would some-how become ruler of the world. This act of attrition against the La Biancas differed from past lynchings in that the couple was killed for being "white" rather than "Italian" or "non-white." It was during this Civil Rights Era that the ethnic minority status of Italian-Americans disappeared before the nation's growing concern for the plight of racial minorities, particularly blacks (Totse.com).

Autumn 1969: Michael Lerner broke new ground writing an article in *The American Scholar* about the bigotry Italian-Americans faced from "upper-class liberals." He made the point that, in the mind of the elite liberal, bigotry against Italian-Americans and other so-called "white ethnics" is not as wrong as bigotry against African-Americans and other racial minorities; hence their indulgence in anti-Italian comments and the like. Richard Gambino expounded on the subject, stating "Unlike the crude bigotry of the old American nativists, the more recent discrimination against Italian-Americans has become respectable. It is no longer the bigotry of redneck types, although this brand still exists. The more damaging bigotry today is that shown by educated middle- and upper-class Americans." Gambino continued, saying that white America found a special scapegoat in Italian-Americans; through the media's sensationalism, Italian-Americans could be blamed for both crime and the suffering of blacks: "The ballyhoo about Mafia drug suppliers permits the liberal anti-Italian bigots to repress in their own minds, or rationalize away, the fact that in many cases their ancestors owned slaves or exploited blacks after their legal emancipation, as Italian-Americans did not. It is very easy, and certainly less painful, simply to see the Mafia—and by extension all Italian-Americans—as the cause of the black problem" (Gambino, 1974: 305, 307). And so Italians were portrayed onscreen and in print as hot headed bigots by the liberal media.

1969-1971: In 1969, reputed mob boss Joe Colombo founded the Italian American Civil Rights League. Representing roughly 100,000 members, the League accomplished what other Italian-American organizations tried to do for 60 years or more: that is, successfully fight discrimination and stereotyping. Unfortunately, Joe Colombo's fight was short-lived, as he was gunned down on June 28, 1971 at the League's second annual Unity Day Rally; he was shot, ironically, in front of a statue of another Colombo—Cristoforo (www.italianinfo.net/joe-page2.htm). Here is a brief background of the Italian American Civil Rights League and the events that led to Colombo's demise: On April 30, 1970, Joe Colombo and 30 Italian-American demonstrators began picketing the FBI's Manhattan office; in no time at all the number of protesters jumped to 5,000 a night, outside the Manhattan headquarters. Writer and former IACRL member Richard Capozzola describes what led to the demonstrations:

"The picketing of the FBI began as a protest against the arrest of Colombo's son, Joseph Jr. by federal authorities, reportedly on direct orders from Attorney General John Mitchell. The charge was that Joe Jr. had conspired to melt down U.S. coins into silver ingots. This was too much for Joe Sr. to take. For many years, Joe endured government badgering and harassment. He never figured on the 'frame' that was set up for his son. The charge was later dismissed when the government's chief witness admitted in open court that he lied in accusing Joseph Colombo, Jr." (www.italianinfo.net/joe-page1.htm).

Two months later, on June 28, 1970, the first Unity Day Rally was held at Columbus Circle; several hundred thousand Italians showed up in a proud and defiant display of solidarity. A sea of red, white, and green flags flooded the streets; innumerable buttons read: "Italian Power," "Kiss Me, I'm Italian," and "I'm Proud to be Italian." Some men even dressed up in gorilla costumes and marched around with signs that said, "The FBI is Using Gorilla Tactics." Thus, Unity Day was both a celebration of things "Italian" and a protest against that which was perceived to be "anti-Italian." Its impact on all of New York was significant: "Many stores, restaurants, and other businesses closed in honor of Unity Day. Activity in the Port New York was scanty as only 10 percent of the longshoremen showed up for work" (www.italianinfo.net/joe-page2.htm).

To the crowd at Unity Day, Joe declared: "I say there is a conspiracy against me, against all Italian Americans—but you and I are together today, under God's eye—and those who get in our way will feel His sting." The crowd cheered for the next few minutes and began chanting the League's slogan in unison, "One! One! One! One!" Weeks after the rally, most New York political leaders stated their support for the League, and some openly condemned the use of the terms "Mafia" or "Cosa Nostra" to describe organized crime (whose illegal members came from all ethnic backgrounds). As a result of the positive attention it received, the Italian American Civil Rights League's power skyrocketed. It successfully began boycotting specific movies, television shows, and commercials that defamed Italian-Americans. It even influenced the producer of *The Godfather* to completely rid the film of any mention of the terms "Mafia" and "Cosa Nostra." And so, the IACRL was doing 3 decades ago what anti-defamation groups like UNICO, Italian American One Voice, and the Sons of Italy's Commission for Social Justice are doing today (www.italianinfo.net/joe-page3.htm).

By early 1971, the Italian American Civil Rights League had acquired enough money to purchase 250 acres in upstate New York. The land was called "Camp Unity" and would be used as a summer retreat for the underprivileged children of New York—children of all backgrounds. During this time, *Joe Colombo* was quickly becoming a national celebrity, appearing on *The Tonight Show* and *The Dick Cavett Show*. All these advances would soon come to an end however. (www.italianinfo.net/joe-page4.htm; www.italianinfo.net/joe-page5.htm).

On June 28, 1971, minutes before Unity Day II was scheduled to begin, a young African-American man named Jerome Johnson gunned down Joe Colombo; seconds later Johnson was shot dead. The press speculated that the mob was behind the shooting (because Colombo was supposedly bringing them too much "heat"), but it is very possible that the government was responsible for Colombo's demise and for the subsequent demise of the IACRL. This latter theory is held by a good number of Italian-Americans who were active in the League. Mobster Frank Costello was even quoted as saying to an inquiring author, "All I can tell you is that no mob guy did the job." Costello further remarked that the so-called "mob guys" were all for the IACRL; after all, they had kids and they did not want to see them stigmatized by anti-Italian stereotypes or hindered by discrimination in any form (even though, ironically, the youngsters' fathers were helping to fuel such anti-Italian sentiment). When one looks at the situation logically, it stands to reason that the government would gun down Joe Colombo—for he defied "the system" peacefully and won. Government agents had even moved in across the street from IACRL headquarters and kept tight surveillance on Colombo and his new organization. Clearly, if Joe was not going to live up to their expectations and bring violence to them, they were going to bring violence to Joe (www.italianinfo.net/joe-page6.htm;www.italian info.net/joe-page7.htm).

Era of Heightened Media Defamation—(1970s to Today)

1970: In their book *Beyond the Melting Pot*, Nathan Glazer and Daniel Moynihan found that the number of Italian-American men employed in "professional or managerial roles" in New York City (8.1 percent) was even lower than the number of black males (8.5 percent) employed in the same positions (Gambino, 1974: 270).

1971: Terry Morris explained in the book *Better Than You* that "social discrimination hits hardest against those who begin to move up the economic ladder than it does the very poor." (And Italian-Americans were of course a group that was moving, rung-by-rung, up the economic ladder.) Morris' theory is logical enough, since those who begin acquiring wealth and small bits of power are more of a threat to those on the ladder's upper rungs than those who are completely powerless. Data was also collected around this time (the early 70s) suggesting that Italian-Americans were still either being totally excluded from urban social clubs, or included as tokens (Gambino, 1974: 348-349).

April 1971: David L. Featherman wrote in the *American Sociological Review* the results of a study done on males from five different ethno-religious groups; the study had been conducted over a ten year period, from 1957 to 1967. The categories were: "Anglo-Saxon Protestant, other Protestants, Jewish, Roman Catholics other than Italian and Mexican Americans, and Italian and Mexican Americans." Out of all the groups mentioned, it was found that Italian- and Mexican-Americans achieved the lowest levels of education, occupation, and income (Gambino, 1974: 268).

August 12, 1971: The New York State Division of Human Rights charged the Flushing Hospital and Medical Center, along with the hospital's Medical Board, with "probable discrimination" against an Italian-American doctor. The hospital committed the following eight offenses against Dr. Ermanno E. Trabucco:

- 1. Told him and others that he formed a Mafia group of doctors (GIM) and refused to place him on the staff.
- 2. That, despite his seniority as a Resident Surgeon, [he] was put on the lowest rung of the ladder.
- 3. That his family was charged higher rates.

- 4. That he was forced to go back to Italy to practice, although he is a duly licensed doctor in New York and an American citizen.
- 5. That Italian-Americans are never promoted to higher positions in the Board of Trustees.
- 6. That he was not readmitted [after he returned from Italy] because he is of Italian background.
- 7. That, the officers [of the Board] have disparaged his accent.
- 8. That pressure has been exercised by members of the Medical Board and Executive Members to withdraw their sponsorship after the sponsors had sponsored his application for readmission (Lagumina, 1999: 300-302).

Dr. Trabucco is one of many Italian-Americans who have been discriminated against in more recent years; they are victimized on account of three main reasons: the old bigotry against Italians never disappeared; Italian-Americans have not displayed the strong group unity that has protected other persecuted ethnicities from attack in the post-Civil Rights Era; and the largely liberal media continues to "cash in" on anti-Italian stereotypes (through the making and marketing of mob-related movies, TV shows and commercials, and through the press' sensationalism and negativity toward all things "Italian").

October 22, 1971: Only two months after Flushing Hospital was charged with discrimination, another anti-Italian complaint was filed with the New York State Division of Human Rights. This time the complainant was an Italian-American who sought employment at Herbert H. Lehman College; Mr. Anthony V. Patti charged the college president, Leonard Lief, "with an unlawful discriminatory practice relating to employment, because of his national origin and creed"—Mr. Patti was denied employment because he was Italian and Catholic (Lagumina, 1999: 302-303).

1972: The major motion picture *The Godfather* was released in the United States.[101]

This movie had a profound effect on the Italian-American community and on American society as a whole. Brilliantly written, directed, and performed, The Godfather carried on the long legacy of the Mafia stereotype and opened new doors to the marketability of onscreen Italian defamation. The movie, directed by Francis Ford Coppola, was adapted from the book by Mario Puzo. That Italian-Americans were the ones behind it, and that mainstream Americans would come to enjoy Mafia movies (and even root for the blood thirsty main characters) marked a great change in American values and in the image Italian-Americans had of themselves. Many Italian-

Americans succumbed to the stereotypes and embraced them because of *The Godfather's* cross-cultural appeal and the interest it spurred (even if misguided) of all things "Italian." Embracing the Mafia image also gave Italian-Americans what they perceived to be a feared and respected identity, and as Coppola and Puzo found out, the image was profitable. So, in a sense, the "if you can't beat 'em, join 'em" mentality prevailed—Italians in the United States had been fighting the criminal stereotype for a century, and where did it get them? After the great success of *The Godfather*, Hollywood created a veritable "Mafia movie industry" which specialized in defaming Italian-Americans for decades to come.[102]

July 10-11, 1972: In a quest to find $4 million in narcotics, thirty federal agents ruthlessly searched the Bronx home of John Conforti. Though Mr. Conforti was the brother-in-law of a drug dealer, he himself harbored no drugs (nor was there any tangible reason to suspect he had). When the agents finished their search, Mr. Conforti's home "had been shorn of its aluminum siding, trim, interior panels, insulation and some shingles"—it had, in effect, been "partly dismantled." The over-zealous agents also "dug deep trenches in the manicured lawn and ripped apart furniture." One non-Italian witness compared the federal agents to gestapos, and the Italian victims to Jews (Lagumina, 1999: 284-285).

September 1972: Indicative of the acceptable bigotry Italian-Americans still faced, the following advertisement for a book was printed in *True* magazine: "Biographies of Italian War Heroes, a great gag, a beautifully hard-bound book with gold stamp lettering—220 pages, each one completely blank. It is a sure laugh-getter for your den or library, for $3.95" (Lagumina, 1999: 309).

January 1973: A study was conducted on American Catholic clergymen and the following was found: Out of 34 archbishops, only 1 was an Italian-American; and of 253 bishops, 5 were Italian-Americans. These figures no doubt reflect the troubled relations that existed for a century between Italian-American parishioners and the Irish-dominated Church (Gambino, 1974: 239).

Another 1973 study was done on the number of Italian-Americans employed by the City University of New York (or CUNY)—the alma mater of thousands of Italian-American students. The following was discovered: "not one Italian-American [was found] among the one chancellor, one deputy chancellor, four vice-chancellors, four university-wide deans, and twenty college presidents in C.U.N.Y."; only 14 of CUNY's 165 deans were Italian-Americans; "only 3 to 6 per cent of the C.U.N.Y. faculty are Italian-Americans, and most of these are in the relatively powerless junior academic ranks"; out of 1,700 faculty members at Brooklyn College (located in the most Italian borough in New York), only 59 were Italian-Americans; and of the 503 faculty members at Queensborough College (a school with a large percentage of Italian-American students), only 46 were Italian-Americans—"and of these only two were full professors and six were associate professors" (Gambino, 1974: 266). As of the mid-1970s, seventy-five percent of all American professors claimed British or other Northern European heritage; this percentage of "Nordic" professors remained constant, more or less, since 1900 (Mangione and Morreale, 1993: 460).

The following information focuses on Italian-American students at CUNY, as of 1973: "The SEEK program, College Discovery Program, Urban Centers, and other programs of the City University which are designed to provide special assistance to students whose circumstances make a successful college career difficult serve about 17,000 students. Of these only two hundred are Italian-Americans. And the number of Italian-American counselors in these programs is proportionately as low. This does not reflect the needs of Italian-American students at C.U.N.Y. It reflects neglect of them and their own diffidence, disorganization, and powerlessness." Around this time, (the early 1970s) it was also discovered that 8.5 percent of the students attending CUNY schools spoke Italian at home; this percentage of students speaking a language other than English was second only to the number of those who spoke Spanish (15.7%). "Of the [Italian-speaking] group 52 per cent were found to have comprehension study problems. (Other figures: Spanish 49 per cent; all others 39 per cent.) Thirty-three per cent of the Italian group had critical reading problems, 22 per cent had vocabulary problems, and 36 per cent had difficulty following directions integral to academic study" (Gambino, 1974: 267). The Civil Rights Era neglect of Italian-Americans (both faculty and students) on CUNY campuses, in addition to the neglect Italian-Americans faced elsewhere, was another reason the sons and daughters of Columbus had to rely on themselves to succeed. One writer sums up the experience of Italian-American students rather well: "At C.U.N.Y. as on all American college campuses the third-generation Italian-American student finds himself precisely as the fewer second-generation students found themselves before him—isolated, alone, disoriented, conflicted, and neglected." As of 1973, a whopping ninety-three percent of all Italian-Americans were not college educated (Gambino, 1974: 268, 271).

Also, in 1973 it was found that out of 60,000 New York City public school teachers, only 10 percent were Italian-Americans; and out of 90 high schools, only 1 principal was of Italian background. The fact that Italians for years have had the third highest dropout rate in the city (behind blacks and Hispanics) has to have been caused, to some degree, by the scarce amount of Italian-American teachers, administrators, and thus role models employed by the system (Gambino, 1974: 271).[103]

1975: Renowned businessman Lee Iacocca wrote of the discrimination he faced at the Ford Motor Company. Business became personal when differences arose between Iacocca and Henry Ford II; Iacocca was treated as an outsider by the company, and Ford hinted that Lee was tied to organized crime. Outraged, Iacocca wrote the following: "I was in the Mafia...I guess The Godfather was enough to persuade him that all Italians were linked to organized crime" (Mangione and Morreale, 1993: 409). The phrase "like father like son" holds true for Henry Ford II in this particular case. His bigoted attitude reminds one of his father's old Nazi sympathies. Perhaps the bigotry was passed down.

1976: The National Center for Urban Ethnic Affairs (founded by the priest and civil rights leader Geno Baroni) discovered in a study of Fortune 500 Corporations based in Chicago that "although 40 percent of the population in the study area were Polish, Italian, African-American, and Latin, they comprised less than 3 percent of the staffs and boards of the corporations examined" (Ashyk, 1999: 50).

1976-1977: "Son of Sam" hysteria swept New York City as 14 young adults were killed or injured (mainly in areas having large Italian populations) over the course of a year. At first, New York City journalists paid no attention to Donna Lauria's murder on July 29, 1976—many of them attributed her death to a Mafia hit (after all, she was an Italian-American and was killed in an Italian section of the Bronx; these facts added up to a "hit" in the press' mind). Little did they know it was the first of 6 murders and 8 maimings committed by David Berkowitz. Nine of the fourteen victims were Italian-Americans (NostalgiaCentral.com, "Son of Sam"; Angelfire.com, "Victims of David").

1981: With more televisions in American homes by the 70s and 80s, and a rapidly growing "Godfather Industry" in Hollywood, anti-Italian defamation increased onscreen. "A [1981] study of prime-time television programs...revealed that denigrating presentations of Italian Americans outnumbered positive ones by a margin of nearly two to one. Those portrayed as professional criminals far exceeded the educated professionals and business executive types. Most Italian American characters held low-status jobs, only one in seven being shown working as an executive, manager, or professional, and the majority spoke improper English, which made them the butt of jokes" (Mangione and Morreale, 1993: 219). Here we see that even though Italian-Americans had been making incredible economic gains since World War II, they were still being portrayed in a negative and lowly manner. This has led me and others to believe that, so long as there is one Italian-American who has dark features and is stereotyped as a member of the "criminal lower class," Italian-Americans as a whole will always have something in common with racial minorities in the United States.

1984: Geraldine Ferraro became the first female/Italian American to run in a presidential election.[104]

Ferraro was running as the Democratic Party's candidate for vice-president. Almost immediately, she "felt the stigma of Mafia attached to her name as newspapers around the country, including the *Philadelphia Inquirer*, the *New York Post*, and the *Wall Street Journal*, insinuated that the Ferraro family was connected with organized crime. That Ferraro had helped form the National Organization of Italian American Women, that she had been an effective congresswoman for years, that there was no evidence for the accusation, was all overlooked." Such mistreatment by the press forced her to respond in earnest, "Because I am Italian, I or my family is suspected of being gangsters" (Mangione and Morreale, 1993: 405). The damage had already been done, however, and there was no way of taking all the hurtful lies and accusations back. Apparently, since it was too risky to attack Ferraro on account of her gender, the press (and probably the Republican strategists), in predictable fashion, launched an all out offensive against her ethnicity. This same ruthless malignancy destroyed the careers and reputations of many Italian-Americans through the years, in politics as well as in other fields.

May 29, 1985: On this date a particularly tragic case of international anti-Italianism occurred in Heysel, Belgium. Thirty-nine Italian soccer fans were killed while attending the European Cup Final. Bad blood had existed for at least a year between Liverpool fans (i.e. the English) and Juventus fans (the Italians). It reached new and deadly heights when rowdy English fans, known as "hooligans," charged the Italian spectators. Violence erupted all over the stadium; it soon turned into the worst day of rioting the soccer world had ever seen. The majority of the 39 killed were trampled while thousands were frantically trying to escape the English wrath. This incident proved that anti-Italian violence is far from dead in the "New Europe" (BBC.co.uk, "The Heysel Stadium Tragedy").

Some have shamefully tried to justify the violence as retribution for the way the Italian authorities handled riotous English soccer fans a year earlier in Italy. Still, others blame "Italian fascists" for provoking the English fans to act (Family.MaltaNet.net). Thus, Anglocentrists of the Old World are similar to their American counterparts, as both believe that people of English stock are always justified in their aggressive acts, and that violence and criminality are imbedded in the genes of Italians and other non-Anglo peoples.

August 23, 1989: A group of approximately thirty Italian-American males assaulted four African-American youths who were looking to buy a car in Bensonhurst, Brooklyn (a predominantly Italian neighborhood). In the scuffle, a black teen, Yusuf Hawkins, was shot dead. This act of violence prompted the Reverend Al Sharpton, a vocal black civil rights leader, to lead demonstrations through Bensonhurst.

The racial tensions that ensued between protesting blacks and residents lining the streets (behind police barricades) provided the media with the proof it needed to confirm that Italian-Americans are inherently racist. Nightly television broadcasts of angry Bensonhursters holding watermelons (an anti-black gesture) and shouting the "N-word" in defiance painted a very negative picture of the community for the rest of America to see (Guglielmo and Salerno, 2003: 192, 203-204; Laurino, 2000: 123-124). A lack of self-control, on the part of some Bensonhurst Italians, was obviously to blame, but so was the media's insistence on portraying the conflict as a simple black and white dispute, heir apparent to the violence that rocked 1960s Birmingham. This was not the same, however. Italian-Americans, unlike white Southerners, do not represent the nation's dominant culture, nor do they hold a prestigious social status in our nation's ethnic and racial hierarchy. Most importantly, Italian-Americans have not had a history of oppressing black people; Italians, like blacks, were more often on the receiving end of prejudice and discrimination. It would therefore have been more accurate if the media treated what happened in Bensonhurst as a minority on minority conflict.

Disgruntled over a lack of affirmative action programs aimed at them and disillusioned with a city government that tended to ignore them, New York Italians unleashed their angst and rage on those minorities they had acquired more power than and on those they felt they could intimidate, like African-Americans and Hispanics. Thus, from the 1980s to the 1990s, Bensonhurst had seen a tragic increase in the number of deadly racial incidents (Laurino, 2000: 122, 130-131). During this period most Italian-Americans did not dare to badmouth the WASP establishment or commit acts of violence against "middle Americans" because 1) they believed they shared the same "values," and 2) Italians wanted to distance themselves demographically and racially from what they perceived to be "crybaby" minority groups who seemed to be encroaching on their territory more and more each day, bringing nothing but urban plight with them. A consistent policy of scapegoating African-Americans for problems such as crime, drugs, and poverty, had been prevalent in the Italian-American community ever since the 1960s when urban renewal decimated entire neighborhoods in the name of "social progress." Historically, scapegoating blacks has been one of the easiest paths toward full assimilation and toward attaining a prestigious social status in the United States. In this regard, it can be said that Italian-Americans have, knowingly or not, learned from history.

Getting back to the 1989 incident, however, I contend that what happened to Yusuf Hawkins could just as well have happened to a non-Italian white person in Bensonhurst. For it is believed the trouble arose when a neighborhood girl told local boys that a gang of her black friends were coming to beat them up (Laurino, 2000: 122-123). Had she substituted the word "Irish" for "black" it is quite possible that the Italian youths would have attacked the first stranger they saw with red hair, freckles, and a light complexion (that certainly would have been the story in the 1930s and before). In that case, no headlines would have been made, but perhaps a small— almost microscopic—article would have been tucked away somewhere in an August 1989 copy of the *New York Times*, describing the sudden demise of one "Shane O'Malley."

April 30, 1990: At the John D. Calandra Institute in New York, a conference was held on "The Education of Italian American Youth." It was revealed at the conference that, "the dropout rate of Italian American public high school students was found to be the third largest in New York City, behind Latinos and African Americans." (This had been a silently acknowledged fact for years.) To help kids with their homework and to provide academic guidance, the Italian American Mentoring Project (or "AMICI") was created (Qcpages.qc.edu, "John D. Calandra...").

September 19, 1990: The movie *Goodfellas* was released in the U.S. This film, directed by Martin Scorsese, was extremely graphic in its depiction of Italian-Americans as cold-blooded Mafia hitmen. In an era of increasing and often gratuitous onscreen violence, *Goodfellas* reinvented and re-popularized the traditional "mob movie," attracting a whole new generation of moviegoers. The third "Godfather" was also released this year, ushering in a whole new decade of mob enthusiasm. This "enthusiasm" and the American fascination with Italian stereotypes led the performer Sammy Davis Jr. to say the following to a largely Italian audience: "If you cats don't get your act together, you won't be riding in the back of the bus, you'll be under it" (Allmovie.com, "Goodfellas," "The Godfather Part III"; SicilianCulture.com, "Sicilian Culture").[105]

January 1992: Future president Bill Clinton was caught on tape saying that New York Governor Mario Cuomo (a fellow Democrat) "acts like" he has Mafia connections. This statement came to light during the notorious Gennifer Flowers scandal; it was the second time a U.S. president (or in this case a future president) was found to have made anti-Italian remarks on scandalous tapes (Italian-American.com, "Bulletproof Bill"; Media Research.org, "Media Should Say Whoops Over Whoopee").

September 9, 1992: In a civil rights dispute dating back to the 1970s a group of Italian-American professors filed a lawsuit against the City University of New York. They alleged that, "they had routinely been discriminated against and denied a series of promotions because of their ethnic background." The case would come to be known as *Scelsa v. CUNY*. A black female judge, Constance Baker Motley, eventually ruled in favor of the professors. On the voluntary self-identification form that is sent out to CUNY job applicants there are now five "protected classes" that are eligible for affirmative action: American Indian/Alaskan Native, Asian/Pacific Islander, Black, Hispanic, and Italian American (Laurino, 2000: 152; Qcpages.qc.edu, "John D. Calandra…").

October 11, 1992: The Columbus Day Parade was cancelled in Denver, Colorado, due to a fear of violence between Italian-American marchers and American Indian protesters—this, on the 500th Anniversary of Columbus' arrival in the New World. The 1990s unfortunately saw escalating tensions between these two ethnic groups over the Columbus Day issue. Essentially the protesters argue that Columbus Day represents the exploitation and genocide of native peoples, while Italian-Americans defiantly maintain Columbus Day is their "ethnic time to shine." The ill will has been especially pronounced in Colorado, since that state was the first to recognize Columbus Day, and since a large number of American Indians live in that part of the country (CNN.com, "Thousands Protest Columbus Day Parades").

1994: The Scorsese film *Casino* was released this year. Many consider this the sequel to *Goodfellas* (even though the stories are unrelated) since Robert De Niro and Joe Pesci teamed up again to bring as much blood and violence as they could to the big screen. Of course, they and other Italian-American actors joined forces bringing a plethora of anti-Italian stereotypes to the screen as well (Allmovie.com, "Casino").

1996-2001: A study was conducted by the Italic Studies Institute that found the following regarding anti-Italian defamation: Of the 1,220 American made films depicting Italians since the sound era (1928), sixty-nine percent portray Italians in a negative light, while 31 percent are positive portrayals; 487 of the films were centered around mob characters (the vast majority of whom—88 percent—were fictitious); another 359 movies (or 29% of the total) included characters who were either boors, bigots, buffoons, or bimbos; and 280 of the mob movies (or 57 percent of them) were released after the 1972 premiere of *The Godfather*, making that particular film's negative influence all too apparent. These revelations are very disturbing, especially when compared to official FBI data which confirms that there has never been more than 5,000 gang members of Italian descent within the United States; that number is less than .0034% of the total Italian-American population (Italic.org, "Image Research Project").

1997: After serving 30 years for a murder he did not commit, Joseph Salvati was released from prison. He and four other Italian-American men (Peter Limone, Henry Tameleo, Louis Greco, and Ronald Cassesso) were wrongfully imprisoned in 1968 for a series of "mob hits" even though J. Edgar Hoover, himself, was aware of their innocence. Sadly, three of the men died before their sentences could be commuted. Peter Limone (like Salvati) was fortunate, however; his freedom came four years later in 2001 (TalkLeft.com, "FBI To Be Sued for $300 Million"; CrimeLibrary.com, "All About the Providence Mob"; TruthInJustice.org, "Man Freed After Serving 32 Years").

December 28, 1998: Just days after the Romagnuolo family celebrated Christmas in their Sunderland, Ontario home, three police officers barged into their house without a warrant and demanded that one of the Romagnuolo boys, twenty-year old Lorenzo, be taken into custody. The youth allegedly threatened eight days earlier to break the legs of Mike Hoskin, the arresting officer, when Hoskin called the Romagnuolo house at 3 am asking for the boy's mother, Linda, yet refused to divulge the reason for the call.[106]

Lorenzo simply did not know who he was talking to on the phone and subsequently lost his temper. This was why the police showed up on the Italian-Canadian family's doorstep (even though 8 days had elapsed since the threat). The officers, however, did not sufficiently explain why they illegally entered the Romagnuolo home, and so Lorenzo's father, Tony, started raising his voice at them in outrage.

This is where things get blurry. It is believed Lorenzo cooperated fully with police, even stating he would go into custody peacefully, yet seemingly out of nowhere eight gunshots were fired by all three officers killing Lorenzo's father instantly and severely wounding his 17-year old brother Rocco. After the deadly barrage Lorenzo's frightened voice was caught on tape asking officer Hoskin why he went for his gun; Hoskin merely replied that he should not bicker with the police—this, from a man who also accused the household puppy "Chico" of unlawful aggression. With that, the twenty year old Lorenzo, his mother, and even his other little brother Michael were all arrested and whisked away in a squad car, while seventeen year old Rocco was sent to the hospital (where he remained for months) and the family patriarch was sent to the morgue (groups.yahoo.com/group/ladolcevita _defamation_database/message/31).

Two years later, on December 19, 2000, a jury decided that the three officers involved in the Romagnuolo case acted in self-defense and were thus not guilty of manslaughter. Just months before this ruling, however, a judge acquitted Lorenzo Romagnuolo of threatening officer Hoskin. All things pointed to a deliberate police cover-up, through the suppression of evidence and the editing of the tape that recorded the fatal incident in December '98. (groups.yahoo.com/group/ladolcevita_defamation_database/message/31). Although the killing of Tony Romagnuolo was a Canadian case, it is relevant to people of Italian descent living all over the diaspora, especially to Italian North Americans—for in the United States and Canada, being "Italian" is still seen as a weakness, a liability, and as a reason to be victimized.

January 1999: HBO's widely acclaimed television drama *The Sopranos* first aired introducing America to fictitious mob boss "Tony Soprano" and his highly dysfunctional family (Tvtome.com, "The Sopranos"). Following in the footsteps of other '90s mob dramas like *Goodfellas* and *Casino*, *The Sopranos* depicted an Italian-American culture that reveled in gratuitous violence, vulgarity, and foul language. And even though there was nothing particularly unique or redeeming about the way this show portrayed Italian-Americana, *The Sopranos* was heralded by the mainstream media as "innovative" and "refreshing." The show's gigantic success season after season, and its even bigger propagation of anti-Italian stereotypes, has led Italian-American activists to make *The Sopranos* the prime target of their anti-defamatory message—a message that begs the question, "Would similar shows about a money-hungry Jewish family or a crack-dealing African-American family receive such societal praise?" It is not likely. Most troubling of all, the show's creator, like Coppola and Scorsese before him, is an Italian-American—David Chase, whose surname was originally "Cesare" (Italystl.com, "The Second Annual Pasta-Tute Award").

January 8, 1999: A 38-year old Italian-American man, Thomas Pizzuto, was physically beaten by two officers at the Nassau County jail in East Meadow, New York. Five days later, he died of a ruptured spleen. Pizzuto, "the father of a son with Down syndrome, was serving a 90-day sentence for driving under the influence when he was assaulted" by officers Patrick Regnier and Edward Velazquez. They attacked Pizzuto after he demanded his prescribed dosage of methadone. Two other officers, Joseph Bergen and

Ivano Bavaro, helped coverup the beating. When the tragic story leaked out, soon thereafter, a federal civil investigation was initiated to detect patterns of violence against inmates in the Nassau County jail (New York *Newsday*, May 27, 2000, p. A3). Sure enough, other inmates (and particularly minority inmates) came forward stating that corrections officers frequently violated their civil rights. The Pizzuto case received a fair amount of media attention at first, but weeks later the horrific NYPD brutalization of Haitian immigrant Abner Louima overshadowed it. While many African-American groups and high profile civil rights leaders came together to protest what the officers did to Louima, I am not aware of any civil rights activists who protested on behalf of Thomas Pizzuto. Even more disturbing, I am not aware of any Italian-American organizations that spoke out against the beating.[107]

The two officers convicted of killing Thomas Pizzuto were each sentenced to eleven years in prison.

March 1, 2000: Five white men were randomly targeted in a racially motivated shooting spree in Wilkinsburg, Pennsylvania; three of the victims died and the other two were critically wounded. The gunman was 39-year old Ronald Taylor, a black man with a history of mental illness and racial hatred. Despite what the media headlines said, Taylor's racism was less anti-white than it was pro-black. In addition to hating "white trash," as he put it, Taylor created a list of "enemies" that included Jews, Asians, Italians, police, and the news media—if his skin was a different color, the KKK would have had a rather "promising" new recruit. But because Taylor was black there was some confusion at first over whether or not one should consider the shootings "hate crimes"; it all went back to the ridiculous age-old question, "Are black people as capable of racial hatred as whites?" In the end, Ronald Taylor's racism could not be ignored. "Ethnic intimidation" was added to the list of charges against him (Post-gazette.com, "Portrait of Wilkinsburg"; CNN.com, "Suspect in Shooting Spree…").

The belief that Jews and Italians possess all the power in the nation is a popular one among modern Afro-centric racists. Although someone of sound mind might assume that only a Ronald Taylor could hold a belief like this, many so-called "educators" subscribe to it as well, peddling this lie on college campuses all over America. One such educated bigot is Dr. Leonard Jeffries. In addition to telling his students that white people are descended from Neanderthals, Jeffries tells them that the Jewish and Italian "Mafias" are responsible for black plight and for Hollywood's stereotyping of African-Americans (Shamash.org). This man (who proves that anyone can get a Ph.D.) is obviously unaware of two simple facts: Jews, next to blacks, were the most active group in the struggle for civil rights, and Italian-Americans (not blacks) are Hollywood's biggest target when it comes to stereotyping. By using the word "Mafia" to describe Italian and Jewish contingents, Jeffries is indulging in a form of hate speech that is no different than that vociferated by white racists and nativists years ago. It is unfortunate, to say the least, that this supposedly intelligent member of academia seems to be the personification of the fascist, isolationist agenda of a growing number of black nationalist groups. We are at a point in American history where coalitions should be built between ethnicities, not walls. Dr. Jeffries' racist lectures should be condemned and protested wherever he goes.

Summer 2000: Zogby International conducted a survey in order to find out "whether or not [American] teen-agers in general and Italian American teen-agers in particular perceive stereotyping on television and in the movies"; 1,264 teens were interviewed in total (591 males and 673 females). Their ethnic and racial backgrounds were as follows:

446 Northern Europeans	321 Italian-Americans
61 Central/South Americans	56 Eastern Europeans
54 African-Americans	28 Asian/Pacific Islanders
10 Middle Easterners	

When the teens were asked to link particular ethnic groups with the roles they would most likely play onscreen, these were the typical responses:

- African-Americans: athletes, gang members, police officers
- Arab-Americans: terrorists, convenience store clerks
- Asian Americans: physicians, lawyers, and CEOs
- Hispanics: gang members, factory workers
- Italian Americans: crime bosses, gang members, restaurant workers
- Jewish-Americans: physicians, lawyers, CEOs, teachers
- Irish-Americans: drunkards, police officers, factory workers.

Not surprisingly, it was found that the teenagers most frequently linked Italian-Americans with crime (44%), and Arab-Americans with terrorism (34%). What was unsettling, however, was that 46 percent of the Italian-American teens believed their ethnicity was accurately portrayed, and almost 30 percent were proud of their onscreen image.

The Zogby study concluded that "Teens learn the less admirable aspects of their heritage from entertainment industry stereotyping [and their] perceptions of other ethnic, religious, and racial groups are shaped by entertainment industry stereotypes"—this is something Italian-American activists have been saying for decades (NIAF, Zogby International, March 1, 2001).

October 9, 2000: Another confrontation between marchers and protesters ruined the festive atmosphere of the Columbus Day Parade in Denver, Colorado; 150 people were arrested by police (CNN.com, "Thousands Protest Columbus Day Parades").

January 5, 2001: The wrongfully imprisoned Peter Limone was finally freed after serving 32 years for a mob hit he did not commit (TruthInJustice.org, "Man Freed After Serving 32 Years").

September 11, 2001: Sustaining approximately a quarter of all fatalities, "Italian Americans were the single largest ethnic group affected by the horrific event[s]" of 9/11. A fund was set up by the Sons of Italy to help the victims' families (SonsofItalyNJ.org).

November 2001: A federal judge, William Yohn, ruled that Italian-Americans were not discriminated against when six of them were excluded from jury duty in the 1980s murder trial of reputed mobster "Joseph Rico" (real name: Joseph Gavel). Yohn said it was acceptable for prosecutors to exclude Italian-Americans since the Supreme Court does not recognize them as a "cognizable racial group." Apparently, individual ethnicities are not protected from profiling in the jury selection process (groups.yahoo.com/group/ladolcevitadefamation.database/message/32).

The National Italian American Foundation strongly protested Yohn's ruling, just as a state appeals court had in 1995 (managing briefly to overturn Rico's conviction). It is believed by a number of individuals that prosecutors violated the defendant's rights by excluding jurors who *they thought* might be more sympathetic towards Rico on ethnic grounds; it is also believed, obviously, that the civil rights of the jurors were violated in the process. The interesting thing is that Joseph Rico is not of Italian background. He took the surname "Rico" to appear more legitimate as a mobster. Surely, the 1931 movie *Little Caesar* influenced him into taking that name (groups.yahoo.com/group/ladolcevita_defamation_database/message/32).

December 2001: Two Pennsylvania men falsely accused the Montgomery County Commissioner, Michael D. Marino, of physically attacking one of them. Jeffrey Hartman told police that his friend, Byron Spallinger, was punched in the mouth by Marino during a scuffle and that several teeth were broken as a result. When both the police and the state attorney general investigated, however, they found "no credible evidence to support the filing of any criminal charges." On April 10, 2002, Marino filed charges of his own in the form of a lawsuit seeking $50,000 in damages. The lawsuit asserted that the false testimony of Hartman and of Spallinger "besmirched Marino's reputation in his community and with his constituents," and it even led to the "public hatred and ridicule of [him]." Marino contends that Mr. Spallinger, his neighbor for many years, has antagonized him ever since he first arrived in the Skippack, Pennsylvania area. Marino also stated that Spallinger made anti-Italian remarks about his heritage on a number of occasions (*Bucks County Courier Times*, Apr. 12, 2002).

Summer 2002: The Italic Institute of America released a disturbing study known as the "Gianelli Report." Upon surveying various political and cultural institutions, the report concluded, "that after 100 years and the accumulation of sizeable wealth, Italian Americans have failed to achieve either political leadership or cultural respectability in the United States." The percentages of Italian-Americans in various "power sectors" are as follows:

- Fortune 500 business executives—3 percent
- Presidents of major universities—less than 1 percent
- Visual media executives for major networks and studios—less than 1 percent
- Ambassadors, congressmen, and those working for the executive branch of the federal government—4 percent
- State governors and lieutenant governors—0 percent
- Mayors of America's fifty largest cities—2 percent
- U.S. military leaders—4 percent
- Press executives—less than 1 percent
- Labor union presidents—0 percent
- Catholic Church leaders—8 percent

Even though this last percentage is the highest (and though Italian-Americans as a whole comprise only 6 to 7 percent of the total American population), it is in no way proportionate to the large number of Italian-Americans who make up 26% of all U.S. Catholics. It just goes to show that the Catholic Church in this country (like other American institutions) is still, after a hundred years, hesitant to put Italian-Americans in positions of power (Italic Institute, "On Image & Defamation," Nov. 2002).

Columbus Day 2002: New York City Mayor Michael Bloomberg marched in a recalcitrant display of solidarity with cast members from HBO's *The Sopranos* (i.e. his "friends"). This came after he publicly disrespected the Italian-American community by refusing to march in the 58th Annual Columbus Day Parade in Manhattan.

For the past couple of years the organizers of the Manhattan parade had banned *The Sopranos* from marching due to the negative image the show puts forth; the mayor knew this. Even his mayoral predecessor, Rudy-Giuliani, a big fan of *The Sopranos*, had enough decency to respect the wishes of the parade organizers (the Columbus Citizen's Foundation). Bloomberg felt it was more important, however, to be with his "Sopranos" friends than to show leadership as a mayor and honor all the Italian-Americans who helped immensely to get him into office. And so, "Bloomie" and friends turned their backs on the largest group to be affected by 9/11, and took to the streets of the Bronx in a pathetic attempt at celebrating the Italo-American holiday (Italic Institute, "On Image & Defamation," Nov. 2002).

C. Conclusion

The one big thing Italian-American history (and the preceding timeline) teaches us is that there was no sudden date that Italians became Americans; nor was there one defining epoch in which they gained acceptance by broader society. This is why, in the timeline, I gradually phase out the word "Italian(s)" and slowly introduce "Italian-American(s)" to describe their evolution and gradual assimilation (though not necessarily their acceptance). Even after the physical persecutions stopped, we see that employment and educational discrimination continued to impede Italian-American advancement for many years. The problem at CUNY, for example, highlights the routine discrimination that Italian-Americans have faced in all parts of the country.

Another major thing our timeline shows us is that the Mafia stereotype has been a perpetual thorn in the side of the Italian-American community. Since the 1880s, the media's perverse obsession with Italian organized crime has led to all sorts of anti-Italian slander, discrimination, and persecution. Though the great "Mafia mystique" grew in notoriety after World War II, due to Senator Kefauver's hearings on organized crime and the creation of stereotypical TV shows and movies, every generation for the past hundred years has seen a major event re-popularize the image of Italian-American criminality: In 1891 it was the lynching of eleven Italians in New Orleans; in 1909 it was Detective Petrosino's murder; in 1931, the movie *Little Caesar*; 1950s—*The Untouchables* (TV show); 1972—*The Godfather*; and, more recently, in the late 1990s and early 2000s it has been *The Sopranos* television series.

Unfortunately, ever since the 1972 release of *The Godfather*, the romanticized concept of the Mafia has been embraced by mainstream America where once it had been detested and even feared. In comparison, the realistic image of Italian-Americans, as industrious law-abiding citizens, seems to have been overlooked or rejected by the majority of Americans for the past thirty years. Although there are a number of reasons for this (not least of which has been Italian-American complacency), one impregnable bloc is chiefly to blame: Hollywood and the media.

It is no secret that these two forces influence the way people think. As we have seen in the Zogby study conducted from 1996 to 2001, onscreen stereotypes greatly influence the way in which young people perceive other people, who are ethnically different from them. Thus, a whole new generation of bigots (and not just anti-Italian ones) is being "programmed" by the many television shows they watch. They are being trained to believe that it is appropriate, even politically correct, to call someone a guinea or wop, and to do "Godfather" impersonations while in the company of people of Italian descent. Indeed, modern anti-Italianism has evolved to such a point that there is a thin line between stereotyping and outright bigotry. What may be an off-color joke about the mob to one person can rightfully be considered sheer racism by another.

To sum up, Italian-Americans have come a long way since the days when they were the second most lynched group in the nation. The transition from pushcart to SUV in a hundred years' time is truly remarkable. However, the bigotry that the immigrant rag picker was exposed to, still lingers over the head of his great-grandson; the bigotry itself might be more subtle and less "redneck," but it is still the same and it is still there. The dehumanization of Italians as heartless criminals is still as acceptable and popular as ever. This keeps the door open for possible future persecutions. And this, of course, is where the true anti-Italian danger lies.

Part II

Italian-Americans: *In-between* on Arrival

25: Waiting on line at Ellis Island

26: Second generation Italian-American school children.

27: Antonio and Kitty, and their son Ralph (my grandfather).

Chapter Three

It is almost inevitable that the Mafia should take an important part in American criminal rackets. Here is a nation-wide organization of outlaws in a sort of oath bound, blood-cemented brotherhood dedicated to the complete defiance of the law where personal advantage or interests are concerned.
The Kefauver Committee, 1951

After World War II, there had been a sharp rise in drug addiction and juvenile delinquency in the United States, according to the Federal Bureau of Narcotics. The Bureau's commissioner, Harry J. Anslinger, went to great lengths to prove that America's "drug problem" was on the verge of a national crisis. Arrest and prosecution figures were produced between 1945 and 1955, showing that the number of drug cases had skyrocketed. These figures are unreliable, however, as many observers did not see any concrete evidence pointing to an increase in drug use. In fact, great inconsistencies appear in the data that the FBN produced. For example, drug addicts who were female and white had greatly outnumbered all others up until the World War II period; but then, suddenly, the majority of drug users were young black males. "And with each periodic hysteria about increases in addiction among youths there would have had to be large inputs of new addicts early in their life spans, with the result that tens or even hundreds of thousands of female, white, and aging victims must simply have vanished conveniently when they were no longer wanted in the count" (www.druglibrary.org, "The Drug Hang Up").

By now, you are probably asking yourself what all this has to do with Italian-Americans and how it relates to their saga. Well, quite simply,

America's fifty-year "war on drugs" has failed miserably and has historically done nothing but aggravate already intense social problems, demonizing and terrorizing minorities in the process. Among the groups demonized and terrorized have been Italian-Americans and African-Americans. Politicians, the media, and law enforcement have targeted both groups as primary sources of illegal drug trafficking, and have indulged in racial profiling and very aggressive "preventative" tactics when dealing with the African-American community.

For Italian-Americans, the root of the modern defamation problem can be found in Senator Estes Kefauver's Crime Committee hearings, held in the early 1950s. Had it not been for these hearings, Italian-Americans might not have been stigmatized by mafia stereotyping, and the "mafia" might have become an obscure, if not totally obsolete, term—quite possibly, *The Godfather* and *The Sopranos* might never have been made. More importantly, the negative effects of these two productions might never have been felt.

What led to the hearings was Commissioner Anslinger's infatuation with drug pushers and users. In 1950, right before the Kefauver investigation began, the Federal Bureau of Narcotics reported that "young hoodlums" primarily controlled the drug trade (as though it had been controlled, at one time, by Catholic school boys!). As an early witness of the Kefauver Committee, Anslinger testified that "Murder, Inc." and the following characters were behind much of the international drug trade: "Waxey" Gordon, "Lepke" Buchalter, "Legs" Diamond, and "Lucky" Luciano (www.drug library.org, "The Drug Hang Up").

There was a problem, however. The public had already heard of Murder, Inc., and Senator Kefauver knew that that was not a term that would capture the frightened imagination of the masses. The term "Mafia," on the other hand, had already proved successful in capturing the public's attention, and even in stirring the citizenry to action (as we have seen in the New Orleans lynching). Thus, Kefauver and Anslinger teamed up, reacquainting millions of Americans with the dreaded yet mysterious "M-word." As Rufus King so eloquently put it, in chapter 13 of *The Drug Hang Up,* "the sinister Italian conspiracy emerged as the exclusive creature of the Narcotics Bureau. The Mafia concept suited the Bureau ideally as a backdrop for its own image-building. It had mysterious foreign roots, overtones of danger and violence, and an exotic quality akin to that of the Chinese tongs....And indisputably there were identifiable Italian-Americans more or less prominently connected with criminal enterprises throughout the country" (www.drug library.org, "The Drug Hang Up"). All Kefauver and Anslinger had to do now was locate other Italian criminals, in addition to Lucky Luciano, and build them up to be veritable anti-Christs; in no time at all, men with names like Costello and Accardo were gossiped about in locales all across the nation. "So why did Kefauver and the Narcotics Bureau go to all that trouble in recreating Mafia hysteria?" you might ask. What did they have to gain? I propose that they had two main goals in mind: 1) solidifying the government's control through aggressive law enforcement (vis-à-vis the Boggs Act, which greatly increased the number of drug-related arrests); and 2) the destruction of Italian-American culture through defamation (i.e. linking legitimate aspects of Italian-Americana to the Mafia). We see a similar story unfolding today with the Department of Homeland Security, as it continues infringing on civil liberties while politicians, pundits, and others continue stereotyping Arabs as degenerate terrorists who apparently "hate freedom."

Truly, by 1951, millions of Italians were interpreted to be a threat to the WASP establishment. The increase in their social mobility after the Second World War alarmed many traditional elites. At this point in time, it was very possible for real Italian culture to become a greater influence on American life than, say, the local pizza parlor.

The Untouchables television series, negative media reporting, and the Kefauver hearings—in addition to the materialistic, conformist culture that developed after the war—all helped to humble the Italian-American community and to make Italians feel ashamed of their heritage. Thus, many abandoned their culture. It is important to remember that Italians, at this time, had no George Lopez to make them feel good about themselves on a weekly basis; neither did they have Italian-language television programs, nor powerful media outlets of any sort. Their culture began to die as a result.

Senator Kefauver never publicly condemned Italian-Americans during his on-camera appearances, but his committee hearings had that effect. Millions of mainstream Americans were tuning in, every so often, to hear what those no good guineas were up to next. It was like the O.J. Simpson case. No one publicly stated that O.J. was an inferior black man, but it was implied many times by the media, through racial sensationalism and by drawing attention to the fact that O.J. had a white wife.

So, what did the Kefauver hearings actually accomplish in the way of fighting crime? The answer: absolutely nothing. For the couple of years it operated, the committee had traveled to fifteen cities, approximately 52,000 miles. It called over 600 witnesses, and compiled 11,500 pages of sworn testimony. "Yet, not one of the 22 contempt of court cases stemming from the investigation held up in court. Of the 221 proposals submitted to U.S. Congress by the committee less than 10% were enacted into law" (www.americanmafia.com, "Televised Gangsters").

If, however, the Commission acted on the secret mission to check the political, social, and educational aspirations of Italian Americans, through the investigation, it achieved more than it had anticipated. Italian Americans were now seen as either criminals or with affiliation to organized crime. No one with a last name ending in a vowel escaped the devastating stereotype.

One man who had learned a lot from the Kefauver hearings was Attorney General Robert Kennedy. He realized, just like Hollywood and the media that one could go far in public life by exploiting mafia hysteria. This led Kennedy to pursue his own investigations of other organized crime figures, like Sam Giancana.

To sum up, there can be no doubt that Italian criminal organizations have existed in the United States for over 120 years—ever since the first immigrants began arriving *en masse*. This is as sure a fact as the criminal enterprises run by Irish, Jewish, "melting pot," and other gangsters. *All* ethnic groups have been represented, historically, in the American underworld. What is unique to the Italian experience, however, is the length to which the media has focused on Italian criminal activity. When one looks at the situation logically, it becomes clear that, at the root of the problem, is an agenda to defame an entire people.

For example, no legitimate proof has ever surfaced supporting the existence of an organization specifically called "the Mafia." Yet, millions of Americans continue to think otherwise. They have been brainwashed by the Dennis Kearneys of the world, the rabble-rousers, the sensationalists, and the Estes Kefauvers—brainwashed into thinking that whenever one person of Italian descent does something crooked, the whole nationality is to blame; that all persons having an -a, -e, -i, or -o at the end of their name are somehow connected to the oath-bound "Mafia" (even if this connection is remote). This oppressive strategy has proven to be successful in curbing Italian-American power and influence. Even Italian-Americans themselves, now far removed from the original immigrating generation, have bought into the lies concerning their heritage. Herein lies the greatest tragedy of defamation.

Chapter Four

Italians are niggaz with short memories
Chuck Nice [108]

A s we have seen to some degree in Chapter 2, the racial status of Italian-Americans has been rather complex and often contradictory through the years. Historically, whenever Italian-Americans had been oppressed or persecuted they assumed an identity that has, in retrospect, been referred to as "black" (though more accurately described as "non-white"). This stands to reason since the Italians' poverty, low social status, resistance to assimilation, and swarthy complexions were all factors which led native whites to equate them with blacks or the "dark other." One might recall how popular the phrase "black dago" was a century ago.

Nevertheless, Italians were considered white in many ways as well. At Ellis Island, even though their complexions were recorded as "dark," their race was almost always recorded as white. (Still, white in this regard was less of a scientific classification than it was an adjective to describe non-blacks and non-Asians—even Hispanics at this time were classified as whites.) Furthermore, it was common knowledge that Western Civilization sprung forth from the virile Italian soil, and that the history of Rome was thus the history of all "Western" nations. What a threat it would have then been for white Americans, a hundred years back, to admit that their civilization was founded by Italic non-whites—by the very ancestors of the dusky Latin immigrants flocking to their shores!

No, it was easier for whites to believe that these Southern Italians, these degenerate Italians, were not even directly descended from ancient Roman stock, but from the Oriental and African slaves of the empire. Realistically, however, one must consider the following if one is to take such racist logic seriously: since there were probably more Germanic and Celtic slaves utilized in ancient Rome (on account of their primitive cultures, as compared to the much more advanced and thoroughly Romanized Near Easterners and North Africans) modern Italians should be all the lighter in skin tone. It amazes me to see online, while in the midst of this supposedly diverse information age, how many individuals still profess their overtly racist beliefs pertaining to the origins of ancient Rome, its downfall, and the inherent inferiority of modern Italians. These types of racists belong to the old "nativist"/Anglo-Nordic school of hatred. Typically, the old school nativists do not subscribe to the belief that race is a social construct.

Then there are those who belong to the modern school of anti-Italian bigotry. These people consider Italians to be completely and totally white, and hold them responsible for the suffering of African-Americans and other "minorities" in America's urban centers. Modern Italophobes can be, either black or white, liberal or conservative. Many Afrocentric racists, whether intellectuals or activists, endorse the belief that Italians and their evil Jewish allies are systematically working together to destroy the African-American community through drug peddling and negative media portrayals. As the timeline showed earlier, the word "Mafia" is used invariably (by the likes of Dr. Leonard Jeffries and other pseudo-intellectual black nationalists) when describing the Italian contingent allegedly working against African-Americans. The timeline also showed that guilt-ridden WASPs (usually of a liberal political persuasion) excelled during the Civil Rights Era in shifting blame on to Italian-Americans for many societal problems, not least of which was black plight. And so, when it comes to race, the one thing that both the "old" and "new" anti-Italian schools agree on is that Italians are a class of degenerate criminals.

That Italians have sometimes been considered non-white, and at other times considered full-fledged "Caucasians," highlights a great deal of ignorance on the part of many Americans. They are ignorant of the true *Mediterranean* identity that Italic people have carried with them for thousands of years. This identity has never been defined in terms so simplistic as "black" and "white"; rather it has been defined by a historical "in-between-ness"— not quite African and not totally European. (In fact, that is what Mediterranean means—"between the lands," or between the European and African continents.) Evidence of this non-black-and-white mentality can be traced back to Roman times when slavery had absolutely *nothing* to do with skin color, and skin color was categorized into many subtle levels, by pigment, and not merely described by those inconclusive extremities—black and white.

Likewise, the Italo-Mediterranean power structure had not been built along black and white lines. Some will naturally try to refute this statement, drawing attention to the historically based social disparities between dark-skinned Southern Italians and light-skinned Northerners. However, one must realize that the social disparities between the two groups of Italians were/are just that—*social*. They did not come about as the result of some form of institutionalized racism against Southerners. The fact that some North Italian bigots try to use the "dark/light" issue to their advantage does not make South Italian plight a racial issue. Knowing, then, that a historical in-betweenness (a *Mediterraneanita*) gripped the Italians' souls, it comes, as little surprise, that the whole "black and white" issue was a totally foreign concept to the newly arrived immigrants. Their lack of experience with this, as well as with other aspects of *Americanita*, contributed even more to the Italian immigrants' sense of detachment, isolation, and in-betweenness.

A. Identity & Assimilation

If one follows the timeline in Chapter 2, one will subconsciously find that there are three main categories of Italian-American identity corresponding to specific time periods. I have given the categories the following names: 1) the period of the Dago/Italian (1880s to 1930s), 2) the period of the Italian-American (1930s to 1950s), and 3) the period of the Italian-American/white (1950s to today). In the first period, Italians (usually immigrants) saw themselves as Italians first and foremost, or at least identified with whatever Italian region they came from; Americans, on the other hand, perceived Italians to be some lower form of life and readily referred to them as "dagoes." Negative remarks were frequently made about them like the following: "The knife with which [an Italian] cuts his bread he also uses to lop off another dago's finger or ear"; "There has never been since New York was founded so low and ignorant a class among the immigrants who poured in here as the Southern Italians" (Lagumina, 1999: 31, 56) —and these statements were made by supposedly intelligent professionals!

Being new to the country, Italians were naturally strange and exotic; though not every American hated this new population, it was apparent to all that Italians were highly visible and out of place—for they were different in their look, dress, language, customs, and religion. At the height of their "strangeness," still during this Dago/Italian period, many similar descriptions of them appear in print (especially prior to World War I). The April 1881 edition of *Harper's Magazine* had this to say of the Italians in New York: "It is no uncommon thing to see at noon some swarthy Italian, engaged on a building in process of erection, resting and dining from his tin kettle, while his brown-skinned wife sits by his side, brave in her gold earrings and beads, with a red flower in her hair" (Moquin, 1975: 40). It would appear that no assimilation took place whatsoever when *Arena* magazine made the following observation sixteen years later of Boston's Italians: "The men are of an olive complexion, short of stature, with prominent cheek-bones and round heads. They uniformly wear low felt hats and ill-fitting clothes, and do not infrequently adorn themselves with earrings. The women, with their gaily-colored headdress and huge ear-drops, are even more noticeable than the men...walking through the streets with large baskets or bundles on their heads..." (Moquin, 1975: 50). Images of impoverished, chaotic Mediterranean humanity come to mind when reading one woman's late nineteenth century account in *Cosmopolitan*: "The [Italian] population swarms; the street is full of swarthy, unkempt men; buxom, handsome women with their babies at their breasts; old crones with bundles on back or head..." (Moquin, 1975: 300). New York's MacDougal Street was said, almost comically, to be "teeming with swarthy babies and their gaily attired mothers" (Mondello, 1980: 185). And so, from the obvious patterns in these descriptions, we can come to a definite conclusion—the Italian "colonies" or "Latin Quarters," as they were called, were what we today would consider to be non-white ghettos. It becomes clear that the modern Central American immigrants to this country—those smallish Spanish-speaking people of three-fourths Indian blood, looked down upon by so many of the descendants of European immigrants (themselves now mixed) —are utterly indistinguishable from the old Italian migrants. The round heads, the swarthy complexions, the ill-fitting clothes, the displaced facial expressions—how many of us can spot Juan and Jorge plodding down the street a mile away? How many Juans and Jorges realize they march in the same exact shoes, on the same exact road, used by streams of Latin migrants who had come before them?

Better yet are the questions that Sal Lagumina posed in his book *Wop!* (1999): "How could Americans fed on a fare of Anglo-Saxon superiority ever accept peoples who looked so funny and behaved so differently, who ate strange and exotic foods, and who wore such colorful but uncouth clothes? How could Americans ever absorb these boisterous, garrulous immigrants and assimilate the crude, simple-minded Italian peasant into urban society?" (53). The answer to these questions, I believe, is simple: America could not accept and absorb such people then, and it still cannot. The only feasible hope for acceptance lies in the *second generation's* willingness to assimilate. As much as we hear that America is a multi-ethnic country that embraces all cultures, it is not.

This is not a criticism but a fact; realistically, a nation needs to have a cultural foundation on which to stand—and the foundation on which the United States was built is of Anglo-Saxon origin. The nation's language, politics, worldview, history, etc., all retain their original Anglo roots. This is not to say that America is not enriched by immigration and that each individual group does not add its own special ingredients to the unique American mix. But to fully function in American society one needs to drop one's old foreignisms and acquire an American identity; one needs to make sacrifices and take on that red-blooded spirit of competition that has made this country great. And no group is more pressured to assimilate or in a more conflicted position than the immigrants' offspring.

This brings us to the next period of Italian identity—that of the true *Italian-American*. This period stretched roughly from the 1930s to the 1950s and was characterized by the second generation's obsession with American conformity. Torn between two cultures, one foreign and one native, one oppressed and one dominant, the children of Italian immigrants learned at an early age that being "ethnic" had its disadvantages. The taunts, the ridicule, the feeling of isolation, not to mention all the physical and verbal abuse they saw their parents endure, were all reasons to abandon that which made them stand out, that which made them different—their heritage. As Jerre Mangione and Ben Morreale wrote in their definitive work, *La Storia* (1993), "Many Italian men and women have at least one childhood memory of an incident on public transportation with a parent speaking in the native tongue. An American passenger looks at them angrily and storms off the car, declaring, 'Can't you speak English!' and 'Goddamn Wops!' A child could feel [the hostility] even in a glance." In this way, Italian men and women were *disprezzati* (despised foreigners), and Italian children were undergoing a process of Americanization, which made them feel ashamed of their parents (221-2).

The public school system's unrelenting, often hostile crusade to impart American culture to the children also aided the long-term assimilation process. Stories abound of fanatical teachers who scolded pupils for speaking Italian, for eating Italian foods during lunch, and even for the seemingly harmless Italianism of talking with one's hands. A legacy that the schools inherited from Ellis Island was the deliberate changing of those students' names which were either too difficult to pronounce or too "ethnic." Teachers did this with the greatest of ease. For example, "Calogero became Charlie; Baldassaro, Ben; Salvatore, Sam or Sal; Luigi, Louie; Gaetano, Guy; Concetta, Connie; Antonio, Tony; Giuseppina, Josephine or Josie" etc., etc. (Mangione and Morreale, 1993: 221-2). My own grandmother, who still goes by the Americanized name Vivian, was an early victim of this school-endorsed "nomenocide"—her birth-name is Vincenza. Some children, when they came of age, went as far as to change their surnames in order to better fit into society; D'Adamo became "Adams," Fontanella transformed into "Fontaine," and so on.

The reader should not get the wrong impression, however. Even with all the adversity mounting around them in the outside world, the immigrant offspring persisted in their foreign ways at home. They still communicated with their parents in Italian, they still ate macaroni and other foods native to Italy, and even when all the other aspects of *Italianita* finally left them, their Roman Catholic faith remained. Thus, the very conflict between the Italian and American cultures was producing, quite unexpectedly, an entirely new culture—one of mixed emotions and dual loyalties; a true hyphenation was setting in.

Perhaps the greatest single act to expedite assimilation came in 1924, when the U.S. finally closed its doors to large numbers of Southern and Eastern Europeans. The so-called National Origins Act shut out those immigrants who had been flooding into the nation—victims of hunger, oppression, pestilence, and more—for a period of over three decades. The time for accepting successive waves of strange foreigners was over; it was now time to assimilate. So, without a steady stream of Italian newcomers to reinforce the truly *Italian* spirit of the Little Italies, there was soon only one direction in which the heritage of the old country could go—down, down, down. With each passing year, Americanization increased by leaps and bounds in the ethnic neighborhoods. Naturally, then, by the 1930s, *Italianita* in the United States reached its peak.

The following, excerpted from an online article, highlights the Depression era problem of Italian assimilation as it relates to the group's racialization by society: "As late as the 1930s, a second generation Italian in New Haven told a researcher that 'our skin gives us away...it is dark and oily.' Another described a conversation with his employer, who called Italians names. When asked why he felt that way about all Italians, the employer said: 'I don't mean you, Henry. You're white.' An American history textbook, again as late as the 1930s, asked whether it would be possible to absorb the 'millions of olive-skinned Italians" into the body of the American people'" (GothamGazette.com). And although it would seem entirely unnecessary (if not ridiculous) by today's standards, it was once said that Italian applicants for clerical jobs often felt obliged to call themselves French or Spanish or Turkish (Higham, 1973: 161). Such was the contempt for Italians and *Italianita* during the first half of the twentieth century; and such was the anti-Italian environment into which they were unconditionally expected to assimilate.

The many Italian immigrants in South America were also racialized (though to a lesser extent), and thus prevented from immediately assimilating into the kindred Latin societies of the various Spanish and Portuguese speaking countries. An article in the December 2003 issue of *National Geographic* confirmed this, stating that the swarthy immigrants from Italy, Spain, the Middle East, and even France "were looked down on by [Argentina's] fair-skinned ruling class and referred to spitefully as *negritos* and, more tolerantly, as *morochos*, or dark-skinned people" (42). I am also reminded of the 1983 movie *Gabriela*, in which Marcello Mastroianni tells a wealthy, fair-skinned Brazilian man that he is half Neapolitan and half Turkish; snobbishly the Brazilian remarks that Neapolitans and the Turks are one and the same. Evidently, anti-Italian/Mediterranean racism was prevalent in both North and South America during the first half of the twentieth century.

Things began to change in the United States around the time of World War II, however. A "whiter" identity was taking shape. Italian-Americans were now ready to take a giant step towards total assimilation. There are three main reasons for this: 1) Italian immigration had already been curbed for two decades; 2) new opportunities, largely produced by the war, were opened up to Italian-Americans and helped them attain a higher level of economic prosperity; and 3) the group's loyalty fell suspect, so they had to go out of their way to prove they were good Americans. In many cases, this meant ceasing to speak Italian at home and in public, changing one's name, and totally forsaking all aspects of one's heritage. That 600,000 Italian-Americans had their civil liberties infringed upon (as discussed earlier) played no small role in convincing many more that being "Italian" was a liability. Hereto, being "white" was obviously interpreted as something good or American.

The hatred of blacks was also interpreted by many (yet not all) to be a natural white American form of expression, and acted as a means for Italian-Americans to distance themselves from other persecuted minorities. As we saw in the 1951 Cicero riots and in the later tensions in Bensonhurst, Italian-Americans turned into persecutors themselves. Nonetheless, these outbreaks should have been interpreted as minority on minority conflicts, if one is to understand their sociological significance; the media, however, chalked up the violence to evil white Italians lynching poor, oppressed blacks—an oversimplification to say the least.

In many respects, the phases of both the Italian- and African-American identities have been rather similar through the years. The "Negro/black" period and the "African-American" period, for example, correspond roughly to the Dago/Italian and Italian-American periods. The historical evidence has also demonstrated that the social status of Italians, during the peak years of their immigration, was not that dissimilar from the social status of blacks (the same ethnic slurs were even hurled at both groups!). The major difference in the two groups' identities is this: African-Americans never made the jump to "white" (sociologically speaking), whereas Italians did.

This is not to say that black people are not on an equal footing with whites today, because in many cases they are—if blacks want to succeed, they can![109] It only means that society still, after some four hundred years, does not yet recognize black people as normal *mainstream* Americans. Italian-Americans, on the other hand, entered the third phase of their identity around the 1950s, secure in their new status as *white* Americans.

B. *Erroneous and Antiquated Racial Beliefs*

If one is not sure by now as to where I stand on the concept of race, let me make one thing perfectly clear: as a social construct race is quite alive in society, yet biologically there is no such thing as the "white" or "black" races. If these terms accurately described legitimate races, only a small minority of people could be included in their ranks. For no one I know is genuinely "white" skinned or "black" skinned. There are, however, various pan-ethnic groups in this world such as the Bantus, Mediterraneans, Mongoloids, and Nordics. Generally speaking, the Bantus inhabit sub-Saharan Africa; Mediterraneans dominate the vast region from the Italian Alps to Libya, and from Portugal to northern India (many can also be found in Latin America); Mongoloids are represented in the many peoples of East Asia (Chinese, Mongolians, Koreans, Japanese, etc.); and the Nordics are, obviously, Northern European peoples.

The degree to which the Mediterranean type is found in all of the above groups (verily, in the billions of diverse people around the world) has convinced me that WE ARE ALL MEDITERRANEANS. To me, the term *Homo Sapiens* could just as well be *Homo Mediterraneus*, especially if one considers that the majority of the earth's people have "intermediate" skin tones (as do Mediterraneans), and that if all six billion of us suddenly merged into one color, we would be light khaki—a Mediterranean hue. Having said that, I wish to stress, even more vehemently, that *I do not believe in the superiority or inferiority of specific groups or "races."* Racial sup-remacy is a primitive, foolish concept that has wrought unfathomable misery upon countless people through the centuries. It must be wiped out wherever it exists and in whatever form it takes.

In America, racism has had an exceptionally ugly past. Quite contrary to the clichéd phrase of universal brotherhood, "liberty and justice for all," it can be argued that the nation was founded on the extermination of Native peoples, the enslavement of blacks, and the cyclical victimization of immigrants. It comes as no coincidence that all of these atrocities, severest during the course of the nineteenth century, occurred around the same time that the race-based eugenics movement gained a pseudo-religious popularity in American society. To justify such immorality as slavery and genocide, White Anglo-Saxon Protestants (and other peoples of Northwestern European heritage) formulated racial beliefs, similar to those found in the Hindu caste system, which maintain that a light-skinned ruling class was predestined to dominate the earth.[110]

Probably the greatest of the early racial theorists, and certainly the most influential, was Johann Friedrich Blumenbach. Living to the age of 87, Blumenbach's works actually spanned both the eighteenth and nineteenth centuries. The German-born anthropologist is chiefly responsible for giving those of us in the English-speaking world our racial classifications. His book, *On the Natural Varieties of Mankind*, first appeared in 1775 (the year the first shot of the Revolutionary War was fired) and we have been using his classifications ever since. Essentially, Blumenbach "divided the human species into five races: the Caucasian or white race, the Mongolian or yellow, the Malayan or brown race, the Negro or black race, and the American or red race" (En.wikipedia.org). When he came across a skull native to the Caucasus mountain region, so the story goes, Blumenbach declared it the perfect, quintessential "white" skull—hence the term "Caucasian."

It is ironic that he would do so, since the people of the Caucasus Mountains are generally similar in physiognomy to the neighboring peoples of the Middle East. In fact, today, many Georgians, Armenians and Chechens, on account of their dark hair and features, are scathingly referred to as "blacks" by contemptuous Muscovites. Nonetheless, Blumenbach's craniometrical research prompted him to apply the term "Caucasian" to the majority of peoples living in Europe, the Middle East, North Africa, and northern India (both Indo-Europeans and Semites alike).

To this day, the U.S. Census Bureau counts Americans of Middle Eastern and North African backgrounds as "Caucasians" or whites. In the biological sense, they are too similar to the peoples of Mediterranean Europe to be listed as "non-whites." Socially, however, many of these people come from non-Christian, Semitic nations and are perceived not to have the same values as legitimate whites; thus, Westerners readily refer to them as "non-whites."

Psychology also plays a great role in the differentiation of "races." For centuries all things "European" or coming from Europe—or, better yet, from that mythical realm of the West— have been classified as "white" (a long-time synonym for that which is "good"), while that which has been traditionally classified as non-European, non-Christian, or non-Western (described by words like Arab and Islamic) has been associated with all that is *non-white*—and, by extension, all that is *not good*. In addition, people all too often look at others' superficial outward appearances and confuse them with racial traits. Many Americans see an Arab woman's *hijab*, or a Latino's skin tone (tanned as the result of extensive outdoor work), or even the different hairstyle and earrings of some exotic foreigner, and immediately they tag such people as "non-whites." The media reinforces American racism everyday with phrases like "the first black" this and "the first Hispanic" that, drawing attention to the race problem yet doing nothing to help solve it. People connect what they read and see first hand, and *psychologically* draw their own conclusions.

Although it is safe to say that the eugenics movement is dead in contemporary American society, the concept of race is not. Today, two types of people can be found on either side of the issue: racists and anti-racists. Racists abound in our society; whether liberal or conservative they tend to categorize people and judge issues by race, even if they say they do not. Though many conservatives certainly have an underlying race prejudice, liberals, I have found, are usually the most blatant of racists making foolish statements like "Hispanics are worse off than whites," contrasting the disparities between "races" that do not exist. In this way, they confuse cultural or social groups with biological ones. Anti-racists, on the other hand, are intelligent enough to realize that our modern conception of "race" is anachronistic and crude. I personally tend to agree more with the anti-racist point of view— that mankind is not divisible into artificial colors and that we are all *humans*, period. Yet, even in this school of thought there is an undercurrent of racism.

For example, the so-called "Race Traitor" website encourages "whites" to abandon their racial status, yet says nothing to blacks or Asians or others about rebelling against their own respective classifications (www.postfun. com; academic.udayton.edu).

This is tantamount to racial hypocrisy. The "Race Traitor" agenda is apparently myopic in its approach to end racism, targeting "whiteness" only. It is thus blinded to the fact that the real enemy is *hatred*—something which all races have indulged in rather copiously (and something, it is safe to say, which will not disappear from human nature any time soon). Until there is an end to such hypocrisy and until we Americans liberate ourselves from rigid, old fashioned racial classifications, misunderstanding will continue to fan the flames of the dreaded "race problem."

C. *"Are Italians White?"—An Online Race Debate*

Below is a debate and discussion that took place in August of 2002 between myself and other members of various online Italian-American groups. The debate, which has been greatly condensed, centered on whether or not Italian-Americans are legitimate "whites"; the subject came up after one woman, who I am referring to as Mrs. A, started an online petition addressed to "White Taxpayer Caucasian Citizens." The clearly racist document called for an end to immigration, bilingualism, minority "complaining," etc., in the crudest of terms. In order to get signatures Mrs. A appealed to the so-called "white ethnics" on various websites. When she found out that the Italian-Americans online wanted nothing to do with her petition (and that Italians are not, in reality, those buffoonish "Moolie"-hating bigots one sees on TV), she was outraged. Mrs. A made a racist backlash taking the position that Italians are simply "white folks" and that a pan-European American solidarity is needed if "we" (meaning whites) are to survive as a racial group in America. Although she claimed to be of partial Italian heritage (a dubious tactic many use in order to persuade a specific group to think a certain way), Mrs. A sounded less like a "European-American" and more like a full-blooded nativist straight out of the 1890s—someone with no room for hyphens in her blood.

Except for myself, I have changed the names of those involved in the discussion so as to protect their privacy. We will now jump into the discussion/debate at the point where Mrs. A began defending her petition; I will leave it for the reader to decide whose point of view makes more sense.

Mrs. A: The entire point of the petition was that WE, AS EUROPEAN AMERICANS, have no voice in Washington because our politicians are too busy importing people to vote for them [and too busy to listen] to us. [Our] constitution was not supposed to guarantee anyone the right to come here, contribute nothing, and be supported by the people who work for a living. As for the petition being racist, EVERY OTHER ETHNIC GROUP in this country has the right to band together...(NAACP, LULAC, La Raza) and [to] try to make things better for their people, often at our expense, both literally and figuratively. The only group of people, branded as racist--if they [are] bold enough to speak out, [are whites]. Everyone else can demonstrate, march, riot, band together, EVERYONE BUT US THAT IS.

Cristogianni: [Mrs. A.] I hardly believe...that a petition addressed specifically to "White Taxpayer Caucasian Citizens" will help [your cause]. this looks profoundly racist, and "David Dukeish," even if it's not the intent of the petition. If you are so adamant about putting an end to illegal immigration, why not simply address the "American people"? It is my opinion that anything having to do with "White Pride" or "European-Americans" (a term David Duke seems to be using a lot these days) has absolutely NO REASON to be posted on Italian-American sites. All it does is affirm in the minds of our defamers that we are indeed bigots off-screen as well.

Mrs. A: Mr. Gianni, I can make the same argument about this website. If we are all "Americans," as you say, then why do we need an "Italian" website, a "German" website, [or] an "Irish" website? There is nothing wrong with people coming together because they all feel that they have something in common. And guess what, Mr. Gianni: we all DO have something in common, besides the fact that we are all of Italian heritage.... [Like] it or not...we are all members of the White, Caucasian (or whatever name you want to call it) race. And we all have in common [the fact] that the WHITE people in Washington who make our laws ARE NOT HEARING OUR VOICES above the din of every minority group that they see as a potential goldmine of votes.

No one is forcing you to sign the petition. But I find it very curious that the moment the word WHITE or Caucasian is mentioned, the petition...is branded as "David Duke-ish" or racist. Why is it okay for a group of African Americans, Hispanics, Martians, etc., to protest [but not us]? I am just trying to help other members of my race, including you, Mr. Gianni. If you choose to live in a dream world where you think that reverse discrimination does not exist, then that is your choice.... Perhaps some day you and I, or future generations of Euro/Americans will be living on a reservation given to [us] by Third World immigrants who have taken over this country, thanks to our politicians, who are fiddling while Rome is burning.

Cristogianni: "Why is it okay for a group of African Americans, Hispanics...to protest?" Because, like Italian-Americans, they are ethnic and of a racial minority, and have no one to stick up for them but THEMSELVES. These groups (Italian-Americans included) have been historically marginalized in society. Your beloved "white people," on the other hand, have always held the power in this country and that's not going to change any time soon. Once the white population in America drops down to 49 percent, I will support your call for an NAAWP. The answer to your other question— "If we are all 'Americans'…why do we need an 'Italian' website, a 'German' website, an 'Irish' website?" The answer is simple. Different ethnicities don't "need" these websites; if they WANT them, they can have them—this is America. (I am an American and I am assuming you are one as well.) That said, your petition should have been addressed to the "American People," not only to "whites." What you and your cronies are doing is alienating the rest of America (specifically, non-whites). And I must say, it's not very "American" of you.

Mr. S: My birth certificate and both my parents' birth certificates say under race, "white." My mother was of English/Welsh ancestry, [and] my father was of Neapolitan ancestry. I am white. Often people on this forum, [and] elsewhere, only speak for themselves and their own personal experiences. [As for skin color,] there are many shades of white ranging from red to pink, vanilla to olive and tan. Olive skin is considered Caucasian, as some of the peoples of India are even considered Caucasian. The "Black" race, as is visible, can range from ebony to tan, and race [is] determined not by skin color but by head index, bone and organ form and above all "features." Some Italian Americans need to get off their NON WHITE kick, though I know there has been an ignorant tendency to [classify] the darker toned…into a "third world" category in the U.S…

Mrs. DF: [Mr. S.] I agree with many of your points. However, my point is that Italians like Arabs, for example, have this dual identity of being "white" and "non-white" when it serves the purposes of others. I am saying that we are an ethnic group that is [perceived not to be] part of the mainstream white public. If we were just plain old white, my brother's friend's car wouldn't have been destroyed and dead animals wouldn't have been left on his porch to chase him out of the neighborhood to which he moved in Arizona. I think that the Italian-Americans who identify so strongly with whites have never felt as if they were treated differently or never ventured out to non-ethnic white America. I think that is valid. We all have different experiences that shape the way in which we see the world. But it is unfortunate for you or anyone [else] to blow off and rationalize the thoughts and experiences of other Italian-Americans [simply] because they do not fit into your mental schema. I agree that "white" is now considered "bad" and [that this mentality was largely propagated] by white radical socialists with an agenda to "bring it all down, man"—a remnant of 60s nostalgia. [But, at the same time, I also believe that the term] "European-American" is a code word for angry white male. My main point was that I don't feel that I am a part of the mainstream white population; when I had taken part in my ivy-league college experience, I felt very different from the others. Not only did I look different, but I valued different things. I was simply on another page due to my heritage and upbringing. To you, this might mean nothing, but to me my experience speaks volumes of the dual identity issues with which Italian-Americans are faced. [Personally,] I am curious as to why you wish to discuss issues concerning Italian-Americans [at all] if you feel so part of the mainstream.

Mr. YL: [Mrs. DF] calls the term "European-American" a code word for angry white male. What bull____! Now we can't consider ourselves European—she's declared it racist!

Mrs. DF: Take a chill pill, [Mr. YL].… I just think that the term Euro-American has its own separate agenda, which does not reflect the history and interests of Italian-Americans. That's my point. Each group has its own agenda. I don't see the need for Italians to join the Euro agenda when we have our own unique concerns. All I want, in this day of preferences, is to have fairness. One day Italian-Americans are denied jobs for being Italian—the next day, for being white. This is how we are different from other groups. I want to see our leadership handle this. We have to go back before we can go forward. Do you know I had a principle tell me she couldn't hire me because I'm white when at first she thought I wasn't white and could hire me? She reneged the job. How do you think that makes me feel? How do you think it feels to be asked what ethnicity you are when you're about to be hired? Where is our payback for the decades of discrimination? Do you know that Italians were lynched in the South? Check into it—Louisiana.… I am tired of fitting into a racial category that does not reflect our history in this nation. I want the truth to be told of the internment and I want the history books to stop being sensitive only to the Japanese. The fact is that people love to laugh at us and the "powers that be" want to use us in their favor. If you can't see this, I don't know how else to make it clear. I am tired of having a dual identity that can be manipulated at will.

Mrs. A: Have you ever wondered why there were no riots during the Depression, when everyone was poor? People stood in line patiently for a bowl of soup. Some people who had lost everything chose to throw themselves out of windows, but they didn't riot, burn down businesses owned by people of other ethnic backgrounds, pull people off of the street and beat them with bricks because they needed to blame someone for being poor. And why weren't there any riots after the O.J. trials? Do any of you on this site actually think the verdict was just? Do any of you REALLY believe that he was innocent? Has anyone seen the news about the two black men in Chicago, one 60, and I can't remember the age of the other one. They had an accident; their van jumped a curb and slammed into some people. THEIR OWN PEOPLE, THEIR OWN RACE, pulled them from the van and beat them TO DEATH. The older one begged for mercy, but got none. And not one person who witnessed this heinous act will come forward. Face it. There are two sets of standards in this country; two sets of acceptable behavior. Perhaps, when WE are the minority (as we will soon be), some of you will be the recipients of this behavior.... And then, if you are still alive, maybe you will think differently. This petition is a lost cause, because people of European heritage are, for the most part, cowards who are afraid to speak the truth about ANYTHING. Yes, there are bad people of all races and good people of all races. The point is that we, as Euro-Americans, have no voice. The only voice, we have: our vote! And guess what? THEY DON'T WANT IT! They would rather import votes than listen to us.

Cristogianni: Why don't you just state what your agenda is and cut all the bull! Your recent post has nothing to do with illegal immigration and everything to do with the hatred of blacks. This is why I refuse to sign your bogus petition. See, it's not really about wanting illegals sent back home or legals learning our language, it's about stirring up white folks (or people you PERCEIVE to be "white folks"). You're nothing more than a rabble-rouser, and you would've fit in rather well during the Nativist Nineties. If in fact you do happen to be part Italian, you're an embarrassment to us all. (And just so you know, calling your "European-American" comrades cowards does not endear you to them.) Furthermore, I would personally like to know if you can define just what exactly a "white" person is. What populations do you believe to be "white"? Is being "white" a constant or does it change over time? Do you realize that Italian-Americans were not always considered "white" in the conventional sense? Or do you conveniently wish to forget this, perhaps brush it under the rug? Can you also tell us what exactly a "Caucasian" is? Are you aware that ACTUAL CAUCASIANS (i.e. people from the Caucasus mountain region such as Armenians, Azeris, and Georgians) have dark features, and often, dark skins? If you fall back on the "All Europeans are white" argument, do you then yourself consider Gypsies, Jews, Turks, and racially mixed Europeans (of which there are a lot now) to be "white"? Perhaps [Mrs. A] is trying to push a Nordic supremacist agenda on us. Let's show a little concern here, paesani!

Mrs. DF: Thank you so very much. I've been getting chewed out by saying the same thing. However, I took it a step further to show how misled some Italian-Americans are by uniting themselves with "European-

Americans"—a code word for angry white males. Their anger toward inequities needs to be redirected from another approach so that Italians, for once, define themselves for themselves. Not white, not non-white, just plain Italian-American. That is why I am on this site. I don't want to hear about the European-American tears. Italian-Americans shouldn't get sucked into that; we should stay within our own group of people—those who understand us because they are "us."

Cristogianni: [Mrs. DF.] you sound very intelligent. If more people understood how persecuted we were as a group from 1890 to 1920, perhaps we would be treated with a little more respect today. Like you, I also have maintained on the Italian-American websites that the "Euro-American party-line" is not the way to go for us. After all, "white people" weren't the ones who cared about Italian issues in the past; they just want to use us as a means to an end. Historically, Italian-Americans have had to fight for everything they've gotten. And if that didn't work, they had to deny their culture to get ahead; they had to change their entire identity to come off more "European" or white. Unfortunately, as you're well aware, some people will just never be able to process these truths.

Mrs. DF: You said it so beautifully. I think there are a great number of self-loathing Italians who, like you clearly pointed out, do not fully grasp what being Italian-American means and has meant. I couldn't agree more with your position. Going with the European-American approach would be our downfall. I think those leaning that way have good intentions, but do not see how we would be getting used by those who have belittled and degraded who we are in the first place. We need to do this ourselves and come at it from our angle. I am willing to do this. My good friend from Brooklyn (who now lives in Arizona) wants to go to Fordham [University] this summer for an institute on Italian American issues. I think the NIAF is organizing it. If I can get myself on a plane, I plan to join her. I miss New Jersey and New York so much, as does she. We are very serious and will not let this go. We also have taken on a publisher and I have been working on the next step. An ESL textbook used in the San Francisco Bay area, and published in Massachusetts, [contains this] excerpt on the Japanese-American internment during WWII: "Italians were not interned because they are white." My friend and I were outraged and contacted the representative of the local publisher; however, this is not enough. We want an additional source created and sent out to every school that is using that book. I am sickened to think of students reading such outright lies. I had said my piece at my own school, yet how many other hundreds of schools are giving their students this garbage? Why are people deliberately denying the fact that

600,000 Italian-Americans had their civil liberties infringed upon during the Second World War? This is outrageous! [That is why] I can never align myself with "European-Americans." There is no other group for me other than Italian-Americans, and I will check "other" on all forms until someone gets it right. **Cristogianni:** Thanks for the initial compliment, [Mrs. DF]. I also check "other" on all official forms. Sometimes, if there is a space, I will write "Mediterranean" or "Italian-American." Other Italian-American friends of mine do this as well. Personally, in an increasingly diverse America, I believe that there should be only one blank line for everyone to describe what they are racially or ethnically. I mean, honestly, what do the words "black" and "white" mean anymore? What does the word "Asian" mean anymore? Should there continue to be only one category for Pakistanis and Japanese? If that's the case, maybe the U.S. should have only two categories: "Aryan" and "Untermenschen." It is really a very complicated time, presently, for immigrants coming into the U.S., and complicated for the U.S. receiving these immigrants. As far as our society has come in the past 35 years with regard to civil rights and "racial justice," it appears that we're still at the same ol' spot trying to figure out who's who racially. Just to give you an example of how crazy a time it is, an Iranian and a Pakistani (though they are geographic neighbors and both speak Indo-European languages) can consider themselves of different "races" in this country, one "Caucasian" and the other "Asian"; for Iran lies in the "Middle Eastern" realm and Pakistan lies in the "South Asian" realm. In addition, while most in this country designate Ethiopians, Eritreans, and Somalis as "black," I've seen with my own eyes how many from each of these groups can easily pass for "Middle Eastern whites." As Cushites, they are located geographically in a northeast African transition zone, between Hamites to the north and Bantus to the south. Many East African skulls are thus closer to "Nordic" skulls than to "Negroid" ones. All this info has led me to believe, personally, that we can't just simply state: "Oh yeah, Ethiopians as a whole are black." My philosophy is that complex times call for complex understanding. The oversimplified words "black" and "white" simply do not fit into the current picture. Finally, as a student of history I also share your outrage when books state that Italians (or other Mediterranean ethnics) didn't suffer abuses on the same scale as those traditionally referred to as "non-whites." This makes my blood boil like crazy! Sadly, there are soooo many books out there saying this. Re-educating people and exposing them to the truth is of course the only way to change things.

Mrs. A: I am outspoken, and I know that what I am about to say will offend some of you, but I am honest. All this talk about checking boxes that say "Italian American" is ridiculous. There are so many different groups and nationalities that are WHITE (the dirty word) in this country that it is amazing that we are doing EXACTLY what the minorities would have us do—fighting among ourselves. The only whites who stick together and help each other are the Jews. Hopefully they learned something from the Holocaust, but obviously, we didn't. We will NEVER right the wrongs of those who came before us. We live in the here and now, NOT IN THE PAST. History is important in that it is a tool, a source of information to help people from repeating the same mistakes over and over again.

The black people are still living in the past. Slavery [in the United States] was wrong. But it still exists in many parts of Africa. And no blacks are slaves in this country, save those who are slaves to an evil government who has made them dependent and stolen their sense of self-worth. Reparations for something that we didn't do and none of them suffer is a ridiculous concept, but one I predict that will come to fruition. The people in this group, MY PEOPLE, the people of my grandparents' homeland, are fighting amongst themselves over whether or not we are white or black, European or not European. It is sad and somewhat (yet not totally) surprising to me. I find it ironic that you want to start a separate, even more EXCLUSIVE petition, when you are denying the very fact that ALL WHITE PEOPLE in this country—whether they are Russian Jew, Polish, German, Irish, Italian, whatever—ARE FACING DISCRIMINATION AND UNFAIR TREATMENT FROM OUR GOVERNMENT. And unless we LEARN from history [about the negative consequences of] apathy and the failure of people to stick together and SPEAK THE TRUTH, we will continue our downward spiral in this country.

Cristogianni: Correction: we are not fighting "over whether or not we are white or black"; we are fighting for the right not to be classified INCORRECTLY as either "white" or "black." Italians have been doing this for over a hundred years now in America; this is nothing new. It's people like YOU who would have us sheepishly accept stereotypes and a classification that many of us don't identify with. I am so sick of this "poor white me" routine I think I'm gonna hurl! I mean when was the last time you were denied ANYTHING for being white? What is all this "unfair treatment" you're ranting about (the fact that there exists affirmative action plans for groups that REALLY need it)? When was the last time you were pulled over because you looked like a "suspicious white person"? How many times have you been rejected for a loan simply because the color of your skin is white? What's unfair is complaining about nonsense (and trying to convince people that "white people don't riot") when there are children dying of hunger at this very minute! What's unfair is white people committing "white flight" in this nation, leaving minority and poverty issues behind them. Poverty knows no color, as there are more white people impoverished in this country than black. (What is your "European-American" group doing about that?) And if you claim not to be a racist, would you just as readily extend your help to a person in need from Compton as you would to someone from Appalachia? I gotta be honest, it doesn't sound like you would. One final point I'd like to make is that white nationalities have neither a necessary reason to band together into a "European-American Union," nor a justifiable reason to do so on purely historical grounds. In other words, contrary to your beliefs, "white people" are doing just fine these days and they have always done rather well when compared to groups such as blacks, Amerindians, Asians, and yes, Italian-Americans. A non-white group such as African-Americans, on the other hand, has every right in the world to band together because their entire identity has been built around the oppression they endured, and so their affiliation with groups like the NAACP is a matter of survival (a relationship forged out of necessity). In addition, it's only natural for black nationalities, such as Jamaicans and Haitians, to join greater African-American organizations because, when they come to this country, they no longer represent the dominant culture in society, and they are immediately affixed to a minority status. This is not the case with immigrating Germans, Swedes, or Irish. Hence the argument that "black nationalities can band together, why can't we?" is not valid here.

Mrs. A: Just how far do you think the Hispanics would have gotten if they had fought over whether they were South American, Costa Rican, Puerto Rican, Mexican, Cuban, Spanish, etcetera? The same goes for the blacks—if they all broke up into little groups with infighting amongst themselves, they would NEVER have gained the attention, or the recognition that they possess as a large group. The same goes for whites, but we're too stupid to see it.

Cristogianni: Uh, excuse me, but Hispanics DO fight over what they consider themselves—perhaps more than any other group on account of their diversity. Obviously, you haven't been exposed to the infighting that plagues this group at times. For instance, many Cubans consider themselves white (on account of the fact that many of their ancestors came straight from Europe, and "black-white" tensions have always been rather pronounced in Cuba); thus, many have had, for quite some time, a particular disdain for the racializing term "Hispanic." Furthermore, in the Southwest there have been cases of people nearly getting killed when using the terms "Hispanic" or "Latino" around Mexican-Americans; this group overwhelmingly prefers to be called "Chicano" or "Mexican-American" (and many show utter contempt for anything European or non-Aztec in their culture).

Remember, "Hispanics" don't form a cognizable racial group in the U.S., and if you think they do, you are much more ignorant than I previously thought; they are rather referred to as an "ethnicity." Hispanics are really just a group of individuals who share a common language, as Americans do with the Brits or Aussies. It's even debatable whether or not Hispanic nationalities can be put into one cultural group. Argentines and Guatemalans differ about as much racially, ethnically, and culturally as Aborigines and Anglo-Australians. Think before you speak.

Mrs. DF: How come there is no response [from Mrs. A] on the selectivity of the term Euro-American? Why isn't her petition being extended to the Jews, Arabs, and Middle Easterners? As Cristogianni pointed out [in an earlier post,] you can't tell the difference between the Lebanese and Southern Italians. Actually, I am darker than my Lebanese friends. They look more "white" than I do.

Cristogianni: It's funny, [Mrs. DF,] most people don't even realize that approximately 60 percent of ALL Arabs in this country are of the Christian faith. Many people could not even tell you who famous Arab-Americans are. The actor Danny Thomas (born Muzyad Yakhoob), singer "Tiny Tim," and presidential candidate Ralph Nader (whom I voted for in the 2000 election) are all of Arab descent.

Mrs. A: Alex, I'll take geography for 100.

I am the continent where the country of Italy can be found.

Q. What is Europe, Alex?...

[As for those of you who do not wish to align yourselves with European-Americans,] I think that no one could deny the fact that we, of Italian blood, ALL COME FROM THE SAME CONTINENT—EUROPE.

Cristogianni: "Europe," as a continent, is a geographical fiction—pick up a globe! In reality, it's a western Eurasian peninsula, which happens to be very important historically and culturally. The original "Europe" only referred to the northern coasts of the Mediterranean, as opposed to the eastern and southern coasts.

Ms. V: I had a guy tell me the other night that he was the only "white" person in this bar I was at. The bar was predominantly Portuguese and Brazilian, with an Italian influence. [Obviously some] WASPs still do not think of certain Hispanics, South Americans, Portuguese, and Italians as white....

My Italian-American friend and I were so insulted by this man's actions and crude comments that [we] had the bouncer come over to escort him away from us. Being young and single, you really do meet them all at bars! **Mr. MI**: Who the heck wants to be "white" anyway? Did you catch the sunburn on George Bush this week? Ouch. Someone give that guy an aloe plant. Quick! Evolution hasn't quite caught up with the Anglos south of the Mason-Dixon. I too have been subtly accosted with the Italians are not white remarks. That's just fine with me, because we Italiani are not. We are Caucasian but so are most Hindus. I like the fact that I can enjoy the sun all day long with my shirt off. So, forget the who's whiter than white debate. Who cares!

This debate and discussion was very stimulating for me. It highlighted the fact that a sense of racial "in-betweenness" can still be found in the collective soul of Italian-Americana. Such feelings may be more suppressed for some, but they are nonetheless there. (Perhaps they can be found now more than ever because national attention is increasingly fixed on the racialized Hispanic community, and because there exists today a higher rate of intermarriage between Italians and non-Italians.) Mr. MI's remark "Who the heck wants to be 'white' anyway?" demonstrates how whiteness has lost its appeal for many Americans and how it is now considered bland and "uncool" to be white. Mr. MI realizes that being white is no longer the only path to success and prosperity in America. There are now a plethora of exotic minorities who can utilize a diverse number of affirmative action plans to take them to the "promised land," so to speak. It is therefore beneficial for Italians to distance themselves from those un-colorful "ethnics" who have traditionally formed the backbone of white America.

Mrs. A's rant, conversely, was essentially a misguided way of expressing frustration with the fact that Italians (along with other select "European-American" groups), having been in America for over a century, are no longer considered an exotic and downtrodden minority—thus there is no preferential treatment for Italians whatsoever. Accordingly, she believes that the group's only salvation lies in forging stronger ties with other white ethnics (or "European-Americans"). This path, however, is steeped in racism; Mrs. A's rant therefore typifies the mentality of the "angry white male"—a mentality, which previously led some misguided Italian-Americans to victimize blacks in Spring Valley and Cicero, Illinois. Her petition ultimately fell on deaf ears not because Italians do not identify themselves as "white" (for many do), but because her politics of victimization were vague and her message was one of alienation. In short, Mrs. A was expecting Italian-Americans to become ardent white supremacists when many are still not comfortable with their white social classification. Her illogical persistence on classifying Italians as white has led me to believe that she is probably the product of a mixed (Italian and non-Italian) marriage, owing her insecurities to suppressed personal feelings of "in-between-ness" and/or inferiority.

Overall, I left the discussion with a sense of optimism. It made me realize that there are other Italian-Americans out there who hold the same beliefs as myself, and who understand that our past victimization, coupled with the modern campaign of anti-Italian media defamation, has helped to form our identity.

D. Forging a "Wog" Identity Down Under

Over the past quarter century Australia has undergone monumental change. Originally, an area of the Southern Hemisphere possessing a homogeneous British culture, Australia has been transformed into a truly diverse nation-continent. Ever since it repealed its racist immigration laws in the 1970s, which only permitted "Anglo-Celtic" peoples to immigrate, large numbers of Southern Europeans, Middle Easterners, and Asians have been flocking to Australia's delectable shores. Out of a current population of about 20 million, there are 1 million Italians there alone. Large numbers of Greeks, Lebanese, Turks, Armenians, and Indians can be found as well.

This new reality, needless to say, irritates many Anglos whose Australian roots go back many generations. The new immigrants, whom Anglos hostilely refer to as "wogs," look different than them, sometimes dress different, speak different languages, and have different religions and customs; it is the same old xenophobic story, yet in a new place, on a "new" continent.

The term, "wog," was originally used by Anglo-Saxons as a racial slur against people of East Indian descent living throughout the British Empire. In more recent times the slur came to include all Mediterranid people bound for Australia—particularly those from Southern Europe and the Middle East. "Go home wogs, we want a white society!" has been the popular greeting which native Australians have given newcomers for three decades. This contemporary Australian nativism, though less bloody, is highly reminiscent of its 1890s American counterpart.[111]

It must be stated, however, that those right-wing racists who comprise a potent force in contemporary Australian politics have already been proven wrong and put to shame for prejudging the "bloody wogs." Within a generation's time frame Italian immigrants and their offspring, in addition to peoples of other Mediterranean backgrounds, rose from lower to middle class status. The Mediterranean community's newly acquired economic success has thus molded them into a powerful ethnic bloc, and has made it possible for "wogs" to enter mainstream society while preserving their vast and varied cultural roots. It is in this present era that the term "wog" has taken on a whole new meaning—it transformed from a slur into a word of ethnic pride (comparable to the African-American transformation of the racial epithet "nigger" into a term of semi-endearment—"nigga"). Being a "wog" is now something to be proud of in Australia. Today, Anglo-Australians are the ones looked down on as bland and "un-ethnic" creatures; they are derisively referred to as "skips."[112]

Anti-immigrant sentiment is still a powerful force "down under," however it is now balanced by ethnic and immigrant rights advocates who are deeply embedded in Australian society.

For proof of Australia's thriving wog culture, one can visit the online magazine "Woglife." It contains all sorts of interesting articles on the new pan-Mediterranean ethnic identity being formed. Past features included information on Italian minority culture, Greek-Italian weddings, Lebanese cooking, Indian music, ethnic humor, immigrant stories, and much more. At the end of each article members of "Woglife" can post their opinions; some posts are many pages long (Wog.com.au). This gives the non-Australian reader good insight into wog-group culture, identity, the group's social status and background, and its political leanings. Although each voice is unique and each "wog" nationality is different, there is generally speaking a shared sense of values and of purpose stemming from their interlocking Mediterranean and Middle Eastern histories, as well as from their racialization by Anglo society. There is, therefore, a distinct tone that exists on the "Woglife" website—one, which boldly announces to the Anglo-Saxon world: WE ARE WOGS, HEAR US ROAR!

Since America has a longer history than Australia of pitting various nationalities against each other, there never has been any real inter-ethnic solidarity in the United States. For instance, whereas an Italian, a Puerto Rican, and an Arab would all be denigrated as "wogs" in Australia, they would separately be considered a "dago," a "spic," and a "rag-head" in America. Their separate patterns of victimization and their greater competition for the same urban and suburban living spaces creates an atmosphere of both aloofness and hostility between the different "wog" groups in the United States. And so there is apparently no sense of *Mediterraneanita* linking the different ethnicities. It is worth noting, however, that Australian visitors to the United States have stated on numerous occasions that they had noticed many "wogs" living in places like Brooklyn, South Florida, and Chicago. To them, there is no major difference between Italians, Hispanics, and Arabs—such peoples are all wogs, period. Personally, I think it is a shame that there is not an American equivalent of wog solidarity and that there is a great lack of inter-ethnic alliances in the United States in general.

E. Conclusion

Identity has always been a rather complicated issue for *all* groups in American society. Though Americans tend to talk of race very simplistically, it never has been a purely "black and white" subject; neither have minority classifications only applied to peoples presently associated with other mythic races such as the Hispanic, Asian, and American Indian groups. All too often, we tend to broadly generalize and lump diverse groups together into "non-white" masses. However, many individual members of these groups, like people of European Cuban and Lebanese Arab descent, have considered themselves "white" for as long as they have been in this country. To say that such people are anything other than lily "white" is, for many, a slap in the face—it is a denial of dignity and of humanity. Thus, outsiders should not decide for others what their race is, or whether they are a minority or not. In a society that is growing more diverse and ethnically mixed by the day, only individuals *themselves* can rightfully affirm who and what they are.[113]

Today the phrase "person of color" is a popular substitute for the archaic "non-white"; it is simply a nicer, more politically correct way of saying *outcast*. I have found this phrase to be exclusionary, as it does not seem to apply to European descended peoples. In reality, we are all "people of color," no matter what our particular backgrounds are; each person on this earth is a totally unique individual whose ancestry reflects the diverse world in which he or she lives. I need only to look at the photos of my great-grandfather, Antonio Borsella, with his English-Irish wife, Kitty, to see that I myself am a person of color—for he resembles a modern-day Guatemalan immigrant and she looks like a typical upper-class Englishwoman.

Naturally then, I, like countless other Italian-Americans, am the confused product of intermixture and forced assimilation. For many, their identity is in question on a daily basis —they do not know who they are ethnically or racially. From my own experience, I can say that I always identified myself proudly as an Italian-American. I never took my ethnicity for granted because I grew up in a section of eastern Long Island that, up until recently, lacked diversity. To me, Italians were *exotic*; they were not the WASPs and African-Americans that I was used to seeing every day in school. Italians were an *in-between* people. Growing up in a non-Italian environment made me curious and enthusiastic about my heritage, unlike someone who grows up surrounded by his/her "own," passively accepting their identity as it is defined by others.

There had been a period in which I considered myself unmitigatedly white, but that was because my parents "said so." Sometimes it was said outright but mainly it was intimated through the differentiation of blacks. As was stated earlier in this book, the most fundamental way to achieve whiteness in America is through the distancing from and the repudiation of blackness. This is true regardless of ethnicity—for there are half Hawaiian and part Korean individuals in my family who, having tread this path to assimilation, identify themselves as white. Still, as far back as I can remember, I always identified with onscreen characters like Rocky Balboa, Tony Manero, and Daniel La Russo. I always identified with the ethnic underdog, and I somehow knew that I could be treated differently or, at worst, persecuted for being Italian. I realized this early on, while still in first or second grade (long before I had heard of the anti-Italian lynchings and mob violence).

Upon going to Italy in February of 1996, I experienced an ethnic re-awakening. Traveling with my high school Latin class, it was the first time I had traveled to a country outside of North America. Being surrounded by *Italianita* made me realize just how different we Americans were and made me appreciate the special beauty of Italy's people and culture. A new appreciation soon blossomed in me for Mediterranean-ness—that is, for all cultures situated around the "Inland Sea." The Mediterranean took shape in my mind as a rich melting pot of civilizations and as the symbolic central point from which all "people of color" (i.e. all human beings) can claim descent; a geographic region incapable of being stereotyped, much like the world as a whole, on account of its infinite diversity. Truly, this re-awakening I experienced was almost religious in nature.

I came back to the United States with a tremendous ethnic pride, looking for more information on my heritage and for more interaction with Italian-Americans. After the '96 trip to Italy, I understood more about myself. By conducting my own research I also found out a great deal about other world cultures, particularly those I deemed "Mediterranean." Eventually, as I came to understand how the histories of all nations were intertwined, I felt obliged to extend the term "Mediterranean" to all peoples. For example, I saw how interconnected the ancient Mediterranean was with Mesopotamia, how connected Mesopotamia was to India, and how Indian civilization greatly influenced Cambodia's Khmer society.[114] The following are just some of the other facts I discovered about the interconnectedness of world cultures: that there exists a close linguistic affinity between the Aryans of northern India and the Baltic peoples; that a common language family existed in ancient times in the Pyrenees, Caucasus, and Hindu-Kush mountain regions; and that the ancient Hibernians and Iberians shared a common past. Such diverse connections are proving to be more certain each day, as many linguists and anthropologists are coming to the conclusion that a common language linked humanity in prehistoric times—this is referred to as the "Nostratic" theory. And so, Mediterraneanness not only provided me with a viable racial identity, but it connected me to the rest of humanity as well. (The concept of unity within diversity prevailed in me.)

The research I conducted after my Italian trip also enlightened me to the great similarities between allegedly "different" ethnicities in the United States; and I found no greater similarity than the one between Italians and Hispanics. As I stated in chapter one: both came from Latin cultures speaking Romance languages; both are Roman Catholic; both have had to endure the same substandard living and working conditions; both have been stereotyped as filthy, criminally prone, ignorant and disloyal to their adopted country; and, finally, both groups have suffered a greater degree of persecution than most other groups. So striking are these similarities that I frequently refer to modern Hispanic immigrants as the "New Italians."[115]

Like Italians, Hispanics also have their own identity problems—some identify more with their Latin/European heritage, and others relate more to their indigenous American past. The Anglo-American refusal to understand this issue further complicates things. For example, how often have we heard a friend or colleague broadly refer to Mexicans, Puerto Ricans, Cubans, Dominicans, and others as "Spanish" merely because these peoples speak their own forms of the Spanish language? These "Spanish people" could look like Sammy Sosa or Karim Garcia, they could be black, yellow, red, white, or a combination of colors—but they are still "Spanish." To me, true Spanish people come from Spain or are the descendants of European-Spanish immigrants in Latin America. The same reasoning maintains that the only true "English" people are those living in Britain, as it would be preposterous for someone to say that Americans, Australians and South Africans are all "English peoples" (despite their diversity) simply because they reside in *English-speaking* countries. If one honestly believes that there is no difference between the peoples of Spain and Latin America (as the racist Mrs. A surely did not), I encourage one to first visit Honduras and then

Spain; while in the latter country, one will find a greater number of natives with freckled faces and flaxen hair than exists in all of Ireland.[116]

As we have seen earlier, Italians (much like Hispanics today) were once depicted as non-whites and described by such terms as "brown-skinned," "swarthy," "olive-complexioned," etc. A popular race-theory book written at the height of Italian immigration highlights this; the book is *The Mediterranean Race*, by the Italian anthropologist Giuseppe Sergi, and it established the premise that Italians are one of many groups connected to the great "Eurafrican" genetic family, otherwise known as the original brown race.[117]

As Italians assimilated, intermarried with others, and turned into legitimate Italian-*Americans* (and then legitimate whites), they were perceived differently. No longer were they thought of as an insular minority population, for they were now a part of the greater American majority. Hispanic-American evolution will probably follow the same course, but this depends on two future factors: 1) an end to massive immigration (illegal or otherwise) and thus an end to the steady flow of newcomers reinforcing the ethnic Hispanic sub-culture, while at the same time preventing assimilation to take place; and 2) an end to ethnic-nationalistic special interest groups that promote balkanization.[118] At the same time, I admit *I do* envy Hispanic solidarity in the United States. It is an undeniable political force that seems to be getting stronger by the day. People of Italian heritage have never galvanized such support, and so they remain an overlooked, underappreciated "white ethnic" group.

To be taken as seriously as Hispanics, Italian-Americans need to get reacquainted with their roots and shake off the "white" stigma. For there are many today who call themselves "Italian" but do not know *anything* about the Italian language (all their *capeeshes* and *fugheddaboutits* aside), and who care nothing at all for the Italian nation or its culture; many who are "fiercely" Italian in the United States do not even have a spouse of Italian ancestry. So in what ways are such people "Italian"? In what ways are they not fiercely "white" instead? Many respond that their heritage and their love of Italian food makes them Italian—but these are, in reality, things that make them *Italian-American*. To be truly "Italian" one must learn or relearn the ancestral language and show concern for Italy and all things genuinely Italian, otherwise one is merely fooling oneself. I am forced to remember an Italian-American friend of mine telling me a few years back that she never felt less Italian than when she was in the presence of a "real" Italian from Italy (an exchange student). This must change if we Italian-Americans are going to survive as a distinguishable ethnic group in this country. We must come to show the same kind of support and concern for Italy that the Jewish-Americans show for Israel; we must show an interest in *Italia* that goes beyond vacationing there every so often with our Irish husbands and wives; we must strive to attain dual citizenship, even if it is difficult to do so at the moment. And organizations like the National Italian American Foundation and the Sons of Italy must be pressured into doing more to promote Italian awareness in the United States.

Part III
Italian-Americans Unite!

28: Italian Power! An Italian woman carrying an enormous box on her head along Bleecker Street, in Lower Manhattan's Little Italy (c. 1912).

Chapter Five

I say there is a conspiracy against me, against all Italian Americans—but you and I are to-gether today, under God's eye—and those who get in our way will feel His sting.

Joe Colombo

When the average American thinks of ethnic groups and activism, Italian-Americans do not usually come to mind. One might recall seeing someone from the Sons of Italy complain about Mafia stereotyping on some late-night news show, but the groups that one normally envisions marching and making a "stink" are blacks and Hispanics. These two groups definitely receive the most media coverage, and so their grievances are taken more seriously than the complaints of others.

But what about Italian-Americans? Are their complaints legitimate? Surely, their history is steeped in persecution, but can they still be considered a persecuted people? To answer these questions we must first take a look at the two biggest issues confronting Italian-American activists today—Mafia stereotyping and the Columbus Day controversy.

A. Italian-Americans vs. Mafia TV

As it has been repeated earlier, the most consistent form of anti-Italian sentiment is Mafia stereotyping. It has been expressed in a number of ways through the years and has led to countless Italian-American "witch-hunts" in the political and business realms; people like Lee Iacocca, Geraldine Ferraro, and Governor Mario Cuomo were all victims of this type of defamation. Historically, newspapers and television have been the two most popular media outlets to broadcast the Mafia stereotype; and although high profile Italian-Americans have been prime targets of defamation, the most popular targets were always the weaker and disorganized working-class individuals. Time after time, lower class Italian-Americans were the recipients of grave injustices as a result of the Mafia stereotype—from the 1891 lynching of the eleven in New Orleans, to the unfair press that Italian-Americans received in the Cicero and Bensonhurst conflicts. The "criminal Italian" is thus a popular image in the American psyche.

Dr. Manny Alfano's Italian American One Voice (an online coalition of Italian-American activists), the Sons of Italy's Commission for Social Justice, and U.N.I.C.O. are the premiere organizations fighting the good fight against ethnic stereotyping. Over the past several years, *The Sopranos* has been the main object of conversation and protest for these groups. Obviously, they do not condone the many negative stereotypes that the show produces, and neither do I, but not everyone sees it our way. The following is an email I received from the Italian American One Voice coalition in November of 2001. It came from a man who I am referring to as "Mr. Jones"; he was of the opinion that *The Sopranos* makes for good TV and does not defame Italian-Americans in the least. Here is what he wrote.

I think that the Sopranos do NOT defame all Italian-Americans. It shows Dr. Melfi and her ex-husband discussing the issue [of stereotyping], and Tony [Soprano] frequently defends Italian-Americans in his dialogue. Please pay close attention to the show and don't attack it. If anything, the Sopranos HIGHLIGHTS the portrayal of Italian-Americans as only mobsters, and defeats that image. Perhaps you should reconsider your opposition to this show, which is, after all, a DRAMA. Thanks for listening.

_____ Jones (former resident of Italy)

And here is my response:

Dear Mr. Jones, I just finished reading your letter in defense of *The Sopranos.* It was brief and to the point, yet I couldn't find any real reasons why Italian-American activists should cease to condemn this "hate-show." I respect the right you have to your opinion, but as far as I'm concerned, this HBO series has no redeeming qualities. Hopefully I can be as pithy as you were in making my points.

1) *The Sopranos* DEFINITELY defames Italian-Americans by portraying them as a brutish and depraved people. I have paid "close attention" to this show (taping and analyzing every episode thus far), so I know what I'm talking about.

2) Dr. Melfi and her ex-husband, Richard, do indeed discuss the issue of defamation. But I've noticed that the Anglo-like doctor often DISMISSES her ex's concerns about it and passes him off as insecure. Doesn't Hollywood and the "all knowing" media treat Italian-American activists this way?

3) As for Tony Soprano "defending" Italian-Americans, how does that help our cause? James Gandolfini plays the part of a professional killer, a crude stereotype. Fictitious characters, like "Tony Soprano," have given our community a bad name.

4) You're right, *The Sopranos* DOES highlight the portrayal of Italian-Americans as mobsters. But the show also revels in this portrayal; it strives to prove that people of Italian descent are exceptionally ignorant and dangerous.

5) In no way does *The Sopranos* defeat the Mafioso image it "highlights" so well. Nor does it defeat any of the other stereotypes it promotes. If you've seen more than one episode, you'd know that African-Americans are depicted as drug-dealers and "gangstas," Jews are either Hasidic or extra money-savvy, and (much like the Taliban) the writers of *The Sopranos* don't try to hide their great contempt for women, based on the many demeaning situations they put them in.

Believe me, Mr. Jones, I've thought long and hard about what Italian-Americans should think of *The Sopranos*. Ultimately, however, I've always come to the same conclusion. We should see it as the racist trash it is, we should be offended by it, and we should do everything in our power to OPPOSE IT, OPPOSE IT, OPPOSE IT! And I, for one, remain steadfast in my opposition (drama or no drama).

Sincerely,
Cristogianni Scarano-Borsella

P.S. What does being a "former resident of Italy" have to do with anything?

Though many people boldly proclaim that *The Sopranos* and other anti-Italian stereotypes are harmless, I say they are not harmless but lead to scapegoating and ethnic profiling. After an hour of watching a show like *The Sopranos*, the viewer is inundated with so many negative stereotypes that they will almost certainly retain some as being true—especially if the viewer is ignorant of real Italian-Americana (which many people are). The show also makes it appealing, sadly, for many Italian-American males to emulate the gestures and expressions of the "guidos" and "goombahs" they see on TV. This is the power of television; probably the most powerful media outlet, it can drastically transform the way individuals think. In the next article, we will demonstrate how Mafia TV is influencing members of our very government.

"There has been substantial controversy over the HBO series 'Sopranos' [and whether or not that show stereotypes] Italian Americans as being members of organized crime. Statistics prove that less than 5% of U.S. organized crime involves Italian Americans.

"Today, we see another injustice involving an Italian American fueled in part by the glamour of the 'Sopranos' that has now influenced police sting operations. It's the case of Dr. Ralph Garritano, a 77-year-old Parlin [New Jersey] physician who now faces 10 years in prison for issuing prescription painkillers to an undercover agent and practicing medicine without a license.

"The Sons of Italy in America Lodge 2621 commends Middlesex County Court Judge Philip Paley for criticizing the unjustified use of negative stereotyping of Italian Americans by the undercover. This case is considered by many legal experts to be one of the worst cases of police entrapment that will go to the jury in December 2001.

"What the jury will hear at the trial sounds like a perfect screenplay from a Hollywood Mafia movie. The undercover 'Vinnie' is an admitted Italian hit man from South Philadelphia who offers the doctor a $10,000 usurious loan to fight [a] protracted child custody battle. The doctor is overheard 9 times refusing the overtures and 8 times refusing to have his ex-wife's boyfriend killed citing he is a religious man.

"The physician, after numerous alleged threats and manipulation, eventually gives the undercover the prescription that results in his arrest. The undercover forgot to turn off the tape and is overheard bragging how he pushed the doctor around and got the prescriptions.

"What is even more appalling is that not one prosecutor ever reviewed the tape or transcript before going to the Grand Jury. Today, Dr. Garritano's medical license has been temporarily suspended [and] has resulted in his being penniless and homeless. To make things worse, he has recently been diagnosed with cancer.

"Italian American leaders have been very critical of negative stereotyping and are concerned that the Garritano case is another illustration [of] how the police will employ the use of Soprano type scenarios to glamorize their prosecution cases before the jury.[119]

The American success of "Mafia TV" also contributes to anti-Italian prejudice abroad; especially in countries that have historically held negative views of Italian immigrants. In Germany, for example, *The Sopranos* has been voted one of the best shows on television. Incidentally, over the past few years there have been many mean-spirited attacks made by German newspapers and politicians, equating Italian Prime Minister Silvio Berlusconi's center-right government with the Mafia. Similar attacks have been made in Canada, where a member of parliament intimated that his rival, who was of Italian background, was connected to the Mafia ("Yahoo! Groups…German"; "Yahoo! Groups…Member").

Children comprise the newest target-audience of "Mafia TV." They are being exposed to anti-Italian stereotypes in cartoons, adolescent television shows, and in pre-teen movies. This is very disturbing when one considers that children are the most impressionable segment of society. Just a couple of recent Hollywood "blockbusters" geared towards kids, and centered around mob storylines, are *See Spot Run* (2001) and *A Shark Tale* (2004).

Some time around the September 11 tragedy, I recall seeing an after-school cartoon which promoted history; it was called "Histeria." This sounds great to someone who is obsessed with history, such as myself. However, the particular episode I saw depicted Marco Polo as a punchy Sly Stallone, and Christopher Columbus as Joe Pesci. Both characters were colored dark brown (bordering black) and were created for no other purpose than to poke fun at the accomplishments of Italians in traditional "olive face" fashion. Another popular children's cartoon, "Dexter's Laboratory," has a character called the Simple-a-Fisha-Man; essentially he is an "evil greedy Italian organ grinder…fat and green with a big nose, and frizzy hair, constantly singing corrupted Italian songs, and churning his mesmerizing organ grinder machine which hypnotizes people and sucks up money and gold" ("Yahoo! Groups… See Spot Run"; "Yahoo! Groups…The Evil").

These kinds of depictions are of course crude, and many adults have the ability to brush them off as nonsense. Children, on the other hand, are predisposed to believe much of what they see. And just as the children of bigots are more likely to retain prejudicial views of others, the children of mob movie fanatics will probably make certain negative assumptions about Italians later in life, if they are not doing so already. This is precisely why we need groups like Italian American One Voice and U.N.I.C.O. to combat ethnic stereotyping.

Still, many people (fellow Italian-Americans included) do not seem to understand or even condone Italian-Americans standing up against defamation. Some even go as far as to deny that stereotyping and negative portrayals exist. In one online club, a man, who we will call "Jerry," posted the following:

"Personally, I don't know anyone who has been discriminated against, in recent years, because of Italian genes. As an ethnic group, we've actually been quite economically successful. My parents did better than my immigrant grandparents, I've done better than my parents and my kids have a great start at exceeding me. This is the case for most families that I know of.

"You want to know about real discrimination and stereotyping talk to Jews and blacks, to name a few. Talk to women. Talk to my Syrian American (born in Detroit) friend whose daughter has been cursed at and spit on by her HS class mates because she's a Muslim and wears a najib ["Jerry" really meant *hajab*—the traditional head scarf].

"I just don't think we have much to complain about, unless you happen to look a little Middle Eastern, like my twenty-year-old son. He was stopped by the police and questioned because someone saw him in the post office mailing large envelopes. There are far more important causes that need my attention.

"Sorry I can't support your cause."[120]

This man utilizes the "economic argument," at the beginning of what he wrote, to justify his position. He essentially states that since Italian-Americans have been economically successful in recent years, and since most of the families he knows are living comfortably, then we *all* must be well off, and therefore stereotyping and discrimination do not trouble our group. However, "Jerry" fails to realize that not all Italian-Americans are "economically successful" today; many are not even members of the middle class. In urban areas, particularly in the northeast, there has been a substantial number of Italian-Americans living in or near the poverty level and, as a result, in New York City, this group has had the third highest school dropout rate (following blacks and Hispanics) for a number of years. And while it is true, that economic success brings social prestige in our society, and thus large-scale persecution eventually disappears, it is just as true that stereotypes and the negative conceptions people have of certain groups are hard to kill. They linger long after a particular group has "made it." This has absolutely been the case for Jews all throughout their history; no matter how successful they become, some always see the Jews as greedy, omnipotent "Christ-killers."

In his online letter, "Jerry" also attempted to discredit the stereotyping and discrimination that Italian-Americans face by throwing around the names of ethnic groups that most people associate with persecution—Jews and blacks. He does not, however, list examples of stereotyping and discrimination that Jews have endured in recent years. Nor does he realize that while stereotyping against Jews might exist to a large extent within certain anti-Semitic circles, persecution against this group in the United States has never equaled the adversity that existed for people of Italian descent (Higham, 1973: 278; Meltzer, 1976: 55).

Jerry's post-9/11 concerns about the ethnic profiling of Arabs and anti-Muslim discrimination are one hundred percent legitimate. In this modern age of terror, Middle Easterners and South Asians are at a greater risk of being attacked in American streets than most other ethnics. They are also stereotyped more often, appearing as either terrorists or store clerks in most movies. But, as if Jerry had a personal grudge against Italian-American activists, he stated at the end of his letter that he cannot support the cause to combat stereotypes. To me, this does not make sense. The following is my online response to Jerry:

Hi Jerry, I appreciate the honesty of your post. But I must take issue with its content.

I believe our "cause" is the cause of all groups; the seemingly endless pursuit to be treated fairly. The "powers that be" in the media don't seem to understand this, and sadly, neither do many of our own people.

Your use of the term "real discrimination" concerns me a bit. It implies that there can be such a thing as "fake discrimination." The truth is discrimination exists on many levels and is WRONG, regardless of the degree of severity. If it's discrimination you're in search of, read up on how Italians were treated during the late 19th and early 20th centuries. Did you know there was a time when Italians were lynched more than blacks? Such "real discrimination" and mistreatment lasted for decades—and frequently there was a direct correlation between the high levels of anti-Italian abuse and stereotyping.

Today, as I'm sure you're well aware, the main grievance many have in our community is that Italian-Americans are being portrayed negatively in movies and television. However, "Soprano-type" shows aren't the only ones to blame; anti-Italian defamation can be found in many places (sometimes it's subtle, sometimes it's not so subtle). This is because Italian stereotypes are still quite popular and accepted in American culture. Many of us are working diligently to educate others as to the evils that stereotypes produce. Is this so irrational a cause to support?

What happened to your son demonstrates how interconnected the "cause" is of all ethnic peoples. Many Italians look "Middle Eastern" (proper term: Mediterranean). That's a fact. So who's to say that many of us aren't just as "at risk" of ethnic profiling as Arabs are? Just yesterday, I was on my way home from grandma's when a cop pulled me over because he didn't see me wearing my seatbelt. But when I rolled down my window, he had to have seen that I was still buckled in! Even so, he ordered me out of my car and proceeded to search it. I didn't get ticketed or charged with anything, but he made sure to ask if I was on my way home. After this incident it hit me. Could I have been a victim of DWI? Driving While Italian? And I only look mildly Italian.

Maybe today we don't have much to complain about, but we still have *something* which, I believe, warrants our complaints, and that is enough for me.

And YES, we have more money than our parents had. YES, we have more political pull. But that doesn't mean we are exempt from discrimination. Just ask the Jews.[121]

"Jerry" responded one last time in an email I received via Italian American One Voice, entitled "Some People Will Never Get It" (Nov. 28, 2001):

"I really have a problem with this so-called stereotyping being such a big deal. I have to really object to the comparisons made between so-called Italian stereotyping with the actual discrimination suffered by blacks and Jews in this country, sometimes at the hands of Italian-Americans.

"I'm a social activist. I can tell you there are far more important things for me to focus on than the masturbatory complaining of a few middle class white Italian Americans who don't like the fiction other white Italian Americans produce. Even though it has some basis in truth.

"If you want to do something important, get involved with how we as a society treat the old, the sick, the poor, the mentally ill. They have a real complaint.

"One thing I'm going to do in response to this is to write Francis Coppola and thank him for making great movies from Mario Puzo's book. Then I'll write Marlon Brando, Al Pacino, Richard Castellano, Talia Shire, Robert Di Niro, and others thanking them for their work. Then I'll start all over with Martin Scorsese and Robert Di Niro, Ray Liotta, Joe Pesci, Lorraine Bracco, Paul Sorvino, [and] Frank Sivero. "This is about all [the] time this subject is worth. I'm done."

"Jerry" is obviously more bitter and hostile in this letter. When he accuses Italian-Americans of mistreating blacks and Jews, he again cites no examples. His argument is again an economic one, as he ridicules the complaints of people he calls "middle class white Italian Americans." Here, Jerry links the socio-economic status of many Italian-Americans with race. In his last letter, Jerry also utilized the economic argument to show how successful Italians are, and how the discrimination they suffer must not be "real." In this letter, it appears that Jerry uses the term "white" to further show how "middle class Italian Americans" do not have any reason—and perhaps they do not have any *right*, in Jerry's mind—to complain. It is an ignorant argument.

Jerry is right when he says that some Italian-Americans do not like the fiction that other big name Italian-Americans produce (like Coppola, Scorsese, et al). It is true that we Italian-Americans are our own worst enemies at times, and that some of us profit extensively from the stereotypes that we buy in to and re-circulate back into society. This is precisely why we need more members of our community to write, produce, and direct shows that portray Italians in a positive light—we need more *positive paesans*, so to speak.

Here was my final response to Jerry, not in an online club, but in a private email:

Dear Jerry,

I've here taken the time to respond to your acrimony in private, as it's only the fair and courteous thing to do. I've read your statements, and I must say that you're quite an enigma to me. Judging by the interests listed on your online profile, you seem to be a well-balanced individual given to liberal causes. But when it comes time to face the liberal cause of Italian-American activists—a cause which advocates fair and balanced ethnic portrayal—you seem to contradict yourself by taking a reactionary position (comparable to the beliefs of Italophobes from years long since past) which looks to deny us our 1st Amendment rights. Why is that? Have we threatened you somehow by standing up for ourselves?

You've made it clear that you "really have a problem" with Italian-Americans who protest media stereotyping. I get that. But you weaken your argument when, in your *attempt* to discredit us, you juxtapose the

SUFFERING of blacks and Jews against the liberal CAUSE of combating ethnic stereotyping and defamation. In addition, you fail to understand that the crusade against wholesale stereotyping (which, in case you haven't noticed, isn't an Italian-American monopoly) is waged on behalf of ALL hyphenated peoples and subgroups, who are commonly stigmatized by mainstream society. (The sooner you realize this, the better.)

You claim to be a social activist. Well, good for you. All the more you should be able to understand where we're coming from. Like yourself, I also believe that we, as a society, should be more mindful of how we treat the elderly, the impoverished, and the mentally infirm. They ALSO have "real complaints." But, as a fellow activist, I cannot honestly say that one group's cause is more important than another's. To me, all injustices committed are wrong and deserve equal consideration. And considering how persecuted Italian-Americans have been in the past (as victims of lynchings, labor abuse, internment, etc.), they *should* speak out against stereotyping in order to avoid repeating that troubled past.

In closing, I'll leave you with a question to ponder, and in it I'll use a minority group that you are probably more sympathetic toward: Suppose people in wheelchairs were constantly depicted as bitter and excessively ignorant gun-toting thugs who preyed upon the rest of society. Would the disabled not have fair grounds to complain?

Sincerely,

Cristogianni Borsella

From my exchange with Jerry, I learned that there are two major ways of dismissing the harmful affects of stereotypes. First, there is the *uninformed* approach to dismissing stereotypes. Jerry's reasoning is a clear example of this; he does not seem to know how persecuted Italian-Americans have been, and how stereotyped this group continues to be. Nor does he seem to realize what kind of damage stereotypes can cause—that they can incite angry mobs to act, as in the case of the 1891 lynching. Secondly, there is the *naïve* approach to dismissing stereotypes—that just because a particular individual does not believe them to be true, everyone else must not believe they are true. This philosophy also maintains that stereotyping is nothing more than "clean fun." The naïve approach, like the uninformed approach, is not cognizant of the dehumanization that stereotypes produce, as in the case of Nazi Germany, where Jews were being compared to rats on a daily basis.

Italian-Americans can protest statements made by *naïve* and *uninformed* people like "Jerry" until they are blue in the face, but education is a much more useful weapon in the fight against defamation. And, fortunately, Italian-Americans have made some positive educational gains in places like New Jersey, where there is a large Italian-American population. Not too long ago, the state's assembly passed a bill establishing the Commission on Italian and Americans of Italian Heritage Culture and Education. "The duties of the commission include giving assistance to and advising public and nonpublic schools on the positive contributions and achievements of Italians…in our society and encouraging a recognition of those values, both cultural and historical, which derive from the Italian heritage" (New Jersey Bill Text, Statement Section).

Educational programs like this are essential to further understanding the Italian-American experience. The commission made it clear that "the culture, history and heritage of Italians and Americans of Italian Heritage are a proper concern for all people." The New Jersey State Legislature also concluded the following: "For the past several decades Hollywood and the communications media have continuously portrayed [Italian-Americans] as mobsters, buffoons and other nefarious characters to such an extent that it appears to be an orchestrated program of cultural dismemberment and disdain which can and will promote ethnic bigotry…. The exposure of our children and others to this unrelenting barrage of negative images has led to the erosion and denigration of Italian-American culture, history and heritage. It has, furthermore, encouraged children to emulate negative role models and promoted the social acceptability of disrespect for and bigotry towards Italians…" (New Jersey Bill Text, Section 1f, 1a and 1b).

It is my hope that the hardships Italian-Americans endured will be taught in detail as well. This subject remains ignored and overlooked. An awareness of anti-immigrant violence, discrimination, lynchings, internment, etc., is of course a proper concern for *all* people. For, we are all the descendants of immigrants, and we must all remember the adversity that our ancestors faced when they immigrated. Thus, by learning from the many blunders and tragedies of our nation's immigration history, we can avoid committing future injustices.

B. *Italian-Americans and the Columbus Day Controversy*

At the present, Italian-Americans are not able to show unity on the issues affecting them because of typical reasons impeding solidarity. A lack of good take-charge leadership, insufficient funding for ethnic programs, general disorganization, and the resulting inability to construct a big enough support base are all contributing factors. Furthermore, some Italian-American organizations tend to alienate or overlook anyone who attempts to step up to the plate. New people and ideas (especially pertaining to solidarity) are met with suspicion or ignored altogether.

The Italic Institute of America is a perfect example of an entire organization that has all the right ideas but is being pushed aside by the larger and older Italian-American groups. For years, the IIA has been developing great educational and activist programs. The Aurora Program—free Saturday classes on the Italian language and heritage for 5th and 6th graders—is probably the organization's greatest achievement. Unfortunately, the entire Italic Institute operates on a shoestring budget and does not receive the support it deserves. Some members of the IIA support combining the larger Italian-American organizations into a single group or coalition of groups, thus centralizing ethnic power. I also think this is a good idea, as unity brings with it many obvious advantages.

For now, however, there are a number of divisions within the Italian-American community, and even more divisions within those divisions. For example: some Italian-Americans are okay with the onscreen stereotyping they see daily in their living rooms and at the local multiplex, yet others are not okay with it. And of those who are okay with the stereotyping, there is probably a considerable number who see nothing wrong with the anti-Columbus/Columbus Day agenda of AIM (the American Indian Movement) and other misguided liberal activists. The Columbus Day controversy is probably the most explosive issue facing Italian-American activists today. In the following article, written three days before 9/11, one gets a feel for the ongoing problem:

Five hundred years after the voyage that made him famous, Christopher Columbus has hit rough waters in a place without an ocean. And as unlikely a port as Denver might be for this cultural storm, the reason resides in history: Columbus Day began in Colorado. "I don't think most people know that," said Glenn Morris, a spokesman for the American Indian Movement, a group that would like the day that began here to end here, too.

On a philosophical level, the clash over Columbus Day has become a question of whether Columbus—heroic explorer to some and barbaric exploiter to others—should be revered or reviled. But at street level, it has become a parade vs. a protest.

"The Italian community feels its rights are being trampled on," said Maria Allen, vice consul of Italy in Denver. "It's a matter of the injustice of it—that's what creates this frustration. And it is a matter of pride. The Italian community wants to hold onto Columbus Day as Columbus Day."

"Columbus oversaw the slaughter of millions of Taino Indian people," Morris said. "He personally began trans-Atlantic slave trade in both Indians and Africans. To say there should be a veneration of Columbus is to say these are the values we respect and the values we expect our children to embrace. To us, that's reprehensible."

Colorado isn't the only place where activists advocate a different historical perspective. South Dakota has replaced Columbus Day with Native American Day; in the California cities of Berkeley, Sebastopol and Santa Cruz, it is now Indigenous Peoples Day.

San Francisco, a city known for its Italian heritage, replaced Columbus Day with Italian-American Day.

Up until 1892, the 400th anniversary of the trans-Atlantic trip, Columbus hadn't attained widespread icon status. In fact, the turn of the century was a time of fierce discrimination against Italians, many of whom labored in the mines of southern Colorado. They were hungry for a hero.

"For them, Columbus was the one name that other Americans would respect," said Tim Noel, a history professor at the University of Colorado at Denver.

"It's very comparable to the struggle for the Martin Luther King holiday," he said. "The Italians wanted a hero that they could point to with pride."

Against that backdrop, Angelo Noce drafted a bill in 1905 calling for a Columbus Day holiday, which Gov. Alva Adams signed. The nation's first Columbus Day celebration, as reported on the front page of the *Rocky Mountain News* on Oct. 13, 1905, took place in Pueblo with the unveiling of a Columbus statue followed by a parade, a banquet and a ball.

"The day became a federal holiday in 1971, another source of Italian pride," Allen said. "Because Columbus Day is recognized and celebrated at a national level, the Italian community feels, 'Why should we give it up?'" she said.

AIM's anti-Columbus Day campaign began in 1989, when AIM activist Russell Means poured blood on the Columbus statue in Civic Center Park. In 1990, the parade began again; protesters agreed not to interfere on the condition that the groups meet and hammer out their differences during the year—a meeting which never took place.

The parade was blocked in 1991, and there were a few arrests. But in 1992, the 500th anniversary of Columbus' voyage, the parade ended before it began.

Despite AIM's promises of a peaceful protest, parade organizers canceled the march after learning that the 120 parade participants were outnumbered 10-to-1 by demonstrators.

Since then, there have been no Columbus Day parades in Denver until last year [i.e. 2000], when tensions ran so high that the U.S. Justice Department stepped in and brokered a compromise that would have called the parade The March for Italian Pride with no mention of Columbus.

But the agreement disintegrated, and police arrested 147 anti-Columbus demonstrators who blocked the parade by sitting in the street.

"Columbus Day started here in Colorado," said Manolo Gonzalez-Estay, a member of the Transform Columbus Day Alliance. "And it will be transformed and end here in Colorado."[122]

And so, the Columbus debate rages over whether this explorer was a great man or a villain extraordinaire. To me, it is not about whether Columbus was a "saint" or a "sinner." People will think what they want about him no matter what facts are presented, either supporting his innocence or his condemnation. To me, the Columbus Day controversy is about losing or retaining an Italian-American day of pride—a day that oppressed Italian immigrants had to struggle to attain, and now a day that reasonably well off Italian-Americans are struggling to retain.

At the same time, lower-class American Indians are fighting to bury Columbus' name once and for all. They are not against Italian-American pride, but they would like to see Italian-Americans dissociate themselves from Columbus. What I believe many are forgetting, however, is that Columbus has been dead for 500 years. He is not, by any stretch of the imagination, the American Indian community's biggest problem—poverty and substance abuse are the Indians' greatest foes. These problems must be solved in the coming years, or else our nation's indigenous peoples will not be joining the rest of America in the 21st century.

Likewise, Italian-Americans will eventually have to ask themselves this question: Is Columbus himself bigger than the Italian-American community, and is all the controversy and parade disturbances surrounding his name worth the trouble for Italians? I, myself, am torn on the issue; my heart says yes—keep Columbus, but my mind says roll with the punches. The smart thing to do, in my opinion, would be to rename Columbus Day "Italian American Pride Day." We, as a community, must not show that we are inflexible when engaged in inter-ethnic relations. Seriously considering opposing views and compromising will win the respect of other groups that we may need to do business with in the future. Besides, Italian-Americans have had more than enough heroes through the years; why should we relegate a day of Southern Italian pride to the cultish glorification of an outdated explorer of Northern Italian extraction? In my mind, it does not make sense.

Another reason we Italian-Americans would be wise to rename our day "Italian American Pride Day" is that any people who try to disrupt the parade would be in violation of the "ethnic intimidation law." The 2001 Columbus Day Parade permit holder, C.M. Mangiaracina, also supported this plan (*Denver Post*, Sep. 19, 2001). However, his position conflicted with the traditional base of the major Italian-American organizations, and so trouble arose. Months before the 2001 parade, the organizations accused Mangiaracina of obtaining a permit without their consent. Ironically, even more bad blood was created when the groups found out that Mangiaracina wanted to honor the victims of 9/11 with a rosary procession that year. One would think this act was very appropriate, considering that the terrorist attacks came only one month before Columbus Day. But apparently, such a display of pious remembrance had nothing to do with being Italian, in the eyes of some (*Denver Post*, Oct. 9, 2001).

Because of their disagreement with Mangiaracina, Italian-American organizational leaders actually told others not to march in the 2001 Columbus Day Parade. As a result, the parade turnout was pathetic, with only forty individuals marching. An irate Mangiaracina had this to say to the *Denver Post* (Oct. 9, 2001): "The Italian community in Denver is a disappointing embarrassment.... I hope they [who refused to march] choke on their meatball sandwiches."

To me, this feud symbolized the renowned ability of Italians to argue and spite each other over anything—even when both sides' intentions were originally good. Others have used this division or regionalist mentality against us in the past. When Italians first immigrated, many Anglos tried convincing the American people that Southern Italians were not "white," like Northerners; then the rumor was spread that Sicilians were not real Italians, but a criminal underclass. These beliefs were promoted by word of mouth, through the press, and largely on account of Italian political disorganization. Having been oppressed by foreigners for 1400 years, Italian unity was lacking. This disorganization is still evident today, when people see Italians fighting against themselves over the one day of the year that is supposed to center around Italian-American solidarity. No doubt, this emboldens the anti-Columbus Day people in their cause.

The exploitation of Italian disorganization is the part of the Columbus Day issue that gets my temper up. Pro-Italian emotions and my *cuore d'italia* override my logical mind. I become possessed, like so many American Indian people in their own right, by the images of my oppressed, impoverished, indigenous ancestors—millions of them—suffering and dying under the thumbs of ruthless imperialists and colonizers. It is in this overly charged emotional state that I turn against the renaming of Columbus Day.

On September 12, 2001, (just one day after the infamous terrorist attacks) I received an email, by way of the Italian American One Voice site, which contained in it a copy of a proposed resolution seeking to abolish Columbus Day. In the email, a Mr. Jonny Bearcub Stiffarm wanted to know if the Denver Mayor's American Indian Advisory Council supported the resolution, as he had. The following is the "Draft Resolution to Support Abolition of Columbus Day":

WHEREAS The man known to us as Christopher Columbus began the invasion of the continents, now known as North and South America, with the intent to pillage and forcefully conquer and convert otherwise spiritual and prosperous human beings, in order to increase his personal wealth and status, and

WHEREAS Christopher Columbus did not "discover America." He was lost, and

WHEREAS Christopher Columbus is responsible for the conscious, purposeful and complete annihilation of the Taino people by torture, rape, murder and diseases such as syphilis and small pox, which were unknown to these continents before his arrival, and

WHEREAS Christopher Columbus was the initiator of [the] trans-Atlantic American Indian and African slave trade on these continents which led to a caste system based on race and which continues today in the form of continuing racism and bigotry and the denial of rights and opportunities to people of African descent and to American Indian people, and

WHEREAS It has recently come to pass that governments and individuals alike have seen fit to acknowledge genocidal-type actions initiated on this continent by Columbus, such as [the] internment of Japanese-Americans during World War II, by reparations to surviving descendants, and
WHEREAS The Italian and Italian American communities have suffered many atrocities due to their heritage and have many true heroes and role

models worthy of respect, and good cause to share the fullness of the Italian culture without glorifying Columbus, and

WHEREAS Columbus Day was first celebrated and sanctioned by the government in Colorado in [1905] and became a national holiday in 1971 and, for all the reasons stated above, should be discontinued in Colorado and the nation.

BE IT RESOLVED that (the name of the organization or group of individuals) does not support the use of the name Columbus in any celebration of culture, language or national origin.

Having read the above resolution, and filled with emotion, I decided to write two personal emails to both Jonny Bearcub Stiffarm and Manny Alfano (the founder of the Italian American One Voice website) entitled "Stiffarm Tries to 'Stiff' Italian-Americans Out of Columbus Day Celebrations." In it I gave my own witty declaration in support of Columbus Day, re-using many of the words and sentences that appeared in the anti-Columbus resolution. It is unapologetically from an Italian-American point of view, and it is my official rebuttal to the anti-Columbians in our society. (Now *this* is my heart speaking:)

An Individual Italian-American's Resolution to Support Columbus Day

WHEREAS The man known to Italian-Americans as Cristoforo Colombo only sought to find a faster route to the East Indies, with the intent to bridge commerce between east and west, and increase the wealth of the Spanish Crown (which exploited Colombo himself, and subsequently betrayed him with imprisonment), and

WHEREAS Cristoforo Colombo did discover America, even if by accident, thus unveiling an entire hemisphere's hidden potential to the rest of the world, and

WHEREAS It is a blatant lie that Cristoforo Colombo is responsible for the conscious, purposeful and complete annihilation of the Taino people (as 1, the government of Spain can be the only one responsible for committing such an atrocity; 2, Taino blood still pumps vividly and vivaciously through the veins of modern peoples such as the Puerto Ricans; 3, some Native tribes, such as the Aztecs, practiced slavery and were excessively bloodthirsty, killing off hundreds of thousands, if not millions—so pre-Columbian civilization was hardly the utopian paradise some would have us believe; and 4, scientists have now discovered that certain diseases, previously thought to have come from Europe, were already in the New World devastating Native peoples), and

WHEREAS Cristoforo Colombo, himself, cannot logically be held responsible for the misfortunes of slavery and racism in the United States, just as he cannot be held personally responsible for the modern oppression or maltreatment of any group in the Western Hemisphere, and

WHEREAS The actions committed and condoned not by Cristoforo Colombo, but by the *conquistadores* and people of Anglo-Saxon stock, led to an accepted and systematic genocide of indigenous people in the Americas, and

WHEREAS It has recently come to pass that governments and individuals alike have seen fit to acknowledge genocidal-type actions initiated on the American continents by the *conquistadores* and Anglo-Saxons, such as the internment and movement restrictions of Italian-Americans during World War II, and

WHEREAS The Italian-American community has suffered countless injustices since its arrival in the New World, such as mass lynchings, police brutality, slave labor, wholesale stereotyping, internment, ethnic profiling, and the utter refusal by other Americans to acknowledge these crimes, and

WHEREAS The Italian-American community has traditionally sought refuge in the strength of Cristoforo Colombo each October, thus celebrating ethnic solidarity and achievement, and

WHEREAS The day of Cristoforo Colombo should continue to be observed and celebrated by any and all who understand the truths stated above.

BE IT RESOLVED that Columbus Day is supported as a national holiday in the United States of America, and shall continue to be supported for many years to come by Americans of Italian extraction and the organizations that represent them.

Thus was my response to Columbus bashers everywhere. In all fairness to Mr. Stiffarm, however, I must mention that he was very courteous in his reply to my resolution. He emailed me saying, "Thank you for your response. The [anti-Columbus resolution] was sent to...the American Indian community and other diverse groups and individuals to see if there was support or no support for [it]. I did not write nor have [a] part in creating the resolution. My council leadership wished to see the reaction of the community. I will forward your response and add it to the results." While I do not believe I was rude in what I wrote, I must confess that Mr. Stiffarm's politeness took me off guard and made me feel a tad guilty for not focusing as much on my manners as I had on my emotions.

One group of individuals who I found not to be as classy as Mr. Stiffarm was the Transform Columbus Day people. Through an email I received from another Italian-American website, they stated the following: "the [Columbus Day] parade represents more than a celebration of Italian culture, or even of Columbus the man. It is a glorification of the colonial tradition...and the privileging of an Italian past that benefited and grew out of that process of subjugation."[123]

The above statement is such an outright lie! It "makes believe" that Italians joined in with the Spanish, French, English and others, in the early colonization of the New World. True history tells a different story, however. With the discovery of the Americas, the Atlantic became the new sea of Western commerce replacing the Mediterranean, and many of the rich Italian city-states went into decline as a result. The newly created European nation-states, like Spain, France and Austria, benefiting greatly from the trans-Atlantic trade, were then able to carve up the Italian peninsula and subjugate the "indigenous people" of Italy for a period extending from the Age of Exploration to the Risorgimento. And although some Italian missionaries and adventurers joined the European expeditions to the New World (and even led these expeditions in some cases), their numbers were very small; a comparable number of Arabs, Jews and black Africans could also be found in these expeditions.

Another statement that attracted my outrage was posted on the Transform Columbus Day website, and was made by the Federation of German Speaking Anarchists, based in Hamburg, Germany. They wrote, "We strongly believe that the Italian heritage and contribution to US society should be celebrated in different ways than linking it to the person of Columbus."[124]

Excuse me for sounding course in what I am about to say, but who in the hell are German anarchists to open their mouths with an opinion about an internal ethnic American issue? If it were up to these guys, nothing less than total chaos would be waiting for us each day that we get out of bed (that is, if they allowed us to have beds). Besides, should they not be more concerned with their own ethnic problems—namely, the way *Sudlaenders* (Mediterranean immigrants like Turks and Italians) are treated in modern Germany?

The vitriolic hate with which Columbus' name is mentioned in Denver, in other parts of America, and all over cyberspace, is growing in intensity. With the possible exception of Adolf Hitler, the earth has never produced a bigger monster than Christopher Columbus, according to fanatics. Forget what the Japanese had done to the indigenous Ainu people in order to take possession of the Japanese islands; forget about the Thai extermination of indigenous cultures when they permanently occupied Cambodian lands; never mind the East Indian caste system which exists and thrives under modern global capitalism; forget about the current funding of anti-black genocide by white Arabs in the Sudan; forget the very fact that history, itself, has been a steady record of one invasion and subsequent annihilation after another—something which all humanity is guilty of perpetrating.

I could obviously list "non-Western" atrocities all day long. But, since these crimes were committed by non-Western peoples, many liberals seem to believe that they were not as bad as some of the horrors initiated by Westerners. After all, according to such liberals, the great bulk of non-Westerners are harmless, superstitious victims of the Third World. They could have never, at one time or other, possessed enough power and riches to do considerable damage to others. And so, once again past truths are distorted by present realities.

The rant of the anti-Columbian liberals signifies a growing problem in contemporary American society, one that has been mentioned earlier in this book. People just do not know their history any more, especially youngsters. Not too long ago I read a statistic somewhere purporting that 40 percent of all high school students believe that the Allies fought with Germany against the Russians in World War II (this, despite the fact that the Second World War can be found on the History Channel virtually 24 hours a day). I hope to God that this statistic is not true because if it is, we are in really bad shape. Insufficient knowledge of the past prevents people from solving modern societal problems that are rooted in history. Couple this with the popular philosophy, born in the 1960s, that "nothing is anyone's fault—that society is responsible" (unless, of course, you happen to be a "dead, white male"), and Columbus becomes a terrific target of our blame. For instead of studying America's race problem intricately and straining those oh-so-tired brain muscles, why not just blame it all on the guy who discovered America in the first place? The best part is, he has been dead for so long that not even his great-great-great grandchildren are able to stand up for him.

I have always said that it is easy to beat up on the dead because they cannot defend themselves. Not liking Columbus and maligning him are two different things. It is everyone's right *not to like* someone, however if people are going to viciously malign a person (whether living or dead), they had better have enough evidence to support the belief that that person is as big a monster as they purport. Otherwise, such people are mere cowards. And in my opinion, the anti-Columbians do not have enough legitimate historical evidence to prove that the "Admiral of the Ocean Sea" was a genocidal maniac. Nevertheless, each October they come out in droves to defecate on the memory of a man who, like it or not, made it possible for others to find political freedom and establish the democratic system of government which all peoples now cherish; at the same time, they spit on the rights of Italian-Americans, preventing them from marching in parades of ethnic pride—parades that have historically given Italian-Americans hope in times of adversity. These, our enemies, *are not* American Indians, they *are not* liberals, they are not non-Italians; they are cowards, and they can be found among all groups and peoples.

So, what is next? After Columbus Day is abolished, will the Knights of Columbus be accused of being a "hate group" unless they change their name, regardless of all the persecution that Catholics have been subjected to in this country? Will Columbus, Ohio, and the nation of Colombia for that matter, have to change their names to accommodate a militant minority? I suppose we shall all find out. What I know for now, however, is that a modern day lynching, with anti-Italian overtones, occurs every October in Denver, Colorado. The victim this time is not Daniel Arata or one of the Walsenburg five—their lynchings took place a little over a century ago when Italians, having no heroes that mainstream America could respect, were spat on and abused in the streets daily (*Rocky Mountain News,* Jul. 27, 1893; Moore, 1906: 841-42). No, the new victim happens to be an Italian hero himself, and he is exhumed annually as the politically correct object of America's hate and scorn. Too bad some of us do not recall what the American Indian James Yellowbank remembers: When Columbus landed on these western shores, he referred to the Indians as "a people of God" (Mangione and Morreale, 1993: 462).

C. Conclusion

Mafia stereotyping and the Columbus Day controversy are definitely the two greatest issues confronting Italian-American activists today. Though verbal and physical abuse undoubtedly occur sporadically in some parts of the country, no longer are Italians beaten by wrathful lynch mobs in the streets; no longer are Italians excluded from colleges and labor unions; no longer is there even a debate on whether or not Italians should be considered "full-fledged Caucasians." Nonetheless, many Italian-Americans, like myself, still do not feel as though we have achieved a full-fledged equal status with mainstream Americans. Our nation's long history of anti-Italian persecution is to blame; the Mafia stereotype and anti-Columbus sentiment are relics of that troubled past deliberately preventing Italian-Americans from being accepted as a respectable American group. Why else would *The Sopranos* continue its reign, as America's best loved TV series? And why else would so much time be vested in proving, each year, that the Vikings, Welsh, Chinese, and others, discovered America years before Columbus?

Now more than ever, Italian-American "in-between-ness" is influencing the group's identity and its struggle for total acceptance. On the one hand, Italians are stereotyped onscreen in a way that is exclusively reserved for non-whites (like criminal blacks and Hispanics), and on the other, Italians are told that they are members of a white European culture whose main hero, Columbus, embodied the values of that culture. (So prevalent is this latter view that many times I wonder if the majority of Americans realize Columbus was not a WASP, that he probably could not speak a word of English, and that he, like other Latins of the day, probably despised Anglo-Saxons.) Naturally, due to the very nature of "in-between-ness," some Italian-Americans feel unabashedly white and others feel more Mediterranean or non-white. This debate has arisen many times in the online clubs, and mirrors the debates of similarly oppressed peoples such as the Irish and Hispanics.

There is no question that the past record of oppression, intimidation, and stereotyping left its mark on Italian-Americans. For at least a couple of generations, many Italian-Americans have felt comfortable being labeled as "goombahs," "guidos" and "Mafiosi"; they believe that these terms—these modern-day equivalents of the older epithets *guinea* and *dago*—accurately describe what it means to be Italian in America. Still others, embarrassed by the type of people above, feel ashamed about their heritage. Not knowing what true Italian and Italian-American culture is, it has somehow been beaten into their heads that *Italianita* is synonymous with buffoonery, criminality, over-eating, Brooklyn accents and chauvinistic male machismo—images the media use, incidentally, in their crusades of ethnic derision. One such ignorant Italian who had bought into the media's crusades was my ex-girlfriend's father, openly admitting that he did not marry an Italian woman because he did not want his children looking like "monkeys."

Here we see a great need for other like-minded Italian-Americans to expand their knowledge about their ethnic history and culture. Since a greater number of Italian-Americans are far removed from the original immigrating generation, and since many have grown up believing that the negative stereotypes represent authentic ethnic culture, it is probably true that Italian-Americans today are more ignorant about their heritage than ever before. It is therefore important for them to learn about the many wonderful gifts that Italic civilization has offered the world, from the time of the Etruscans to today. Large-scale stereotyping will then diminish, as more Italian-Americans come to respect their *true* heritage and their Italian "selves." A great outcry for inspirational movies on the lives of extraordinary Italians, like Antonio Meucci, Vito Marcantonio, Giuseppe Garibaldi, and Carlo Tresca, will force Hollywood and broader society to re-examine their popularly held views of Italian-Americana. This ethnic reawakening will have commanded the respect of other Americans.

Obviously, for the plan to work, *Italian-Americans* are the ones who need to initiate the changes. They must not forget where they came from, but they must also be determined to empower themselves, by seeking education and by utilizing the hard work ethic passed down to them by their immigrant forbears. Ethnic empowerment is essential if a group is going to survive recognizably in American society.

Staying involved in Italian-American organizations, and treating one's relationship with one's heritage--like a marriage (i.e. being there through thick and thin)—is a key way to ensure ethnic survival. I once told my Italian professor that I would participate in the *Circolo Italiano* club events wherever and whenever they were held—even if the club only had three members and met several towns over. Other Italian-Americans must have this kind of passion if our ethnic group is to survive.

"Just" being a member of an Italian-American organization is preferable to turning one's back on one's heritage altogether, however make no mistake—our organizations, today, appeal literally to dying members (to the elderly sons and daughters of immigrants and to the immigrants themselves). If you go to many Sons of Italy or Bella Italia Mia clubs, for example, you will seldom see people under 40 years of age. Thus, the ethnically aware must become more active; both young and old should become *activ-*

ists—especially the young, since they are the future leaders of the Italian-American community. The question naturally follows: In what way do we become activists? Marching down 5th Avenue and creating a ruckus is not, necessarily, what I mean by activism (although we should not totally shy away from this form of activism either); being the foremost promulgators of our heritage *is* what I mean. Writing letters of protest via email and making calls to companies that put out stereotypical commercials *is* what I mean when I say that we should become activists. For if we ourselves do not actively combat the negativity, while at the same time accentuate the positive and promote the innumerable glories of Italic civilization, who else will?

We owe it to ourselves and our downtrodden immigrant forbears to study our past, apply *Italianita* to our present, thrive in an Italian-American future, and then repeat the process again and again. I believe these are the most effective ways to preserve our heritage and identity, while ensuring that the anti-Italian persecution of the past never again rears its ugly head.

Chapter Six

*I lived in a plenty tough neighborhood. When some-
body called me a "dirty little Guinea," there was
only one thing to do—break his head. When I got
older, I realized that you shouldn't do it that way. I
realized that you've got to do it through education.
Children are not to blame. It is the parents. How can
a child know whether his playmate is an Italian, a
Jew or Irish, unless the parents have discussed it in
the privacy of their homes."*

Frank Sinatra[125]

Compared to other Americans, people of Italian background have experienced a disproportionately large number of hardships and tragedies. The "Timeline of Tears" has emphasized this fact. However,
even greater than their defeats, Italian-Americans have enjoyed innumerable successes as well. The resilient determination displayed by individuals such as Rocky Marciano, Frank Sinatra, and Fiorello LaGuardia,
have mirrored the broader Italian-American community's resolve to "make
good" in the Land of Opportunity—even if succeeding meant breaking
down barriers, or denying oneself certain luxuries so that one's children
could eventually attain a greater degree of wealth and prestige. Breaking
down barriers has certainly never been a rarity for Italian-Americans. In the
past hundred years, virtually every occupation has been enriched by Italian-
American men and women.

Their names might not stick out today, but Tony Lazzeri and Ernie Or-
satti were two of the first Italians to achieve fame as major league baseball
players, in the 1920s. Around this time, as Italian males were fighting boys
of other ethnic backgrounds in the streets daily, a promising young fighter

named Tony Canzoneri won world titles in three different weight classes (featherweight, junior lightweight, and lightweight); he is regarded as one of the greatest boxers that ever lived. The early success of these forgotten athletes made it possible for the more famous Italian-American sports stars to emerge in the 1940s and '50s (athletes with names like Di Maggio, Rizzuto, Marciano, LaMotta, etc.). Soon, entire sports teams, particularly in baseball, consisted of Italian majorities, and avid fans paid as little attention to this fact as their descendants do today, while looking over the field dotted with Dominicans (Mangione and Morreale, 1993: 375-6).

In the world of entertainment, no single Italian-American pioneer was bigger than Frank Sinatra. Although even Sinatra was influenced by the styles of lesser known singers, like Russ Colombo and Carlo Buti, his radio and cinematic breakthrough acquainted mainstream Americans with genuine Italian-American performers. Because of his good looks and golden voice, ordinary Americans embraced Sinatra as one of their own; this shattered the previously held belief that Italian singers could only sing in opera houses or ethnic theaters. Thus legendary singers, like Dean Martin, Vic Damone, Julius LaRosa, and Al Martino, can all owe their success, in no small part, to the breakthrough success of Frank Sinatra (Mangione and Morreale, 1993: 390-1).

In some ways, Sinatra was highly symbolic of the second generation. Fully assimilated, yet undoubtedly ethnic, both his style and persona were half American and half Italian. Sinatra was extremely aware of this, and of who he was; that is why he championed the cause of fellow Italian-Americans in his public and private life. He remembered the abuse he received at the hands of other children when he was young. The words "guinea" and "dago" left a hurtful mark on Sinatra, as they had on many other Italian-Americans. And like so many other Italian-Americans, Frank Sinatra had also been accused of being affiliated with organized crime because of his outspokenness (Mangione and Morreale, 1993: 390-1).

In the realm of business, many enterprising Italian-Americans stand out. Among the earliest to amass great wealth, and to be accepted on an equal level with mainstream businessmen, were Amadeo Pietro Giannini, the founder of the Bank of America, and Amedeo Obici, the founder of the Planters Peanut Company. Both men started out as humble fruit peddlers, yet through hard work and incredible business savvy, they went on to become millionaires. With all the adversity that hindered the success of Italian-American entrepreneurs, A.P. Giannini and Amedeo Obici were of course two exceptions; they somehow rose above the discrimination and prejudice that they encountered, and in the process, they paved the way for future Italian-Americans to succeed, like CEOs Lee Iacocca and Carly Fiorina (Mangione and Morreale, 1993: 198-9, 406-7).

Italian-American political pioneers also had humble origins, first starting out as labor leaders and radicals. Coming from oppressed and exploited backgrounds, the people of the *Mezzogiorno* tended to vote left of center when they arrived in the United States. Naturally, many longed for the day when they would be free of their ruthless employers and treated as equals in American society. This widely shared sentiment empowered popular figures like Carlo Tresca, Arturo Giovannitti, Joe Ettor, and Salvatore Ninfo. Italian-American labor leaders thus caught the attention and ire of big business.

However, as the overall number of Italian-Americans grew in urban centers, during the first half of the twentieth century, there was a need for legitimate politicians to represent them—politicians who resembled them in appearance, speech, level of income, and in *ethnic background*. Working-class Italian-Americans needed to know that other Italian-Americans were looking out for their best interests on the local, state, and eventually national levels. First to step up were the inner-city leaders like Fiorello LaGuardia, Vito Marcantonio, and Pete Cacchione. Then, by the 1960s and '70s, Italian-American politicians were finally visible on the state and national levels.

As Italian-Americans gained more affluence, after World War II, their voting habits turned increasingly conservative. The anti-leftist trauma they suffered during the Palmer Raids and the McCarthy era, coupled with their desire to distance themselves from Irish Democrats and encroaching minorities, probably played no small part in why Italian-Americans started voting Republican (Mangione and Morreale, 1993: 397-405).

By the time Italian-American leaders appeared on the state and national levels, like New York Governor Mario Cuomo and Supreme Court Justice Antonin Scalia, they represented Americans of *all* backgrounds; there was no further need to exclusively address insular Italian issues. Italian-Americans were finally attaining lofty positions of power, and were succeeding in whatever professions they pursued. Assimilation seemed to have caught up with the second and third generation, and writers began predicting that Italian-Americans would soon find themselves in the "twilight of ethnicity." This is a premature assumption, however.

Just because Italian-American issues do not receive as much attention or air-time as black and Hispanic issues, does not mean that Italian-American identity is ready to be stamped out. There are still many, many Mediterranean faces all over this country who are continuing to practice the traditions that have been passed down to them. Even among people who are only "part

Italian," interest in their ethnicity is up. The Italian language is currently one of the most studied languages in the U.S., and all people, regardless of political ideology or demographics, seem to share a post-Civil Rights Era interest in investigating their "roots."

It should not be overlooked, however, that Italian-Americans are still underrepresented in many fields. Yes, they can be found in large supply on construction sites and on sports teams, yet how many can be found in the Fortune 500 and in Ivy League schools? How many can be found in positions of leadership within the American Catholic Church? The truth is, not too many. Thus, their fully integrated status is still in question, even as they continue intermingling with non-Italians.[126]

Issues such as these go unnoticed in our society because there is a lack of influential Italians in the media, and the Italian-American community is itself divided along political, economic, and even religious lines. I suppose the community is influenced by broader societal fragmentation, however the belief that Italian-Americans were at one time genuinely united is pure fiction. Even under the old Roman Empire, the various Italic peoples were not willfully united in the same way that a New Yorker and Californian are united as Americans. Rather, they were forced to unite under the dominion of Rome; and so the Samnites still regarded themselves as Samnites, and the Latins still regarded themselves as Latins. In more recent times, we notice the many regional contrasts between Calabrians and Tuscans, Lombardians and Sicilians, Neapolitans and Venetians: hence, the absurdity of a fully united population inhabiting the Italian peninsula.

Nevertheless, a common "Italic" past has linked these peoples culturally, linguistically and genetically, thus establishing a viable Italian identity. Maintaining a viable Italian identity in the diaspora is much harder, however, for obvious reasons. If *Italianita* is to survive in the United States, Italian-American youth must be given a good enough reason to carry on their families' timeless traditions. They must be taught Italian and Italian-American history, and they must learn about important historical figures from the time of *Romulo e Remo* to Silvio Berlusconi, from Giovanni Caboto to General Anthony Zinni. Finally, more initiative must be taken on the part of adults to depict this history in book and movie format. *Avanti!*

Epilogue

Writing this book was a wonderfully informative and exciting journey for me. It transplanted my state of mind to a time, not too long ago, in which Italians were victimized on a daily basis in the United States. Writing this book also reminded me that the modern troubles affecting the Italian-American community, such as stereotyping and ethnic disorganization, are mere symptoms of a continuing anti-Italian legacy. Nonetheless, these "symptoms" can potentially facilitate a new era of persecution, especially as our society continues fragmenting itself along ethnic lines, downplaying the importance of history in the lives of all people, and gravitating towards accepting the kind of anti-immigrant nativism that plagued our country a century ago.

As I stated in the preface, I wrote this book with love for all who remember and respect history, and resentment for those who dismiss it. The cyclical victimization of immigrants is a subject that most Americans spend little time thinking about, but for me it is an obsession. Every couple of generations or so, a new immigrant group comes along in large enough numbers to win the resentment and fear of the Anglo establishment. Meanwhile, the older ethnic groups, having had more time to assimilate, rally around the anti-immigrant battle standard so as not to merit the disapproval of mainstream America and lose their place on the societal totem as a result. Over and over again this cycle has repeated itself in American history; from the time when the allegedly "inferior" Irish began persecuting newly arrived Italian and Jewish immigrants, to our own times when Italian-Americans make prejudicial remarks about the Muslim and Hispanic communities. To me, this ethnic-immigrant cycle of victimization is unfortunate, yet ridiculous at the same time. It amazes me to see how fast the majority of Americans forget—or, rather, how fast they want to forget—that they were yesterday's *undermenschen*; and herein lies the root of the problem.

Like Elie Wiesel said at the beginning of his book *From the Kingdom of Memory*, "I fear forgetfulness as much as hatred and death," and verily so do I. Forgetfulness opens the door to ignorance, and ignorance makes it possible for the same old historical mistakes to occur again and again. We must therefore clamp the door shut to forgetfulness. The history of past atrocities must be taught zealously through the nation; we as a people must *never forget* about the genocide of Indigenous Americans, the enslavement and systematic terror waged against African-Americans, the lynchings and discrimination against Italian-Americans, nor must we turn our back on the continuing legacies of anti-Semitism, anti-Hispanic sentiment, and Muslim profiling. To the educated, all of these injustices are invariably linked.

Compared to fifty years ago, I suppose, we are a more "tolerant" society—and certainly, compared to 100 years ago, we are not as willing to go out lynching—but are we more *accepting*? I am not so sure. What I *am* sure about is that toleration is not a particularly democratic ideal. By definition, toleration assumes that people, on account of their differences, are naturally inclined to dislike and even despise one another. True acceptance, on the other hand, occurs when diverse people realize that their infinite and undeniable similarities outweigh their superficial differences.

Today, Americans are pushing for globalization and a smaller world like no other people. Their thinking, however, remains local, constructing man-made walls along racial lines, border lines, political lines—all Maginot lines destined to fail, all Hadrian's Walls destined to crumble. It is my undying hope that a greater number of Americans will not give in to fear and xenophobic behavior in the 21st century, and that they will answer the call of their God-given mission to combat injustice, so that America will become a more open and accepting and, ultimately, a freer place in which to live.

Appendices to Chapter 2, Section B

The following four appendices list the number of Italians legally executed between the years 1873 and 1962. The lists are organized chronologically and include the victims' names, the methods by which they were executed, and the locations of their death. The three main methods of execution were hanging, electrocution, and gas. The definitive "Before the Needles" website was the source from which I extracted all my information—it is an extremely helpful site for those doing research on American executions.

Appendix I

(Executions 1873-1899)

1	May 15, 1873:	Luigi Lusignani/hanging/Morris, New Jersey.
2	Jan. 9, 1874:	Jacob Machella/hanging/Hudson, New Jersey.
3	May 11, 1883:	Angelo Cornetti/hanging/Westchester, New York.
4, 5	Apr. 17, 1885:	Raffaele Capone and Carmine Santore/ hanging/ Penobscot, Maine.
6, 7, 8	Nov. 14, 1885:	Giovanni Azzaro, Augustine Gilardo, Ignacio Sylvester (this last surname is undoubtedly Anglicized)/hanging/Cook, Illinois.[a]
9	May 28, 1886:	Antonio Nardello/hanging/Washington, D.C.
10	Jan. 5, 1888:	Phillip Palladoni/hanging/Fairfield, Connecticut.[b]
11	Mar. 28, 1892:	Jeremiah Cotto/electrocution/Brooklyn, New York.
12	Nov. 14, 1892:	Angelo Petrillo/hanging/New Haven, Connecticut.
13	Jun. 6, 1893:	Sapione Martello/electrocution/Saratoga, New York.
14	Jun. 29, 1893:	Pietro Buccieri/hanging/Berks, Pennsylvania.
15	Dec. 4, 1893:	John Delfino/electrocution/Brooklyn,New York.

16	Dec. 14, 1893:	Angelo Zappie (probably a misspelling)/ hanging/Allegheny, Pennsylvania.
17	Aug. 7, 1894:	Harry Manfredi/hanging/Schuylkill, Pennsylvania.
18	Jul. 1, 1896:	Crescenzo Meroloe (probably a misspelling)/ hanging/Lackawanna, Pennsylvania.ᶜ
19	Jun. 22, 1897:	Giuseppe Constantino/electrocution/Oneida, New York.
20	Jul. 27, 1897:	Pasquale Dadario/hanging/Philadelphia, Pennsylvania.
21	Dec. 3, 1897:	Giuseppe Fuda (spelled "Gussippi" on the website)/hanging/Fairfield, Connecticut.
22	Dec. 17, 1897:	Nicodemo Imposino/hanging/Fairfield, Connecticut.

Source: "Before the Needles...Executions in America Before Lethal Injection," Rob Gallagher (website manager), downloaded Apr. 10, 2003.
http://users.bestweb.net/~rg/execution.htm
http://users.bestweb.net/~rg/execution/New%20York.htm
http://users.bestweb.net/~rg/execution/Connecticut.htm
http://users.bestweb.net/~rg/execution/Illinois.htm
http://users.bestweb.net/~rg/execution/Maine.htm
http://users.bestweb.net/~rg/execution/New%20Jersey.htm
http://users.bestweb.net/~rg/execution/Pennsylvania.htm
http://users.bestweb.net/~rg/execution/DC.htm

Appendix II

(Executions 1900-1920)

1	Feb. 26, 1900:	Antonio Ferraro/ electrocution/Brooklyn, New York.
2	Apr. 6, 1900:	William Pepo/hanging/Teton, Montana.
3	Nov. 15, 1900:	Isaac Birriola/hanging/Tioga, Pennsylvania.
4	Feb. 6, 1901:	Lorenzo Priori/electrocution/New York, New York.
5	Aug. 29, 1901:	Joseph Zachello/electrocution/Staten Island, New York.
6	Dec. 17, 1901:	Luigi Storti—the first man to die in the electric chair in Massachusetts. (Interestingly, the records show that the first Italian to be executed in the state of Massachusetts was Cassumo Garcelli in 1784.)
7	May 25, 1903:	Antonio Triola/electrocution/New York, New York.
8	Nov. 23, 1903:	Carmine Gaimari/electrocution/New York, New York.
9	Feb. 23, 1904:	Michael Pallone/hanging/Jefferson, Pennsylvania.
10	Apr. 21, 1904:	Tomasso Aiello/hanging/Jefferson, Pennsylvania.
11	Aug. 30, 1904:	Antonio Giorgio/electrocution/Allegany New York.
12	Sep. 5, 1904:	Giuseppe Versacio/electrocution/ Allegany, New York.
13	Dec. 13, 1904:	Nelson Boggiano/electrocution/Erie, New York.
14	Feb. 20, 1905:	Frank Rimieri/electrocution/Brooklyn, New York.
15	Mar. 23, 1905:	Reno Dardaia/hanging/Allegheny, Pennsylvania.
16	Apr. 28, 1905:	Sam Aspara/hanging/Orleans, Louisiana.

17	May 5, 1905:	Frank Guglielmo/hanging/Multnomah, Oregon.
18	Jul. 25, 1905:	Francesco Cefali/hanging/Jefferson, Pennsylvania.
19	Sep. 15, 1905:	Frank Pasquale/hanging/Pierce, Washington.
20	Jan. 26, 1906:	Nicholas Murdaco/hanging/Hudson, New Jersey.
21	Feb. 10, 1906:	Jerry Rosa/hanging/Bergen, New Jersey.
22	Mar. 22, 1906:	Giuseppe Marmo/hanging/Essex, New Jersey.
23	Jul. 12, 1906:	Giovanni Mallina/hanging/Fayette, Pennsylvania.
24	Sep. 6, 1906:	Ricardo Forte/hanging/Chester, Pennsylvania.
25, 26 27, 28	Jan. 3, 1907:	Stephen Carlui, Joseph Celioni, Anthony Delaro, and Severio Rodelli/hanging/Lancaster, Pennsylvania.
29	Feb. 26, 1907:	Francis Godina/hanging/McKean, Pennsylvania.
30	Apr. 30, 1907:	Joseph Boccia/hanging/Northampton, Pennsylvania.
31	May 21, 1907:	Carlo Giardi/electrocution/Tompkins, New York.
32, 33	Aug. 8, 1907:	Georgio Quagenti and Giovanni Graziano/hanging/Allegheny, Pennsylvania.
34	Aug. 27, 1907:	Carmene Renzo/hanging/Indiana, Pennsylvania.
35	Dec. 11, 1907:	Saverio Di Giovanni—the first man to die in the electric chair in New Jersey.
36	Jan. 23, 1908:	Saverio Curcio/hanging/Lackawanna, Pennsylvania.
37	Jan. 29, 1908:	Salvatore Garrito/hanging/Berks, Pennsylvania.
38	Mar. 5, 1908:	Luigi Feruchi/hanging/Philadelphia, Pennsylvania
39, 40	Mar. 9, 1908:	Antonio Strollo/electrocution/New York, New York; Michael Tomasi/ electrocution/ Hunterdon, New Jersey.
41	Mar. 23, 1908:	Joseph Paolucci/hanging/Washington, D.C.

42	Apr. 7, 1908:	Joseph Talrico/hanging/Philadelphia, Pennsylvania.
43, 44	May 5, 1908:	Frank Paese/hanging/Dauphin, Pennsylvania; Dominic Ramunno/hanging/Jefferson, Pennsylvania.
45	Jul. 14, 1908:	Rosario Sergi/hanging/Lawrence, Pennsylvania.
46	Jul. 15, 1908:	Giuseppe Alia/hanging/Denver, Colorado.
47	Jul. 20, 1908:	Angelo Laudiero/electrocution/New York, New York.
48	Jul. 24, 1908:	Lorenzo Rossi/hanging/Hartford, Connecticut.
49	Sep. 11, 1908:	Constantino Borsei/hanging/Los Angeles, California.
50	Nov. 16, 1908:	Andrea Del Vermo (male) /electrocution / Oneida, New York.
51	Dec. 22, 1908:	Giacento Ricci/electrocution/ Middlesex, New Jersey.
52	Jan. 11, 1909:	John Montessana/electrocution/Essex, New Jersey.
53	Jan. 18, 1909:	Sabino Millilio/electrocution/Hudson, New Jersey.
54	Jan. 26, 1909:	Rocco Racco/hanging/Lawrence, Pennsylvania.
55	Feb. 1, 1909:	Salvatore Governale/electrocution/New York, New York.
56, 57	Feb. 24, 1909:	Giuseppe Campagnolo and Raffaele Carfaro/ hanging/ New Haven, Connecticut.
58	Mar. 16, 1909:	Salvatore Randazzio/electrocution/ Cattaraugus, New York.
59	Mar. 25, 1909:	John Karaffa (or "Caraffa")/ hanging/Cambria, Pennsylvania.
60	Apr. 30, 1909:	Antonio Cipolla/hanging/Sacramento, CA.
61	Jun. 29, 1909:	Joseph Pagano/hanging/Cameron, Pennsylvania.
62	Jul. 6, 1909:	Giuseppe Sanducci/electrocution/ Allegany, New York.
63, 64	Jul. 8, 1909:	Bruno Carboni and Joseph Veltre/ hanging/ Indiana, Pennsylvania.
65	Jul. 16, 1909:	Leonardo Gebbia/hanging/St. Charles, Louisiana.

66	Jul. 29, 1909:	Nicholas De Marzo/hanging/ Lackawanna, Pennsylvania.
67	Nov. 22, 1909:	Teodoro Rizzio/electrocution/Oneida, New York.
68	Dec. 2, 1909:	Ferdinand Rosena/hanging/Lawrence, Pennsylvania.
69	Jan. 3, 1910:	John Barbuto/electrocution/Orange, New York.
70	Jan. 14, 1910:	Carl Bortunna/hanging/Orleans, Louisiana.
71	Feb. 23, 1910:	Carlo Giro/electrocution/Brooklyn, New York.
72	Jun. 21, 1910:	Antonio Fornaro/electrocution/Rensselaer, New York.
73, 74	Jun. 23, 1910:	Frank Chicarine and Nick Marengo/hanging/ Montgomery, Pennsylvania.
75	Jul. 25, 1910:	Giuseppe Gambaro/electrocution/New York, New York.
76	Aug. 9, 1910:	Petro Silverio/electrocution/Passaic, New Jersey.
77, 78	Jan. 6, 1911:	Dominick Ferrera and Vincent Leonardo/ electrocution/Albany, New York.
79	Feb. 23, 1911:	Antonio Pacito/hanging/Philadelphia, Pennsylvania.
80	May 3, 1911:	Joseph Nesce/electrocution/Seneca, New York.
81	Jun. 26, 1911:	Joseph Nacco/electrocution/Niagara, New York.
82	Jul. 17, 1911:	Giuseppe Serimarco/electrocution / Westchester, New York.
83	Nov. 20, 1911:	Pietro Falletta/electrocution/Westchester, New York.
84	Jan. 8, 1912:	Philip Mangano/electrocution/New York, New York.
85	Jan. 16, 1912:	Antonio Luciano/electrocution/Essex, New Jersey.
86	Mar. 8, 1912:	Frank Oteri/hanging/Iberville, Louisiana.
87	Mar. 12, 1912:	Mariano Bellini/electrocution/ Middlesex, New Jersey.
88	Mar. 18, 1912:	Domenico Di Pasquale/electrocution/ Monroe, New York.
89	Mar. 20, 1912:	C. Caruso/electrocution/Greene, New York.

90	Mar. 29, 1912:	Andrea Tanganelli (male)/hanging/New Haven, Connecticut.
91	May 6, 1912:	Salvatore Condido/electrocution/Rockland, New York.
92	May 23, 1912:	Antonio Romezzo/hanging/Lancaster, Pennsylvania.
93	May 28, 1912:	Nicolo Consuli/electrocution/ Rensselaer, New York.
94, 95	Jul. 8, 1912:	Santo Zanza (of the "Croton Lake murder") and Giuseppe Cerelli/electrocution/ Westchester, New York.
96, 97	Aug. 12, 1912:	Joseph Ferrone, Salvatore De Marco,
98, 99	Aug. 12, 1912:	Lorenzo Cali, Angelo Giusto (or "Guista"),
100,	Aug. 12, 1912:	Vincenzo Cona, and Filepo (or "Filippo")
101	Aug. 12, 1912:	De Marco electrocution Westchester, New York. (Five of these men were connected with the "Croton Lake murder," yet none actually committed the murder—Santo Zanza, executed on July 8, was said to have done it. Most of the five men executed on August 12 did not even know someone was killed, during their botched robbery, until police informed them later on. Nonetheless, the five Italians were executed for murder, making this case a historic one.)
102	Nov. 22, 1912:	Dominic Salvaggio/electrocution/Erie, Ohio.
103	Dec. 16, 1912:	Matteo Dell Omo/electrocution/ Brooklyn, New York.
104, 105	Feb. 10, 1913:	Donato Cardillo and Joseph Garfalo (or "Garofalo")/ electrocution/Westchester and Suffolk, New York (respectively).
106	Feb. 20, 1913:	Frank Romeo/executed by firing squad/Carbon, Utah.
107	Apr. 29, 1913:	Dominick Petrelli/ hanging/ Westmoreland, Pennsylvania.
108	May 5, 1913:	William Linglui/electrocution/New York, New York.
109	May 21, 1913:	Raffaele Ciavarella/electrocution/Oswego, New York.
110	Jun. 2, 1913:	Gregorio Patini/ electrocution/Westchester, New York.

111	Jul. 2, 1913:	Andrew Manco/electrocution/Orange, New York.
112	Aug. 4, 1913:	Antonio Grace/electrocution/Orange, New York.
113	Nov. 25, 1913:	Louis Pellazi/hanging/Indiana, Pennsylvania.
114	Dec. 4, 1913:	Rosario Gigliotti/hanging/McKean, Pennsylvania.
115	Feb. 10, 1914:	Antonio Fiore/electrocution/Essex, New Jersey.
116	Feb. 20, 1914:	Harry Rasico—the first man to die in the electric chair in the state of Indiana. Incidentally, he died in Vigo County, named after an early Italian explorer of the mid-west.
117	Apr. 13, 1914:	Frank Cirofici/electrocution/New York, New York.
118	May 26, 1914:	Raffael Longo/electrocution/Union, New Jersey.
119	Jun. 22, 1914:	Pietro Rebacci/electrocution/ Westchester, New York.
120	Jun. 30, 1914:	Joseph Buonomo/hanging/Fairfield, Connecticut.
121	Jul. 14, 1914:	James Linzi/hanging/Bucks, Pennsylvania.
122	Aug. 31, 1914:	Giuseppe De Gioia/electrocution/Erie, New York.
123	Dec. 9, 1914:	Michael Sarzano/electrocution/Erie, New York.
124	Dec. 22, 1914:	Stefano Ruggieri/electrocution/ Somerset, New Jersey.
125	Feb. 26, 1915:	Vincenzo Campanelli/electrocution/ New York, New York.
126	Mar. 8, 1915:	Rocco Tassone—the second man to die by electrocution in the state of Pennsylvania (Lancaster County).
127	Mar. 22, 1915:	Giuseppe Gino/electrocution/Erie, New York.
128	Apr. 5, 1915:	Nicholas Mondolo/electrocution/ Fayette, Pennsylvania.
129	May 11, 1915:	Biago Falzone/electrocution/Hampden, Massachusetts.
130	May 31, 1915:	Vincenzo Buoninsegno/electrocution/Oneida, New York.
131	Jun. 30, 1915:	Joseph Ferri/electrocution/Nassau, New York.

132	Aug. 13, 1915:	Frank Grela/hanging/Hartford, Connecticut.
133, 134	Sep. 3, 1915:	Antonio Salemne and Pasquale Vendetti/ electrocution/Monroe and Brooklyn, New York, respectively.
135	Nov. 26, 1915:	Frank Grano/hanging/Worcester, Maryland.
136	Feb. 4, 1916:	Giuseppe Marendi/electrocution/ Brooklyn, New York.
137	Mar. 10, 1916:	Pasquale Zuppa/hanging/New Haven, Connecticut.
138	Apr. 10, 1916:	Michael Louisa/electrocution /Schuylkill, Pennsylvania.
139	Jun. 2, 1916:	Giovanni Supe/electrocution/ Westchester, New York.
140, 141	Jun. 26, 1916:	Thomas Chichirella and Gaspar Marturanto/ electrocution/Cambria, Pennsylvania.
142	Jun. 30, 1916:	Oresto Schilitano/electrocution/New York, New York.
143	Dec. 4, 1916:	Dominick Digiso/electrocution/ Schuylkill, Pennsylvania.
144, 145	Jan. 5, 1917:	Francisco Vetere and Joseph Castelli/hanging/ New Haven, Connecticut.
146, 147	Mar. 27, 1917:	Calogero Pettito and Francesco Nicolisi/ electrocution/ Salem, New Jersey.
148	May 17, 1917:	Antonio Impoluzzo/electrocution/New York, New York.[d]
149, 150	Nov. 16, 1917:	Stephen Buglione and Giovanni Donvanso/ hanging/Hartford, Connecticut.
151	Jan. 4, 1918:	Pasquale Biondo/electrocution/ Summit, OH.
152	Feb. 1, 1918:	Charles Burnetti/electrocution/Stark, Ohio.
153	Feb. 9, 1918:	Giovanni Iraca/electrocution/ Burlington, New Jersey.
154	May 27, 1918:	Giuseppe Polito/electrocution/ Westmoreland, Pennsylvania.
155, 156, 157	Jun. 17, 1918:	Frank Dusso, Carmine Pisaniello, Carmine Lanzillo/hanging/New Haven, Connecticut.
158	Aug. 30, 1918:	Giuseppe Roberto/electrocution/Erie, New York.
159	Jan. 20, 1919:	Tony Mulferno/electrocution/Clarion, Pennsylvania.

160,	Feb. 21, 1919:	Rosario Borgio and Frank Mazzano/
161		electrocution/Summit, Ohio.
162	Mar. 21, 1919:	Giovanni Ferraro/electrocution/ Cattaraugus, New York.
163	May 19, 1919:	Patsy Medio (male)/electrocution/ Somerset, Pennsylvania.
164,	Jun. 27, 1919:	Joseph and Erasmo Perretta/hanging
165		Hartford, Connecticut.

| 166 | Jul. 24, 1919: | Paul Chiavaro/electrocution/Summit, Ohio. |

167	Aug. 19, 1919:	Frank Laviere, Michael De Palma, Gerino
168	Aug. 19, 1919:	Palmieri/electrocution/ Middlesex, New
169	Aug. 19, 1919:	Jersey.
170	Jan. 2, 1920:	Raffaelo Durazzio/hanging/Cook, Illinois.
171	Jan. 8, 1920:	Vincenzo Esposito/electrocution/ Schenectady, New York.
172	Jan. 14, 1920:	Frank Campione/hanging/Cook, Illinois.
173	Mar. 5, 1920:	Daniele Cerrone/hanging/New Haven, Connecticut.
174	Mar. 31, 1920:	Vincenzo Damico/electrocution/ Summit, Ohio.
175	Aug. 16, 1920:	Francesco Feci/electrocution/Bristol, Massachusetts.
176	Dec. 9, 1920:	Joseph Milano/electrocution/Bronx, New York.
177	Dec. 10, 1920:	Nicholas Vianna/hanging/Cook, Illinois.
178	Dec. 13, 1920:	Jennaro (or "Gennaro") Sansone electrocution/Erie, Pennsylvania.

Source: "Before the Needles...Executions in America Before Lethal Injection," Rob Gallagher (website manager), downloaded May 3, 2003.
http://users.bestweb.net/~rg/execution.htm
http://users.bestweb.net/~rg/execution/New%20York.htm
http://users.bestweb.net/~rg/execution/Pennsylvania.htm
http://users.bestweb.net/~rg/execution/New%20Jersey.htm
http://users.bestweb.net/~rg/execution/Connecticut.htm
http://users.bestweb.net/~rg/execution/Ohio.htm
http://users.bestweb.net/~rg/execution/Louisiana.htm
http://users.bestweb.net/~rg/execution/Illinois.htm

http://users.bestweb.net/~rg/execution/Massachusetts.htm
http://users.bestweb.net/~rg/execution/California.htm
http://users.bestweb.net/~rg/execution/Colorado.htm
http://users.bestweb.net/~rg/execution/Indiana.htm
http://users.bestweb.net/~rg/execution/Maryland.htm
http://users.bestweb.net/~rg/execution/Montana.htm
http://users.bestweb.net/~rg/execution/Oregon.htm
http://users.bestweb.net/~rg/execution/Utah.htm
http://users.bestweb.net/~rg/execution/Washington.htm
http://users.bestweb.net/~rg/execution/DC.htm

Appendix III

(Executions 1921-1941)

1	Jan. 7, 1921:	Joseph Deli/electrocution/Cuyahoga, Ohio.
2	Jan. 24, 1921:	Domenico Diaco/electrocution/ Delaware, Pennsylvania.
3	Feb. 11, 1921:	Settimi De Santis/hanging/Williamson, Illinois.
4, 5	Apr. 15, 1921:	Sam Cardinella and Joseph Constanzo/ hanging/Cook, Illinois.
6	Apr. 18, 1921:	Antonio Insano/electrocution/Jefferson, Ohio.
7	May 5, 1921:	Michael Casalino/electrocution/ Queens, New York.
8	Jun. 17, 1921:	Felix Birbiglia/hanging/Orleans, Louisiana.
9	Aug. 29, 1921:	Frank Moto/electrocution/Cuyahoga, Ohio.
10	Sep. 1, 1921:	Angelo Giordano/electrocution/New York, New York.
11	Nov. 9, 1921:	Frank Ligrengi/hanging/Cook, Illinois.
12	Nov. 28, 1921:	Frank Palma/electrocution/ Lackawanna, Pennsylvania.
13	Jan. 30, 1922:	James Di Salvo/electrocution/Clarion, Pennsylvania.
14	Feb. 27, 1922:	Michael Marano/electrocution/ Philadelphia, Pennsylvania.
15	May 9, 1922:	Samuel Purpera/electrocution/ Cuyahoga, Ohio.
16, 17	Jun. 8, 1922:	Albert Librero and Luigi Ebanista/ electrocution/Rockland, New York.
18	Jun. 14, 1922:	Dominick Benigno/electrocution/ Cuyahoga, Ohio.[e]
19	Jun. 26, 1922:	James Di Stefano/electrocution/Blair, Pennsylvania.

20	Jun. 29, 1922:	Michael Rossi/electrocution/Westchester, New York.
21	Jul. 20, 1922:	Peter Nunziato/electrocution/Queens, New York.
22, 23	Sep. 25, 1922:	Antonio Puntario and Peter Erico electrocution/Luzerne, Pennsylvania.
24	Feb. 15, 1923:	Joseph Zampelli/electrocution/Queens, New York.
25, 26	Apr. 26, 1923:	Joseph Alfano and Michael Fradiano/ electrocution/ Queens and Bronx, New York (respectively).
27	Jun. 15, 1923:	Casper Pastoni/hanging/Cook, Illinois.
28	Jun. 29, 1923:	Mauro Parisi/hanging/Fresno, California.
29	Aug. 30, 1923:	Raffaele Amendola/electrocution/ Oneida, New York.
30	Dec. 6, 1923:	Emilio Semione/electrocution/Erie, New York.
31, 32	Dec. 10, 1923:	Marcantonio Daniele and Angelo Fragassa/ electrocution/Washington, Pennsylvania.
33	Dec. 13, 1923:	Harry Santanello/electrocution/ Broome, New York.
34, 35, 36.	Jan. 4, 1924:	Nick Salamante, Philip Connizzaro, Richard Ferri/hanging/Harrison, West Virginia.
37, 38	Jan. 29, 1924:	Antonio Turco and Angelino Carlino/ electrocution/ Sussex, New Jersey.
39	Feb. 15, 1924:	Samuel Muratore/hanging/Harrison, West Virginia.
40	Mar. 10, 1924:	Dominick Delfino/electrocution/ Lackawanna, Pennsylvania.
41	Apr. 10, 1924:	Antonio Viandante/electrocution/ Onondaga, New York.
42	Apr. 29, 1924:	Louis Rossi/electrocution/Mahoning, Ohio.
43, 44, 45, 46, 47, 48.	May 9, 1924:	Joseph Rini, Joseph Giglio, Andrew Lemantia, Joseph Bocchio, Roy Leona, and Natale Deamore/ hanging/ Tangipahoa, Louisiana.[f]
49	Jun. 12, 1924:	Alberigo Mastrota/electrocution/ Queens, New York.

50	Jun. 24, 1924:	Vincenzo Caparra/electrocution/ Jefferson, Ohio.
51	Jul. 15, 1924:	Tony Briglia/electrocution/Gloucester, New Jersey.
52	Aug. 8, 1924:	Euzebo Vidrine/hanging/Evangeline, Louisiana.
53	Jan. 8, 1925:	John Emieleta/electrocution/Suffolk, New York.
54	Jan. 16, 1925:	Frank Lanciano/hanging/Cook, Illinois.
55	Jan. 22, 1925:	Nicholas Ferranti/electrocution/ Broome, New York.
56	Jan. 30, 1925:	Peter Vergolini/electrocution/Lake, Indiana.
57	Apr. 20, 1925:	Angelo Gelfi/electrocution/ Westmoreland, Pennsylvania.
58	Apr. 30, 1925:	John Farina/electrocution/Brooklyn, New York.
59, 60	Jun. 1, 1925:	John Torti and Tony Burchanti electrocution/Lackawanna, Pennsylvania.
61	Sep. 4, 1925:	Cosmo Ferranto/electrocution/ Cuyahoga, Ohio.
62, 63	Sep. 21, 1925:	Tony Pezzi and Michele Bassi/electrocution/Cambria, Pennsylvania.
64	Dec. 15, 1925:	Daniel Genese/electrocution/Somerset, New Jersey.
65	Jan. 1, 1926:	Tony Vettere/hanging/Silver Bow, Montana.
66	Jan. 29, 1926:	Luigi Rapito/electrocution/Cayuga, New York.
67	Apr. 16, 1926:	Raymond Costello/hanging/Cook, Illinois.
68	Jun. 28, 1926:	Angelo Cicere/electrocution/ Westmoreland, Pennsylvania.
69	Aug. 19, 1926:	David De Maio/electrocution/ Westchester, New York.
70, 71	Aug. 26, 1926:	Cosimo Brescia and John Garguila/ electrocution/Brooklyn and New York, New York (respectively).
72	Dec. 27, 1926:	Paul Fasci/electrocution/Lackawanna, Pennsylvania.
73	Jan. 11, 1927:	Peter Doro/electrocution/Essex, New Jersey.
74	Feb. 17, 1927:	Tony Paretti/electrocution/Brooklyn, New York.

75	Mar. 7, 1927:	William Juliano (or "Giuliano")/electrocution/Philadelphia, Pennsylvania.
76, 77	Mar. 17, 1927:	Giuseppe Provenzano and Giuseppe Friia/electrocution/Monroe, New York.
78	Aug. 5, 1927:	Salvatore Merra/electrocution/Essex, New Jersey.
79, 80	Aug. 23, 1927:	Nicola Sacco and Bartolomeo Vanzetti—after 7 years on death row they were put to death in the electric chair in Norfolk and Middlesex, Massachusetts (respectively). The man who confessed to the crime for which Sacco and Vanzetti were executed, Celestino Madeiros (of Portuguese background), was also put to death the same day in Middlesex.
81, 82,	Nov. 18, 1927:	Louis Capozzi, Christopher Barone,
83, 84.	Nov. 18, 1927:	and Joseph and Nick Juliano (or "Giuliano")/ electrocution/Essex, New Jersey.
85	Dec. 13, 1927:	Thomas Costello/electrocution/ Hillsborough, Florida.[g]
86	Dec. 16, 1927:	George Ricci/electrocution/Brooklyn, New York.
87	Mar. 9, 1928:	Joe Genna/hanging/Beauregard, Louisiana.
88	Jun. 22, 1928:	Sam Mareno/electrocution/ Washington, D.C.
89	Jan. 14, 1929:	Tony Luccitti/electrocution/ Washington, Pennsylvania.
90	Feb. 20, 1929:	Anthony Grecco/electrocution/Cook, Illinois.
91	Jun. 24, 1929:	Angelo Lazzarini/electrocution/Beaver, Pennsylvania.
92	Aug. 29, 1929:	John Fabri/electrocution/Onondaga, New York.
93	Dec. 3, 1929:	Charles Trippi/electrocution/Essex, Massachusetts.
94, 95	Dec. 13, 1929:	Antone Negra and George Costello/ hanging/Merced and Alameda, California (respectively).
96	Dec. 20, 1929:	Mario Croce/hanging/Mendocino, California.
97, 98	Jan. 10, 1930:	Joseph Marrazzo and Frank Pannatiere/electrocution/Mercer, New Jersey.

99, 100	Jan. 30, 1930:	Michael Sclafonia and Frank Plaia/electrocution/Nassau, New York.
101	Feb. 3, 1930:	Giuseppe Guida/electrocution/Bucks, Pennsylvania.
102	Feb. 21, 1930:	Frank Di Battista/hanging/Hartford, Connecticut.
103	Mar. 28, 1930:	Louis Galvano/hanging/New Castle, Delaware.
104	Jun. 30, 1930:	Frank Tauza/electrocution/Luzerne, Pennsylvania.
105	Jul. 7, 1930:	James Flori/electrocution/Philadelphia, Pennsylvania.
106, 107 108.	Jul. 22, 1930:	Joseph Rado, Louis Malanga, and Victor Giampietro/electrocution/Essex, New Jersey.
109, 110, 111.	Jul. 25, 1930:	Carl Nasello, John Messino, and Tony Mangiaracina/hanging/St. Louis City, Cooper, and Jackson, Missouri (respectively).
112	Aug. 12, 1930:	Henry Lorenzo/hanging/Hartford, Connecticut.
113	Dec. 12, 1930:	Italo Ferdinandi/electrocution/Nassau, New York.
114	Dec. 29, 1930:	Joseph Calabrese/electrocution/Essex, New Jersey.
115	Jan. 16, 1931:	Charles Rocco/electrocution/Cook, Illinois.
116	Jan. 30, 1931:	Fred Massa/electrocution/Crawford, Ohio.
117, 118	Feb. 26, 1931:	Anthony Luciano and AnthonyVelluchio/ electrocution/Montgomery, New York.
119	Apr. 10, 1931:	Daniel Grosso/electrocution/Union, New Jersey.
120	May 25, 1931:	James Romeo/electrocution/Stark, Ohio.
121	Jun. 29, 1931:	Peter Spirellis/electrocution/Schuylkill, Pennsylvania.
122, 123, 124.	Jul. 2, 1931: Jul. 2, 1931:	Nicholas Leonelli, Ferdinand Mangiamele, and Fred Carmosino/ electrocution/Bronx, New York.
125	Jul. 20, 1931:	Bonaventura Nardella/electrocution/ Passaic, New Jersey.
126	Aug. 17, 1931:	Frank Cantilla/electrocution/Cambria, Pennsylvania.

127	Dec. 30, 1931:	Peter Giordano/electrocution/Salem, New Jersey.
128,	Jan. 7, 1932:	Joseph Caricari and Alphonso Carrato/
129	Jan. 7, 1932:	electrocution/Westchester, New York.
130	Jan. 14, 1932:	Joseph Senna/electrocution/Bronx, New York.
131,	Mar. 31, 1932:	Dominick Scifo and Peter Sardini/ electrocu-
132	Mar. 31, 1932:	tion/Queens and Brooklyn, New York (respectively).
133	May 13, 1932:	Frank Franco/hanging/Santa Clara, California.
134	Jun. 8, 1932:	Eugene Compo/electrocution/Essex, New Jersey.
135,	Jul. 2, 1932:	Dominick Odierno and Frank Giordano/
136	Jul. 2, 1932:	electrocution/Bronx, New York.
137,	Jul. 15, 1932:	Alfred Cozzi and Alfred Corbellini/ electrocu-
138	Jul. 15, 1932:	tion/New York, New York.
139	Jul. 20, 1932:	Giuseppe Di Dolce/electrocution/Union, New Jersey.
140	Jul. 22, 1932:	Luigi Raffa/electrocution/Bronx, New York.
141	Mar. 20, 1933:	Giuseppe Zangara/electrocution/Dade, Florida.[h]
142	Apr. 28, 1933:	Tony Rotunno/electrocution/Trumball, Ohio.
143	Dec. 29, 1933:	Frank Vacchiano/electrocution/Lucas, Ohio.
144	Jan. 5, 1934:	Peter Alosi/hanging/Lassen, California.
145	Feb. 6, 1934:	Albert Bruno/electrocution/Lucas, Ohio.
146,	May 18, 1934:	John Capaci and George Dalleo/
147	May 18, 1934:	hanging/ Jefferson, Louisiana.
148,	Jun. 7, 1934:	Anthony Marino and Frank Pasquale /
149		electrocution/Bronx, New York.
150	Jun. 14, 1934:	Ross Caccamise/electrocution/Monroe, New York.
151	Jul. 12, 1934:	Frank Canora/electrocution/Rockland, New York.
152,	Aug. 9, 1934:	Vincent Saeta, Sam Foraci, and Anna Antonio
153, 154.		(female)/electrocution/Albany, New York.
155	Jan. 11, 1935:	Mike Lami/hanging/Sacramento, California.
156	Jan. 15, 1935:	John Favorito/electrocution/Bergen, New Jersey.
157	Jan. 24, 1935:	Giuseppe Leonti/electrocution/New York, New York.

158	Feb. 2, 1935:	Walter Legenza/electrocution/Richmond City, Virginia.
159	Feb. 7, 1935:	Alfred Giallarenzi/electrocution/Onondaga, New York.
160	Feb. 21, 1935:	Vincent Deleo/electrocution/Clinton, New York.
161, 162	Mar. 15, 1935:	George Di Stefano and Connie Scarpone (male) /electrocution/Mercer, New Jersey.
163	Apr. 8, 1935:	William Talarico/electrocution/ Philadelphia, Pennsylvania.
164	Jun. 21, 1935:	Leonard Belongia/gas chamber/Weld, Colorado.
165	Jun. 27, 1935:	Leonard Scarnici/electrocution/ Schoharie, New York.
166	Jul. 3, 1935:	William Deni/electrocution/ Philadelphia, Pennsylvania.
167	Sep. 9, 1935:	Dominick Iacobino/electrocution/ Lackawanna, Pennsylvania.
168	Dec. 6, 1935:	Ellis Latona/hanging/Los Angeles, California.
169	Jan. 9, 1936:	Amerigo Angelini/electrocution/New York, New York.
170, 171	May 29, 1936:	Vincent De Martino and Frank Russo/ electrocution/Brooklyn, New York.
172	Jun. 4, 1936:	Damiano Consentino/electrocution/ Brooklyn, New York.
173, 174	Jan. 7, 1937:	Joseph Bolognia and Theodore Didionne/ electrocution/Brooklyn, New York.
175	Jan. 21, 1937:	John Fiorenza/electrocution/New York, New York.
176	Apr. 13, 1937:	Frank Pramera/hanging/Brooke, West Virginia.
177	Aug. 26, 1937:	Louis Apicello/electrocuted/Brooklyn, New York.[i]
178	Jan. 6, 1938:	Salvatore Ossido/electrocution/ Brooklyn, New York.
179	Jan. 7, 1938:	Adam Ricchetti/gas chamber/St. Louis, Missouri.
180	Jan. 15, 1938:	Anthony Dallao/hanging/Orleans, Louisiana.

181,	Jan. 18, 1938:	Anthony and Frank Di Stasio/electrocution/ Suffolk and Worcester, Massachusetts (respectively).
182		
183	Jan. 28, 1938:	Angelo Giancola/electrocution/St. Clair, Illinois.
184	Jan. 31, 1938:	Antonio Peronace/electrocution/ Northumberland, Pennsylvania.
185	Mar. 28, 1938:	Fred Reibaldi/electrocution/ Philadelphia, Pennsylvania.
186	Apr. 1, 1938:	Albert Faria/electrocution/Essex, New Jersey.
187	Nov. 3, 1938:	Carl Ferrito/electrocution/Cuyahoga, Ohio.
188	Dec. 21, 1938:	Stephen Figuli/electrocution/Franklin, Ohio.
189,	Jan. 5, 1939:	Charles Sberna and Salvatore Gatti/ electrocution/New York, New York.
190		
191	Jan. 12, 1939:	Vincente Forte/electrocution/Brooklyn, New York.
192	Jan. 26, 1939:	Dominick Guariglia/electrocution/New York, New York.
193	Sep. 29, 1939:	Pete Catalina/gas chamber/Chaffee, Colorado.
194	May 17, 1940:	Virgilio Spinelle/gas chamber/Los Angeles, California.
195,	Jan. 14, 1941:	Anthony Cirasole and Joseph Di Marco/ electrocution/Cuyahoga and Crawford, Ohio (respectively).
196		
197	Jan. 20, 1941:	Herman Petrillo/electrocution/Philadelphia, Pennsylvania.
198	Feb. 13, 1941:	Arcangelo D'Agosto/electrocution/ Brooklyn, New York.
199	Feb. 20, 1941:	Joseph Carosella/electrocution/Nassau, New York.
200	Mar. 31, 1941:	Paul Petrillo/electrocution/Philadelphia, Pennsylvania.
201	Jun. 5, 1941:	Peter Salemi/electrocution/Brooklyn, New York.
202	Nov. 21, 1941:	Juanita Spinelli/gas chamber/ Sacramento, California. (Spinelli was the first woman to die in the gas chamber.)

Source: "Before the Needles…Executions in America Before Lethal Injection," Rob Gallagher (website manager), downloaded May 5, 2003.

http://users.bestweb.net/~rg/execution.htm
http://users.bestweb.net/~rg/execution/New%20York.htm
http://users.bestweb.net/~rg/execution/Pennsylvania.htm
http://users.bestweb.net/~rg/execution/New%20Jersey.htm
http://users.bestweb.net/~rg/execution/Ohio.htm
http://users.bestweb.net/~rg/execution/Louisiana.htm
http://users.bestweb.net/~rg/execution/California.htm
http://users.bestweb.net/~rg/execution/Illinois.htm
http://users.bestweb.net/~rg/execution/Massachusetts.htm
http://users.bestweb.net/~rg/execution/West%20Virginia.htm
http://users.bestweb.net/~rg/execution/Missouri.htm
http://users.bestweb.net/~rg/execution/Colorado.htm
http://users.bestweb.net/~rg/execution/Connecticut.htm
http://users.bestweb.net/~rg/execution/Florida.htm
http://users.bestweb.net/~rg/execution/Delaware.htm
http://users.bestweb.net/~rg/execution/Indiana.htm
http://users.bestweb.net/~rg/execution/Montana.htm
http://users.bestweb.net/~rg/execution/Virginia.htm

Appendix IV

(Executions 1942-1962)

1	Jan. 22, 1942:	Arturo Renna/electrocution/Bronx, New York.[j]
2, 3	Feb. 19, 1942:	Harry Maione and Frank Abbandando electrocution/Brooklyn, New York.
4, 5	Mar. 12, 1942:	William and Anthony Esposito/electrocution/New York, New York.
6	Mar. 23, 1942:	Angie Ciangetti (male)/electrocution/Volusia, Florida.
7	Jun. 30, 1942:	Paul Giacomazza/electrocution/ Middlesex, Massachusetts.
8	Sep. 10, 1942:	Carlo Barone/electrocution/Brooklyn, New York.
9	Sep. 18, 1942:	John Pantano/electrocution/Cook, Illinois.
10	Jan. 14, 1943:	Edmund Sileo/electrocution/Brooklyn, New York.
11	Jan. 21, 1943:	Frank Castellano/electrocution/New York, New York.[k]
12	Jan. 6, 1944:	Joseph Mascari/electrocution/Madison, New York.
13	Jan. 21, 1944:	Louis Valle/electrocution/Nassau, New York.
14	Mar. 2, 1944:	Vincent Solami/electrocution/Brooklyn, NewYork.
15	Mar. 4, 1944:	Louis Capone/electrocution/Brooklyn, New York.
16	Mar. 20, 1944:	Michael Musto/electrocution/Blair, Pennsylvania.
17	May 3, 1944:	Carlo De Caro/electrocution/Hartford, Connecticut.

18	Jun. 3, 1944:	Louis Parisi/electrocution/New York, New York.
19, 20 21	Jun. 29, 1944:	Peter De Lutro, Frank Di Maria, and Alex Bellomo/electrocution/New York, New York.
22	Jun. 18, 1945:	Nicholas Rossi/electrocution/Hartford, Connecticut.
23	Nov. 30, 1945:	Albert Simeone/gas chamber/Los Angeles, California.
24	Jan. 1, 1946:	Arthur Tommaselli/electrocution/Hartford, Connecticut.
25	May 9, 1947:	Phillip Bellino/electrocution/Suffolk, Massachusetts.
26	Jul. 10, 1947:	Salvatore Di Cristofaro/electrocution/ Erie, New York.
27	Aug. 29, 1947:	Joe Caetano/gas chamber/Humboldt, California.
28	Jul. 1, 1948:	Anthony Papa/electrocution/Nassau, New York.[l]
29	Jan. 7, 1949:	Robert Battalino/gas chamber/Jefferson, Colorado.
30	Jan. 18, 1949:	Eugene Gambetta/gas chamber/Washoe, Nevada.[m]
31	Mar. 3, 1949:	Santo Bretagna/electrocution/New York, New York.
32	Jun. 27, 1949:	Ralph Cordasco/electrocution/Essex, New Jersey.
33	Nov. 26, 1949:	James Morelli/electrocution/Cook, Illinois.
34	Jan. 5, 1950:	Frank Bruno/electrocution/Brooklyn, New York.
35	Jan. 9, 1950:	Edward Di Pofi/electrocution/ Allegheny, Pennsylvania.
36	Sep. 25, 1950:	Alexander Niemi/electrocution/ Delaware, Pennsylvania.[n]
37	Jan. 15, 1953:	Joseph Paonessa/electrocution/ Dutchess, New York.
38	Mar. 30, 1953:	Dominick Daerse/electrocution/ Westmoreland, Pennsylvania.
39	May 17, 1954:	Joseph Bibalo/electrocution/ Susquehanna, Pennsylvania.
40	Jul. 15, 1954:	Frank Pedrini/gas chamber/Washoe, Nevada.

41	Jun. 3, 1955:	John Santo/gas chamber/Los Angeles, California.
42	Feb. 28, 1957:	Leonardo Salemi/electrocution/New York, New York.
43	Aug. 7, 1958:	Anthony La Marca/electrocution/ Nassau, New York.
44	Mar. 23, 1962:	Vincent Ciucci/electrocution/Cook, Illinois.

Source: "Before the Needles...Executions in America Before Lethal Injection," Rob Gallagher (website manager), downloaded May 5, 2003.
http://users.bestweb.net/~rg/execution.htm
http://users.bestweb.net/~rg/execution/New%20York.htm
http://users.bestweb.net/~rg/execution/Pennsylvania.htm
http://users.bestweb.net/~rg/execution/California.htm
http://users.bestweb.net/~rg/execution/Connecticut.htm
http://users.bestweb.net/~rg/execution/Illinois.htm
http://users.bestweb.net/~rg/execution/Massachusetts.htm
http://users.bestweb.net/~rg/execution/Nevada.htm
http://users.bestweb.net/~rg/execution/Colorado.htm
http://users.bestweb.net/~rg/execution/Florida.htm
http://users.bestweb.net/~rg/execution/New%20Jersey.htm

In the last twenty year period (1942-1962) there was a marked decrease in executions because Italian-American socio-economic prosperity increased dramatically. Since Italian-Americans were no longer at the very bottom of the social ladder, the drive to commit crimes out of desperation was not as strong as it had been. Nevertheless, on average, two Italians were still being executed each year. In total, from the 1870s to the 1960s, 446 Italians were *legally* executed in the United States; this figure does not include, of course, those who were lynched. Thus, for a period of ninety years (almost a century), approximately five Italians were executed annually.

As one can see, the "Before the Needles" website is a very informative source on American executions. However, after reading all the names of the Italians put to death (446 by my calculations), I resent the fact that they were not represented as a separate group on the website. The "races" represented were: White, Black, Asian, Native American, and Hispanic. After "whites" and "blacks," people of Italian background were the most executed group. Virtually every month, for a successive number of years, one could find Italians lined up, waiting to be executed in multiple places throughout the United States. It is very disappointing that the "Before the Needles" website overlooked this fact, especially since it went to great lengths to show the numbers of "minorities" executed, and to sort out who was who racially. And if some would assume that Italians were executed merely as "white men," they are obviously ignorant of Italian-American history—a history in which Italians were treated as non-whites for many years, and were one of the greatest targets of white anger, next to African-Americans.

It also bothers me that Hispanics are represented erroneously by *race* on the website (just as they are racialized by society). In truth, the term "Hispanic" does not denote race (although it is currently popular to think otherwise), rather it is a broad cultural term denoting people who speak Spanish and whose families follow the customs and traditions of Latin America and the Iberian peninsula. Much like Americans, Hispanics can be of *any* color (not just the mythic "brown" associated with them in modern times). And like many confused modern-day Americans, the "Before the Needles" website does not even seem to know what constitutes being Hispanic. On Maryland's execution list, for example, I noticed that the names "Sanchez" and "Perez" were listed as "white." (See, http://users.bestweb.net/~rg/execution/ Maryland.htm.) What I found particularly insulting on other states' lists were question marks next to names that were very "Latin," yet clearly Italian, as if to say: "Not sure whether this guy's a 'white Italian' or a 'Hispanic.'" I voice my discontent because I believe it is unfair that Italians are not afforded their own status on the website (and also that they are not given a special box to check on racial forms), especially since they suffered so much and were treated like so few groups in this country—their numbers alone (446 executed) warrant recognition. Hence, racial and ethnic hypocrisy.

Works Cited

Books

Angle, Paul M. 1992. *Bloody Williamson: A Chapter in American Lawlessness*. Chicago: University of Illinois Press.

Aquila, Richard. 1999. *Home Front Soldier: The Story of a GI and His Italian American Family During World War II*. Albany, New York: State University of New York Press.

Ashyk, Dan, Fred Gardaphe, Anthony Tamburri, Eds. 1999. *Shades of Black and White: Conflict and Collaboration Between Two Communities*. Staten Island: American Italian Historical Association.

Baiamonte, John V. 1986. *Spirit of Vengeance: Nativism and Louisiana Justice, 1921-1924*. Baton Rouge: Louisiana State University Press.

Caso, Adolph. 1984. *Mass Media vs. The Italian Americans*. Boston: Branden Books.

_____. 1979. *They Too Made America Great*. Boston: Branden Books.

_____. 2002. *To America and Around the World*. Boston: Branden Books.

Cordasco, Francesco, Ed. 1975. *Studies in Italian American Social History*. Totowa, New Jersey: Rowman and Littlefield.

Cordasco, Francesco, Eugene Bucchioni. 1974. *The Italians: Social Backgrounds of an American Group*. Clifton, New Jersey: Augustus M. Kelley, Publishers.

Cutler, James Elbert. 1905. *Lynch Law: An Investigation into the History of Lynching in the United States*. New York: Longmans, Green, and Co.

Foerster, Robert F. 1969. *The Italian Emigration of Our Times*. New York: Arno Press.

Fox, Stephen. 1990. *The Unknown Internment: An Oral History of the Relocation of Italian Americans During World War II*. Boston: Twayne Publishers.

Gambino, Richard. 1974. *Blood of My Blood: The Dilemma of the Italian-Americans*. Garden City, New York: Anchor Press/Doubleday.

_____. 1998. *Vendetta: The Story of the Largest Lynching in U.S. History*. Toronto: Guernica Editions, Inc.

Guglielmo, Jennifer, Salvatore Salerno, Eds. 2003. *Are Italians White? How Race Is Made in America*. New York: Routledge.

Higham, John. 1973. *Strangers in the Land: Patterns of American Nativism 1860-1925*. New York: Atheneum.

Hosokawa, Bill. 1969. *Nisei: The Quiet Americans*. New York: William Morrow and Company, Inc.

Ingalls, Robert P. 1988. *Urban Vigilantes in the New South, Tampa, 1882-1936*. Knoxville, Tennessee: University of Tennessee Press.

Iorizzo, Luciano J., Salvatore Mondello. 1980. *The Italian Americans*. Boston: Twayne Publishers.

Katz, William Loren, ed. 1969. *NAACP: Thirty Years of Lynching in the United States 1889-1918*. New York: Arno Press.

Krase, Jerome, Judith De Sena, Eds. 1994. *Italian Americans in a Multicultural Society*. New York: Forum Italicum.

Lagumina, Salvatore J. 1999. *Wop! A Documentary History of Anti-Italian Discrimination in the United States*. Toronto: Guernica.

La Sorte, Michael. 1985. *La Merica: Images of Italian Greenhorn Experience*. Philadelphia: Temple University Press.

Mangione, Jerre, Ben Morreale. 1993. *La Storia: Five Centuries of the Italian American Experience*. New York: HarperPerennial.

Meltzer, Milton. 1976. *Taking Root: Jewish Immigrants in America*. New York: Farrar, Straus and Giroux.

Mondello, Salvatore. 1980. *The Italian Immigrant in Urban America, 1880-1920, As Reported in the Contemporary Periodical Press*. New York: Arno Press.

Moore, Joan W. 1970. *Mexican-Americans*. Englewood Cliffs, New Jersey: Prentice-Hall, Inc.

Moore, John Bassett. 1906. *A Digest of International Law (vol. 6)*. Washington: Government Printing Office.

Moquin, Wayne, ed. 1975. *A Documentary History of the Italian Americans*. New York: Praeger.

Murphy, Eugene and Timothy Driscoll. 1974. *An Album of the Irish Americans*. New York: Franklin Watts, Inc.

Nelli, Humbert S. 1976. *The Business of Crime: Italians and Syndicate Crime in the United States*. New York: Oxford University Press.

Orsi, Robert Anthony. 1985. *The Madonna of 115th Street: Faith and Community in Italian Harlem, 1880-1950.* New Haven: Yale University Press.

Pisani, Lawrence Frank. 1957. *The Italian in America: A Social Study and History.* New York: Exposition Press.

Sergi, Giuseppe. 1967. *The Mediterranean Race: A Study of the Origin of European Peoples.* New York: Humanities Press.

Simpson, George Eaton and J. Milton Yinger. 1965. *Racial and Cultural Minorities: An Analysis of Prejudice and Discrimination,* Third Edition. New York: Harper & Row.

Sung, Betty Lee. 1967. *Mountain of Gold: The Story of the Chinese in America.* New York: The Macmillan Co.

Vecoli, Rudolph J., ed. 1987. *Italian Immigrants in Rural and Small Town America.* Staten Island: American Italian Historical Association.

Online Resources and Articles

"All About the Providence Mob," by Allan May, http://www.crimelibrary.com/gangsters_outlaws/family_epics/pr Providence_mob/3.html?sect=16, Courtroom Television Network, LLC, downloaded May 29, 2003.

"The Autobiography of Mother Jones: Chapter XIII," http://womenshistory.about.com/library/etext/mj/bL_mj13.htm About.com, downloaded Jun. 18, 2003.

"Before the Needles," Rob Gallagher (website manager), http://users.bestweb.net/~rg/execution.htm, originally downloaded Oct. 25, 2002.

"Book Reviews 2002," by Anthony Buccino, http://www.anthonysworld.com/rev02.html, downloaded Apr. 18, 2003.

"Bulletproof Bill," by Warren Swartz, http://www.italian-american.com/descrim1.htm, downloaded Sep. 29, 2003.

"Casino" http://www.allmovie.com/cg/avg.dll?p=avg&sql=1:135453, downloaded Sep. 30, 2003.

"Chapter IV" (on the Latimer Massacre), by William Brinton, http://www.us-history.info/chap_4.html, downloaded Mar. 20, 2003.

"Charles Manson's 1992 Parole Hearing," http://www.totse.com/en/law/justice_for_all/manson92.html, Totse.com, downloaded Jun. 2, 2003.

"Cherry Mine Disaster," http://putnam.k12.il.us/Cherry2.htm, downloaded Mar. 9, 2003.

"Colorado Coal Field War Project," http://coloradodigital.coalliance.org/cfphoto.html, downloaded Mar. 20, 2003.

"Contadini in the New World Paese," by Dr. Paul Loatman, http://www.mechanicville.com/history/articles/Contadini%20in%20the%20New%20World%20Paese.htm, downloaded Apr. 1, 2003.

"The Croton Lake Murder," by Mark Gado, http://www.crimelibrary.com/classics5/croton/2.htm http://www.crimelibrary.com/classics5/croton/5.htm http://www.crimelibrary.com/classics5/croton/6.htm http://www.crimelibrary.com/classics5/croton/9.htm http://www.crimelibrary.com/classics5/croton/10.htm http://www.crimelibrary.com/classics5/croton/11.htm http://www.crimelibrary.com/classics5/croton/12.htm http://www.crimelibrary.com/classics5/croton/13.htm http://www.crimelibrary.com/classics5/croton/14.htm downloaded Oct. 25, 2002.

"Daniela Gioseffi: Book Review…" http://www.gioseffi.com/Gioseffi6.html, downloaded May 28, 2003.

"Dawson-New Mexico Ghost Town," http://www.ghosttowns.com/states/nm/dawson.html, downloaded Mar. 12, 2003.

"The Drug Hang Up, America's Fifty-Year Folly: Chapter 13, Chairman Kefauver and the Mafia Myth," by Rufus King, http://www.druglibrary.org/special/king/dhu/dhu13.htm downloaded Dec. 19, 2004.

"FBI Joins Long Island Firebombing Probe," http://1010wins.com/topstories/winstopstories_story_190075432.html, 1010 WINS.com, downloaded Sep. 20, 2003.

"FBI To Be Sued For $300 Million," http://www.talkleft.com/archives/000759.html, downloaded Oct. 8, 2003.

"The Following Was Excerpted From Howard Zinn's A People's History of the United States (pgs 346-349)" http://www.spunk.org/library/places/us/sp000937.txt, downloaded Mar. 20, 2003.

"The Godfather Part III," http://www.allmovie.com/cg/avg.dll?p=avg&sql=1:20079

downloaded Sep. 29, 2003.

"The Golden Age of Immigration Is Now," by Nancy Foner, http://www.gothamgazette.com/commentary/63.foner.shtml, downloaded Dec. 14, 2001.

"Goodfellas," http://www.allmovie.com/cg/avg.dll, downloaded Sep. 29, 2003.

"Grand Lodge of New Jersey," http://www.sonsofitalynj.org/events.htm, downloaded Oct. 12, 2003.

"The Heysel Stadium Tragedy, 1985," http://www.bbc.co.uk/dna/h2g2/alabaster/A713909, BBC MMIII, downloaded Jun. 30, 2003.

"The Heysel Tragedy—A Hidden Agenda?" http://family.maltanet.net/hawk/html/Heysel.html, downloaded July 2, 2003.

"Hidden Italian Heritage," http://www.heritage.nsw.gov.au/heritagenews/dec98/6_art.htm, Heritage Council of New South Wales, downloaded May 17, 2003.

"Hillel-Jewish Students Mailing List," http://shamash.org/listarchives/hillel/log9303, downloaded Oct. 8, 2003.

"Hispanic American Timeline," http://srd.yahoo.com/goo/timeline+hispanic+discrimination /3/T=1025394976/F=7d3ae292cd8b4c2e85d049b20ee5b162/ (Taken from *Hispanic-American Almanac*, Gale, 1997, http://www.gale.com/freresrc/time.htm, downloaded Jul. 12, 2002.

"Hispanic Contributions to World History," Don Nicholai Hermosillo (contributor), http://www.neta.com/~1stbooks/tragic2.htm, Hispanic America USA, Inc., downloaded Mar. 20, 2003.

"Huddled Masses: The History of Our Immigrant Church," by Moises Sandoval, http://www.uscatholic.org/2000/07/hm0007.htm, Claretian Publications, downloaded Feb. 16, 2003.

"Image Research Project: Italian Culture on Film (1928-2001)," http://www.italic.org/imageb1.htm, Italic Studies Institute, downloaded Sep. 30, 2003.

"The Immigration Act of 1924," http://www-personal.umd.umich.edu/~ppennock/doc-immigAct.htm, downloaded Apr. 5, 2003. (This article was originally titled "Our New Nordic Immigration Policy" and was found in the *Literary Digest*, May 10, 1924, pp. 12-13.)

"Immigration Restriction Act of 1924," http://nkasd.wiu.k12.pa.us/vhs/discush1924.html,downloaded Apr. 6, 2003.

"Inscription on the Ludlow Massacre Memorial," http://ehcitizens.org/cbmgas/rb_road_tour_1/LudlowMassacreMemo rialInscription.htm, downloaded Oct. 16, 2002.

"The Italian-American Website of New York," http://www.italian-american.com/nixon.htm, Joe Anastasio (website manager), downloaded May 28, 2003.

"Italian Immigrants in Springfield," by Kaitlin Moredock, http://www.lib.niu.edu/ipo/ihy991219.html, downloaded Apr. 10, 2003. (Originally published in *Illinois History: A Magazine for Young People*, Dec. 1999.)

"Italians Interned in Australia During WW2," http://home.st.net.au/~pdunn/pow/italiansinterned.htm, Peter Dunn (website manager), downloaded May 17, 2003.

"Italian Studies: Italian/American Timeline," http://artsci.shu.edu/italianstudies/timeline-italianamer/1900.htm, Seton Hall University, downloaded Mar. 27, 2003.

"Johann Friedrich Blumenbach," http://en.wikipedia.org/wiki/Johann_Friedrich_Blumenbach, Wikipedia, downloaded Feb. 5, 2004.

"John D. Calandra Italian American Institute: Who We Are," http://qcpages.qc.edu/calandra/whoweare/whojohn.html, downloaded Sep. 24, 2003.

"Knock-Knock! 'Who's There?'—'It's the FBI!'" by Richard Capozzola, http://www.italianinfo.net/knock-knock.htm, downloaded Apr. 18, 2003.

"Latino Laborers Targeted," http://www.natcath.com/NCR_Online/archives/090701/09070 1d.htm, downloaded Oct. 6, 2002.

"The Lawrence Strike of 1912 and the IWW," by Philip C. Muth, http://www.loyno.edu/history/journal/1987-8/muth.htm, downloaded Mar. 10, 2003. (This article was originally published in *The Student Historical Journal*, Loyola University, vol. 19, 1987-1988.)

"The Life of an Italian Immigrant in the Early 1900s," by Cecilia P., http://www.wf168.frnkln.k12.il.us/fchs_Lh003.htm, downloaded Apr. 3, 2003.

"List of Men Killed in the 1914 Eccles Explosion" (pp. 1-3), http://www.rootsweb.com/~wvcoal/ecles1.htm, http://www.rootsweb.com/~wvcoal/ecles2.htm, http://www.rootsweb.com/~wvcoal/ecles3.htm, downloaded Mar. 26, 2003.

"Ludlow Massacre," http://www.holtlaborlibrary.org/ludlow.html, Holt Labor Library, Shannon Sheppard (website manager), downloaded Mar. 20, 2003.

"The Ludlow Massacre and the Birth of Company Unions," by Stephen Millies, http://www.hartford-hwp.com/archives/45b/030.html, downloaded Mar. 20, 2003. (Originally published in the *Workers World,* Jan. 26, 1995.)

"The Ludlow Massacre," http://www.pbs.org/wgbh/amex/rockefellers/sfeature/sf_8.html, PBS Online/WGBH, downloaded Mar. 20, 2003.

"The Ludlow Massacre," http://www.umwa.org/history/ludlow.shtml, UMWA website, downloaded Mar. 20, 2003.

"The Ludlow Massacre: Monument," http://www.umwa.org/history/ludlow2.shtml, UMWA website, downloaded Mar. 20, 2003.

"Lynching and Criminal Justice: The Midwest and West As American Regions," by Michael J. Pfeifer, http://academic.evergreen.edu/p/pfeiferm/lynching_ criminaljustice.html, downloaded May 13, 2003.

"Manchester's Little Italy at War 1940-1945: Enemy Aliens or a Reluctant Foe," by Paul Di Felice, http://www.italian-heritage-ancoats.org.uk/italart2.htm#Issue1, downloaded May 16, 2003.

"Man Freed After Serving 32 Years," by Martin Finucane, http://www.truthinjustice.org/limone.htm, The Associated Press, downloaded Oct. 6, 2003.

"Man Guilty of Beating Long Island Laborers," http://www.optonline.net/...4,channel%3D32&article %3D205562,00.html, downloaded Oct. 6, 2002.

"Massacres and Atrocities of WWII," by George Duncan,
http://members.iinet.net.au/~gduncan/massacres.html,
downloaded May 18, 2003.

"Massacres of History," by Howard Zinn,
http://www.thirdworldtraveler.com/History/Massacres_History.
html, downloaded Mar. 20, 2003.

"Media Should Say Whoops Over Whoopee," by Tim Graham,
http://www.mediaresearch.org/realitycheck/1998/fax1998
129.asp, Media Research Center, downloaded Sep. 29, 2003.

"Memorial Day Massacre," by Howard Fast,
http://www.trussel.com/hf/memorial.htm, downloaded Apr. 11,
2003.

"The Messina-Reggio Earthquake: 1908," by Frank Ardvini,
http://www.ardvini.net/tales/tales15a.htm, downloaded May 16,
2003.

"Milwaukee's Italian Flavor Runs Deep," by Bob Tanzilo,
http://www.onmilwaukee.com/buzz/articles/italians.html?page=1,
OnMilwaukee.com, LLC, downloaded Mar. 26, 2003.

"Mine Workers Strike in Telluride,"
http://www.rmpbs.org/byways/telldoc1.html, Rocky Mountain
Public Broadcasting Network, Inc., downloaded Mar. 26, 2003.

"1914 No. 5 Eccles Mine Explosion,"
http://www.rootsweb.com/~wvcoal/ecles.html, downloaded Mar.
26, 2003.

"1924 Coal Mine Disaster,"
http://www.rootsweb.com/~wvmarsha/mine.htm, downloaded
Apr. 3, 2003.

"(Not) Only Irish Need Apply," by Dermot McEvoy,
http://publishersweekly.reviewsnews.com/index.asp?layout=article&
articleid=CA169022, Publishers Weekly/Reed Business Information,
downloaded Apr. 8, 2003.

"Our Parish History,"
http://www.mtcarmelparish.com/our_parish_history.htm,
downloaded Feb. 16, 2003.

"People & Events: The Rise of the Ku Klux Klan in the 1920s,"
http://www.pbs.org/wgbh/amex/flood/peopleevents/e_Klan.html,
PBS Online/WGBH, downloaded Apr. 6, 2003.

"Portrait of Wilkinsburg Shooting Suspect Shows History of Mental
Illness and Hate,"
http://www.post-gazette.com/regionstate/20000303taylor1.asp,

Post-Gazette.com, downloaded Nov. 5, 2000.

"Race Traitor," http://www.postfun.com/racetraitor/welcome.html, downloaded Feb. 9, 2004.

"Race Traitor: What We Believe," http://academic.udayton.edu/race/01race/traitor.htm, downloaded Feb. 9, 2004.

"Re: Involvement," http://messages.clubs.yahoo.com/ clubs/i...=italianamericans&sid=16309052&mid=2469 Nov. 27, 2001.

"Re: Involvement," http://post.clubs.yahoo.com/clubs/ itali...lianamericans&sid=16309052&mid=2474&n=1 Nov. 27, 2001.

"The Second Annual Pasta-Tute Award," http://www.italystl.com/ misc/m01i46.htm#top, downloaded Oct. 30, 2003.

"Sicilian Culture...Edward James Olmos—Quandry, Conundrum, Conclusion and Questions," by Richard Annotico, http://www.sicilianculture.com/news/Olmos.htm, Sep. 29, 2003.

"Son of Sam," http://www.nostalgiacentral.com/pop/sonofsam.htm, NostalgiaCentral, downloaded Jun. 2, 2003.

"The Sopranos," http://www.tvtome.com/tvtome/servlet/ShowMainServlet/ showid-314/, downloaded Sep. 25, 2003.

"The Story of the Triangle Fire: Part 6," http://www.ilr.cornell.edu/trianglefire/narrative6.html, Kheel Center for Labor-Management Documentation and Archives, Cornell University/ILR, downloaded Mar. 9, 2003.

"Suspect in Shooting Spree Had Long List of Enemies, Police Say," http://www.cnn.com/2000/US/03/03/wilkinsburg.shootings.01, CNN.com, downloaded Oct. 1, 2003.

"Televised Gangsters," by John William Tuohy, http://www.americanMafia.com/Feature_Articles_171.html, AmericanMafia.com , (Rick Porrello, webmaster), downloaded Dec. 19, 2004.

"Thousands Protest Columbus Day Parades," http://www.cnn.com/ 2002/US/central/10/12/columbus.day.parade/, CNN.com, downloaded Sep. 30, 2003.

"Transform Columbus Day," http://www.transformcolumbusday.org/ alliancestatements.htm, Jul. 18, 2004.

"Transform Columbus Day," http://www.transformcolumbusday.org/faq. htm#first%20amendment, Jul. 18, 2004.

"Una Storia Segreta: The Italian American Internment During World War II," http://www.fierimanhattan. org/bulletinboard/ unastoriasegre ta/unastoriasegreta.html, Fieri Manhattan, downloaded Apr. 18, 2003.

"Victims of David," http://www.angelfire.com/oh/yodaspage3/victims.html, downloaded Jun. 2, 2003.

"Wartime Violation of Italian American Civil Liberties Act," 106th Congress, 1st Session, on H.R. 2442, Oct. 26, 1999, http://commdocs.house.gov/committees/ judiciary/hju60413.00 0/hju60413_0.htm, downloaded Apr. 15, 2003.

"When Speaking Italian Was A Crime," by Michael San Filippo, http://italian.about.com/library/weekly/aa102500d.htm, About, Inc., downloaded Apr. 15, 2003.

"Who Shot Joe Colombo and Killed the Italian American Civil Rights League?" by Richard Capozzola,
http://www.italianinfo.net/joe-page1.htm,
http://www.italianinfo.net/joe-page2.htm,
http://www.italianinfo.net/joe-page3.htm,
http://www.italianinfo.net/joe-page4.htm,
httw.italip://wwaninfo.net/joe-page5.htm,
http://www.italianinfo.net/joe-page6.htm,
http://www.italianinfo.net/joe-page7.htm, downloaded Jun. 6, 2003.

"Woglife," http://www.wog.com.au, downloaded Feb. 10, 2004.

"Yahoo! Groups…" http://groups.yahoo.com/group/ ladolcevitadefamation database/message/31, downloaded Sep. 3, 2003.

"Yahoo! Groups…"
http://groups.yahoo.com/group/ladolcevita_defamation_database/ message/32, downloaded Oct. 13, 2003.

"Yahoo! Groups…The Evil Simple-A-Fisha-Man Organ Grinder," http://groups.yahoo.com/group/ladolcevita_defamation_database/ message/20, Francesca L'Orfano (site manager), Dec. 12, 2002.

"Yahoo! Groups…Media Uses 'Sopranos' Popularity to 'Smear' Italian Government,"
http://groups.yahoo.com/group/Italian_American_One Voice/message/752, Manny Alfano (site manager), Jan. 19, 2002.

"Yahoo! Groups…Member of Parliament Hon. Alfonso Gagliano Accused of Having Links to Organized Crime," http://groups.yahoo.com/group/ladolcevita_defamation_database/ message/38, Francesca L'Orfano (site manager), Feb. 25, 2002.

"Yahoo! Groups…'See Spot Run'"
http://groups.yahoo.com/group/ladolcevita_defamation_dat

abase/message/17, Francesca L'Orfano (site manager), Dec. 12, 2002.

"Yahoo! Groups…The Zogby Report National Survey: American Teen-agers and Stereotyping," http://groups.yahoo.com/group/ladolcevita_defamation_dat abase/message/43, downloaded Oct. 1, 2003.

Newspapers and Periodicals

Bucks County Courier Times, "Marino Sues, Claiming False Accusations," by Greg Coffey, April 12, 2002.

Buffalo Daily Courier, "Raiding the Italians," and "A Search for Knives," March 5, 1888, p. 4.*

Charities, "The Italian Foreman as a Social Agent," by Gino C. Speranza, 1903, vol. 11, pp. 26-28.

Denver Post, "Columbus Boycott Planned," by Arthur Kane, Sep. 19, 2001. "Forty March on Columbus Day," by Sheba R. Wheeler, Oct. 9, 2001.

Forum, "Italian Immigrants and Their Enslavement," by S. Merlino, April, 1893, vol. 15, pp. 183-190.

Italian Tribune, "Uncle Floyd Vivino's Italian American Serenade," August 1, 2002.

————. "Uncle Floyd Vivino's Italian American Serenade," February 6, 2003.

The Marion Daily Republican, "First Public Lynching in History of County Took Place Thursday," June 11, 1915. "Leona's Store Dynamited," June 11, 1915. "John Garavalgia is on Trial for His Life," June 14, 1915.

The Marion Evening Post, "Perry County Has Lynching," October 13, 1914. "Cooper Fourth Feud Victim," October 14, 1914. "Lynched

---

* Interestingly, in this same paper (right next to the column on "Raiding the Italians"), there was mention of a Bohemian saloon-keeper who was shot and killed. Before slipping into a state of unconsciousness, the Bohemian said that a policeman named John Slater fired at him. However, it was later found out, after the cop was nearly lynched by outraged locals, that a different man had fled the scene of the crime. Apparently both the Bohemian and the cop received justice (even if not immediately). If an Italian, on the other hand, was placed in the Bohemian's shoes, there probably would not have been such an outcry for justice on the part of white natives.

Man's Victim is Dead," October 14, 1914. "State Troops to Willisville," October 14, 1914.

National Geographic, "And Still They Tango," by Alma Guillermoprieto, December 2003.

New York Newsday, "Ex-Officers Get 11 Years," by Andrew Metz and Robbin Topping, May 27, 2000, p. A3.

Outlook, "Forced Labor in West Virginia," by Gino C. Speranza, June 13, 1903.

The Pennsylvania Magazine of History and Biography, "The Buena Vista Affair 1874-1875," by Herbert G. Gutman, July, 1964, pp. 254, 257-8, 265-272.

Pittsburgh Daily Dispatch, "Narrow Escape From Lynching for an Italian," June 27, 1899.

The Pittsburgh Post, "Drove Out the Italians," March 21, 1894.

Rocky Mountain News, "Arata Lynched," July 27, 1893. "Columbus Day Began in Colorado. Aim Would Like the Holiday to End Here, Too," by Lisa Levitt Ryckman.

The Tampa Tribune, "Strike of 1910 Turned Violent," by Leland Hawes (staff writer), News Bank Info-web, Metropolitan edition, Baylife section, p. 4.

The Vicksburg Evening Post, "Lynch Law," March 29, 1886.

Yale Law Journal, 25, May 1916, pp. 561-581, Charles H. Watson.

Reports

"The Italian Massacre at Walsenburg, Colorado 1895," Conrad Woodall, Presented to the American Italian Historical Association, Chicago, Nov. 1987.

"Italian Prisoners of War and the Enemy's Barbarity," Torino: Unione Tipografico—Editrice Torinese, 1918.

New Jersey Bill Text, Assembly No. 3693, State of New Jersey, 209th Legislature, Introduced June 21, 2001, Statement Section and Text Sections 1a, 1b and 1f.

"On Image and Defamation: A Report to the Membership," Executive Council of the Italic Institute of America, Floral Park, New York, Nov. 2002.

"Report to the Congress of the United States: A Review of the Restrictions on Persons of Italian Ancestry During World War II," Washington, D.C., United States Department of Justice, Nov. 2001.

"'Soprano' Sting Operation Railroads Physician," Press Release, Order Sons of Italy in America, Frank Sinatra Lodge 2621, Englishtown, New Jersey, Aug. 27, 2001.

Films

Casino. Dir. Martin Scorsese. Perf. Robert De Niro, Joe Pesci, Sharon Stone. Prod. Universal, 1994.

Gabriela. Dir. Bruno Barreto. Perf. Marcello Mastroianni, Sonia Braga. Prod. Ibrahim Moussa and Harold Nebenzal, 1983.

The Godfather. Dir. Francis Ford Coppola. Perf. Marlon Brando, James Caan, Al Pacino. Prod. Paramount, 1972.

The Godfather Part III. Dir. Francis Ford Coppola. Perf. Al Pacino, Andy Garcia, Talia Shire. Prod. Paramount, 1990.

Goodfellas. Dir. Martin Scorsese. Perf. Robert De Niro, Ray Liotta, Joe Pesci, Paul Sorvino. Prod. Warner Bros., 1990.

The Italian. Dir. Reginald Barker. Perf. George Beban, Clara Williams. Prod. Thomas Ince, 1915.

Italian-American Internment: A Secret Story. Dir. Stephen Kroopnick. Narr. David Ackroyd. Prod. A & E Television Networks/The History Channel, 2000.

Little Caesar. Dir. Mervyn LeRoy. Perf. Edward G. Robinson, Douglas Fairbanks Jr., Glenda Farrell. Prod. Warner Bros., 1931.

Scarface: The Shame of a Nation. Dir. Howard Hawks. Perf. Paul Muni, Ann Dvorak. Prod. United Artists, 1932.

Photographic Sources

Figure 1: Library of Congress, Prints and Photographs Division LC-USF33-002911-M1.

Figure 2: Library of Congress, Prints and Photographs Division LC-USZ62-30404.

Figure 3: Library of Congress, Prints and Photographs Division LC-USZ62-41516.

Figure 4: Library of Congress, Prints and Photographs Division LC-USF3301-013289-M2.

Figure 5: Library of Congress, Prints and Photographs Division LC-USF34-037023-D.

Figure 6: Library of Congress, Prints and Photographs Division LC-

DIG-nclc-05054.

Figure 7: Library of Congress, Prints and Photographs Division LC-USZ62-72436.

Figure 8: Library of Congress, Prints and Photographs Division LC-USZC4-12142.

Figure 9: Photo appears courtesy of the Barbato Borza Archive and Mr. Barbato Borza.

Figure 10: Library of Congress, Prints and Photographs Division LC-USZ62-90521.

Figure 11: Photo appears courtesy of the Chicago Historical Society and Roosevelt University's "History of Chicago" web-page, http://www.roosevelt.edu/chicagohistory/mod2-chap1.htm.

Figure 12: Library of Congress, Prints and Photographs Division LC-USZ62-79432.

Figure 13: Library of Congress, Prints and Photographs Division LC-USZ62-122655.

Figure 14: New York Public Library, Digital Collections, Mid-Manhattan Picture Collection, Image ID # 800775.

Figure 15: New York Public Library, Digital Collections, Mid-Manhattan Picture Collection, Image ID # 805500.

Figure 16: Library of Congress, Prints and Photographs Division LC-USZ62-87776.

Figure 17: Library of Congress, Prints and Photographs Division LC-C2688-687.

Figure 18: Library of Congress, Prints and Photographs Division LC-USZ62-73448.

Figure 19: Photos appears courtesy of the Westchester County District Attorney's Office.

Figure 20: Library of Congress, Prints and Photographs Division LC-USZ62-64731.

Figure 21: New York Public Library, Digital Collections, Mid-Manhattan Picture Collection, Image ID # 801552.

Figure 22: Library of Congress, Prints and Photographs Division LC-USZ62-120716.

Figure 23: Library of Congress, Prints and Photographs Division LC-USW3-013946-D.

Figure 24: Library of Congress, Prints and Photographs Division LC-DIG-ppmsca-01846.

Figure 25: Library of Congress, Prints and Photographs Division LC-USZ62-26543.

Figure 26: Library of Congress, Prints and Photographs Division
LC-USW3-013495-D.

Figure 27: Photos are the personal property of the author.

Figure 28: Library of Congress, Prints and Photographs Division
LC-USZ62-75167.

Endnotes

[1] In addition to being armed camp guards who were used to intimidate Italian laborers, it is believed a number of blacks participated in the 1891 lynching of 11 Italians in New Orleans.

[2] It was once discovered that forty Italian families inhabited five small houses in Lower Manhattan; see Mangione and Morreale, p. 132.

[3] Being at the very bottom of the social ladder, Italians would work for much lower wages. They even replaced black workers in a variety of menial labor jobs and on southern plantations. As might be expected, with a great number of Italians arriving in America each year, there was an increase in "bottom-rung" job competition between them and African-Americans. Booker T. Washington and other observers at the time feared that the introduction of Mediterranean laborers in the South would exacerbate racial tensions and eventually create a three-way problem between blacks, whites, and Italians. (See *The Booker T. Washington Papers,* vol. 9, pp. 508-510, 571, Apr. 1908/vol. 10, pp. 363-364, Aug. 1910, University of Illinois Press; see also Emily Fogg Meade, "Italian Immigration into the South," *A Documentary History of the Italian Americans,* ed. Wayne Moquin, pp. 59-60, New York: Praeger, 1975.) Washington's attitude was not surprising since blacks were also influenced by anti-immigrant prejudice. That notwithstanding, there are many accounts of black-Italian cooperation in the "New South"; both groups were known to live and work side by side. The "black-white" thing did not define their early relationship since Italians did not come to this country with either a pre-existing race prejudice or a "white" self-identity, and since blacks considered the down-trodden Italians as ambiguous *others.* When cultural (not racial) misunderstanding led to occasional violence between the two groups, it was seldom reported. The press only showed concern when white natives were embroiled in conflicts with minorities. (See Jean Ann Scarpaci, "Immigrants in the New South: Italians in Louisiana's Sugar Parishes, 1880-1910," *Studies in Italian American Social History,* ed. Francesco Cordasco, p. 142, Totowa, New Jersey: Rowman and Littlefield, 1975.) For it was commonly believed a hundred years ago that White Anglo-Saxon Protestants were worth more than others. (Again, the lives of minorities were cheaply valued.)

[4] Even the issues concerning Italian/Hispanic illegal immigration parallel one another. There was a particular fear that, Italian "desperadoes," bandits, and *Mafi-*

osi were entering America through the "back door," just as today there is growing concern that an illegal Mexican element is wreaking havoc in the nation. Interestingly, the ethnic slur "wop" was created as an acronym for Italian illegals; it stood for "without papers."

[5] In 1890s New York, it was discovered that 473 of the 474 foreign bootblacks were Italian; the number of native-born bootblacks was only 10. (See Robert F. Foerster, *The Italian Emigration of Our Times*, New York: Arno Press, 1969, pp. 334-335.)

[6] The reader should understand that Italians and Americans did not give the word "African" the same exact meaning. To Italians, Africans were depicted and thought of primarily as Arabs or Berbers (from that part of Africa closest to Italy). To Americans, the word "African" is a generic name for "blacks" (or people whose origins lie in sub-Saharan Africa).

[7] For more on the inferiority of the Mediterranean race and the supremacy of Anglo-Saxons, see Madison Grant's long winded racial manifesto, *The Passing of the Great Race*, New York: Charles Scribner's Sons, 1916.

[8] In his book, *The Italian Emigration of Our Times*, Foerster cites the following quotes made by random individuals: "One 'white man' is as good as two or three Italians!"; "It makes no difference whom I employ, negro, Italian or white man" (p. 408).

[9] While observing an Italian minding his own business, one man said in concordance with the beliefs of his time, "These Italians are the worst of the lot [of immigrants]. They are a dangerous element. Stick a knife in you in a minute. Look at the villainous-looking fellow standing right there on the box, smoking a cigar. Why, criminal instinct is written in every line of his head and face. See the bravado in the way he holds his shoulders and the nasty look in his uneasy eyes." (See Michael La Sorte, *La Merica: Images of Italian Greenhorn Experience*, Philadelphia: Temple University Press, 1985, p. 144). Jack London, the writer, confessed that his mother had held the same view. For he had heard her say, "if one offended an Italian, no matter how slightly and unintentionally, he was certain to retaliate by stabbing one in the back." (See Salvatore J. Lagumina, *Wop! A Documentary History of Anti-Italian Discrimination in the United States*, Toronto: Guernica, 1999, p. 126.) Anti-Italian statements that circulated by word of mouth, such as these, were probably more damaging than those in print, since children and impressionable others heard ordinary adults (whom they looked up to) spreading them.

[10] The *New York Times* specialized in its negative depiction of Italians, as it still does today (though more subtly). (Again, see Lagumina's *Wop!*) Many other papers frequently attacked Italians as well. The *Baltimore News* went on record stating, "The disposition to assassinate in revenge for a fancied wrong is a marked trait in the character of this impulsive and inexorable race." (See John Higham's *Strangers in the Land: Patterns of American Nativism 1860-1925*, New York: Atheneum, 1973, p. 90.) Whenever an Italian either committed a crime, was suspected of committing one, or was the victim of one, his "race" came into question.

[11] The *straniere* (or "foreigners") who ruled sections of Italy included Germanic

"barbarians," Byzantines, Arabs, Normans, Spaniards, Austrians, and the French.
[12] It should be noted that these secret societies were regarded more as liberation groups than "criminal organizations" by Italian natives—comparable to the way many modern Muslims view Hamas or the Al-Aqsa Martyrs Brigade.
[13] Substandard quarters awaited Italians wherever they ventured. In the rural districts of Western Europe, along the French-German border, life was especially harsh. There, "dwellings" (if they could be called that) constituted one room huts having mud floors, straw to sleep on, no windows, and nothing else but pungent, nauseating odor. In many cases, poultry was also raised inside the huts. As many as 20 people would jam into a single space. Italian quarters were also the most primitive in major European cities like Paris. (See Foerster, *The Italian Emigration of Our Times*, p. 144 and the footnotes on pp. 166 and 168.)
[14] The same anti-Italian perceptions also existed in the Northern European nations that Italians migrated to. In early twentieth century Germany, where Italian immigrants very rarely became citizens and were far removed from mainstream society, they were described as dirty, primitive creatures who were ever ready to resort to "revolver and stiletto." (See Foerster, *The Italian Emigration of Our Times*, pp. 140-142, 161, 163-164, 421-422.) Influencing the Germans' prejudice were the same factors that influenced Americans, such as the international rumors about the "Mafia," racial doctrines supporting the inferiority of darker peoples (such as Southern Europeans and Jews), and the belief that Italian workers were all strikebreakers and wage depressors. To this day in Germany, there is still bigoted opposition to Mediterranean immigration. Turks, Italians, and various Balkan peoples are frequently the targets of neo-Nazi rage.
[15] As far as hypocrisy is concerned, the words of Dr. Lawrence Frank Pisani ring especially true: "Frontiersmen who depended on their own justice in preference to civil authority were self-reliant; Italians who did the same were lawless."
[16] For the inhospitality of the largely Anglo-, Irish-, and German-descended ship workers, see La Sorte's *La Merica*, pp. 23-25; see also Lawrence Frank Pisani, *The Italian in America: A Social Study and History*, New York: Exposition Press, 1957.
[17] Again, see La Sorte, pp. 51-52.
[18] One would think that the American Catholic Church would have welcomed the Italian newcomers as co-religionists and perhaps even given them more of a warm reception than other groups since they came from the birthplace of Catholicism—Italy; but the opposite is true. The American Catholic Church was dominated by people of Irish descent who differed from the Italians in their religious customs and ways of worship. The Mediterranean Catholicism that Italians practiced, rooted in traditions predating Christ himself, was scorned by Irish Catholics and considered a combination of heresy and "African savagery." Ignorant of Southern Europe's geo-political realities, Irish Catholics also blamed the Italians (powerless and impoverished though they were) for breaking the Pope's grip on central Italy during Unification; it was not the Southern Italians who pushed for Italian Unification however—many died trying to prevent it. Since the Irish started moving up in society when Southern Italians began immigrating, there was a sim-

ple Darwinian need to deflect as much racism as they could (initially aimed at them) on to the Italians. The segregation of parishioners, Italian-Irish neighborhood wars, and mutual distrust were the result.

[19] See La Sorte, p. 139.

[20] And yet Foerster also said the emigrant's Italy was "whatever country will give him his bread." (See *The Italian Emigration of Our Times*, p. 428.)

[21] For source information and a list of those executed, see the Appendices to Chapter 2, Section B.

[22] Luciano Iorizzo and Salvatore Mondello state in their book *The Italian Americans* (Boston: Twayne Publishers, 1980, p. 290) that four Italians were killed in Buena Vista, Pennsylvania, on December 17, 1874. Personally I believe they somehow misread what occurred on November 29, since I have not seen any sources that make mention of December 17. It is possible, however, that they may have stumbled across an entirely different bit of information. What occurred in Buena Vista demonstrates the interwoven relationship between anti-immigrant feeling and labor violence in nineteenth century America. It is a unique case in that the immigrants actually fought back—*and militantly*. Around the time of the Buena Vista incident, anti-Italian labor hostility was on the rise in other parts of the world as well. In the early 1880s bloody anti-Italian riots took place in Marseilles, France. (See Foerster, p. 141.)

[23] Though anti-Italian depictions and prejudice picked up speed when Italians began arriving in large numbers in the 1880s, there is evidence of a pre-existing Italophobia. (See Lagumina, *Wop!*, pp. 23-51.)

[24] It appears that the New Orleans papers were much more familiar with Spanish names than with Italian ones; Hispanic names were often passed off as being Italian. For example, one murdered "Sicilian" was given the name "Manuel Mangeloa." (See Humbert S. Nelli, *The Business of Crime*, New York: Oxford University Press, 1976, p. 33.) Such an error is understandable given the fact that the Hispanic presence in New Orleans had predated the Italian arrival by hundreds of years, and since both groups are "Latin" and thus very similar to Anglo eyes.

[25] There is not much information on this lynching. All that is known is the victim's name, the place he was lynched, and the date it occurred. (See "Louisiana Lynchings," http://users.bestweb.net/~rg/lynchings/Louisiana%20Lynchings.htm "Before the Needles" website, downloaded May 13, 2003.)

[26] Two years before the founding of the Society of St. Raphael, Mother Cabrini began her charitable work with Italian immigrants in both North and South America; the first American citizen to be canonized, Cabrini is remembered as the patron saint of immigrants. (See Mangione and Morreale, *La Storia*, p. 119.)

[27] This lynching was also lacking additional information and can be found on the "Before the Needles" website; see "Kentucky Lynchings," http://users.bestweb.net/~rg/lynchings/Kentucky%20Lynchings.htm, Rob Gallagher (web manager).

[28] The son of a carpetbagger, Hennessy was a murderer himself who had many political enemies. He actually killed his main rival for the position of police chief

in October of 1881. Nine years and two days later (symbolically on the ninth anniversary of his opponent's demise) it was his turn to be gunned down. Obviously his attackers were more powerful than the insular Italians implicated in his death. (See Mangione and Morreale, *La Storia*, pp. 202-205.)

[29] It is interesting to note that post-World War II Hispanic immigrants, namely Puerto Ricans, inherited this same stereotype from their Italian predecessors. The only difference was that the press did not "flay" the Hispanics alive with their own "switch-blades," as they had done to the Italians for so many years.

[30] On March 18, 1891, just four days after the eleven were lynched, NAACP records show that a man named "Nograde Bela" was lynched in Branchville, Virginia. (See William Loren Katz, ed., *NAACP: Thirty Years of Lynching in the United States 1889-1918*, New York: Arno Press, 1969, p. 100.) Whether or not the man was Italian is impossible to tell; this early NAACP source contains many errors in the spelling of names and places. However, given the time frame of the lynching and the fact that the man's name "sounds Italian," it is quite possible that "Nograde Bela" was indeed an Italian.

[31] Before he became president, Theodore Roosevelt boasted that the lynching of the Italians in New Orleans was "a rather good thing"; he stated this at a party where there were, as he said, "various dago diplomats." Senator Henry Cabot Lodge (1893-1924) was probably the most vociferous of the Italian haters in the political sphere. (See Richard Gambino, *Blood of My Blood: The Dilemma of the Italian-Americans*, Garden City, New York: Anchor Press/Doubleday, 1974, p. 118-119.) In 1911, Governor Parker of Louisiana (one of the men who had helped organize the New Orleans lynch mob in 1891) stated that Italians were "just a little worse than the Negro, being if anything filthier in [their] habits, lawless, and treacherous." (See: John V. Baiamonte, *Spirit of Vengeance: Nativism and Louisiana Justice, 1921-1924*, Baton Rouge: Louisiana State University Press, 1986, p. 63).

[32] In some instances Italian laborers were fired upon and murdered when trying to escape the work camps; a case like this occurred in the Adirondacks. (See Francesco Cordasco and Eugene Bucchioni, *The Italians: Social Backgrounds of an American Group*, Clifton, New Jersey: Augustus M. Kelley, Publishers, 1974, pp. 393-394; see also, S. Merlino, "Italian Immigrants and Their Enslavement," *Forum*, vol. 15, April 1893, pp. 183-190.)

[33] In September of 1892, according to NAACP records, a man named "Gabriel Magloire" was lynched in Avoyelles, Louisiana; the man is listed as black. However, the "Before the Needles" website lists the man's surname as "Magliore." If this latter spelling is accurate—and given the fact that Italians were racially ambiguous a century ago, especially in Louisiana—it is quite possible that he was of Italian background. (To compare the data, see: Katz, *NAACP*, p. 69, and "Louisiana Lynchings," http://users.bestweb.net/~rg/lynching/Louisiana%20Lynching.htm). The two sources differ in the spelling of four more persons who may have had Italian blood: "__Ella" (see Katz, p. 69) or "Ella__" (see "Louisiana Lynchings"); "Joseph

Dazzele" (see Katz, p. 70) or "James Dandy" (see "Louisiana Lynchings"); "Nicholas Dublano" (see Katz, p. 71) or "Nicholas Deblanc" (see "Louisiana Lynchings"); "Christopher Chamblers" (see Katz, p. 43) or "Christian Chalma" (see "Alabama Lynchings"). Also in 1892, in Logan County, Oklahoma, "__Cora" was lynched (see Katz, p. 86) —yet another person who might have been of Italian background. Further research should be conducted to see if there were a number of Italians listed as "Negroes" in the records of those lynched a hundred years back (especially in the South). Naturally, the Anglicization of victims' names should also be investigated.

[34] That same year (1893), in France, "at the salt works of Aigues-Mortes, the French miners savagely attacked their Italian competitors, killing fifty and wounding a hundred and fifty." Virulent anti-French demonstrations took place in Italy, and there were even threats made to burn down the French Embassy. Many anti-Italian conflicts broke out in France during this period. (See Foerster, p. 141.) Two Frenchmen, writing after the Aigues-Mortes episode, declared, "Because of the strength of their emigration movement, their endurance in hard labor, their docile obedience to the orders of boss or employer, their sobriety and the native misery which allows them to accept low wages, the Italians are the Chinese of Europe." (See Foerster, p. 142). Obviously the Frenchmen were comparing the Italian workers of Europe to the Chinese workers in America. However, if these two men were more knowledgeable of the Italian experience in the United States, and how much the Italian population had suffered there, they would have realized that the Italians of Europe were in fact the *Italians* of America.

[35] On May 30, 1893, a man named Celio Lucero was lynched in San Miguel County, New Mexico. (See Katz, p. 83.) Although he might have possessed some Italian blood, Lucero was most likely of Mexican background. It is evident that the NAACP source is inconsistent when listing Hispanics by race. For example, all of the Hispanics lynched in Arizona and New Mexico (on pages 48 and 83) are recorded as white (i.e. in light print), yet the Mexicans lynched in Oklahoma (p. 86) are listed as black (in bold print). Still, in Texas (pp. 95-99) some Hispanics are listed as white while others appear to be "inbetween" (i.e. a combination of bold and light print). So one can see how Hispanics have been considered an ambiguous "other," racially, for many years.

[36] I have not found a detailed account of the lynching. (See the "Before the Needles" website, "Kentucky Lynchings," http://users.bestweb.net/~rg/Lynchings/ Kentucky%20Lynchings.htm.)

[37] In *Blood of My Blood*, Gambino stated (on page 118) that six Italians were lynched—this is a common mistake made by other sources as well. It is most probable that they accidentally included a German prisoner who was left unharmed by the attacking party. It should also be known that while five Italians were attacked, two managed to escape the lynching. John Higham, in *Strangers in the Land*, erroneously stated that 6 Italians were massacred. (See page 90.)

[38] On January 7, 1895, a man named Spencer Costello was lynched in Madison County, Mississippi; he is listed as black. (See Katz, p. 76, and "Mississippi Lynch-

ings," http://users.bestweb.net/~rg/Lynchings/Mississippi%20Lynchings.htm.) Also in 1895, someone recorded by the NAACP as "Floantina Suitta" was lynched in Catula, Texas (see Katz, p. 96). This person is listed as a female. Both of the above cases should be looked into further.

[39] A farming community consisting of forty Italian-American families founded Tontitown. The town was named after the Italian explorer Enrico Tonti. (See Gambino, *Blood of My Blood*, pp. 103-104; see also Pisani, pp. 77-78.)

[40] Although, it has been documented that the rate of Italian prospectors knifed and shot at, while looking for gold in California, was rather high. (See Mangione and Morreale, p. 193.)

[41] See Appendix.

[42] Occurring some time in 1900, a man named John Gambola was lynched in Hackensack, New Jersey. Suspected of murder, he was the only man lynched in New Jersey between 1889 and 1918. (See Katz, p. 83.) Three other men were lynched that same year; they were from Florida, Indiana, and Mississippi (respectively): James Barco, John Rollo, and Dago Pete. All three are listed as black men. (See Katz, pp. 55, 64, 77; see also the "Before the Needles" website at the following three locations:
http://users.bestweb.net/~rg/lynchings/Florida%20Lynchings.htm
http://users.bestweb.net/~rg/lynchings/Indiana%20Lynchings.htm
http://users.bestweb.net/~rg/lynchings/Mississippi%20Lynchings.htm.)
While it is possible that these men were indeed African-Americans, it is not inconceivable that they were swarthy Italians mistaken for blacks. One must remember that this was an era in which Italians were frequently called "black dagoes." (See Gambino in both his works: *Vendetta*, p. 56, and *Blood of My Blood*, p. 107.)

[43]This was obviously a very confusing time historically, as Italians were simultaneously being classified as pro-labor radicals and prideless scabs.

[44] The NAACP source (Katz) is very inaccurate when it comes to listing lynched Italians. As was mentioned earlier, it misprints names, dates, places, etc. When reporting the attack on the three in Erwin, it listed a "John" and "Victor" *Ameo* (instead of Giovanni and Vincenzo Serio). In addition, the NAACP listed a "Salvator Libereo" as being lynched in Montana on July 16. (*Salvatore Liberto* was, of course, only wounded in Erwin, Mississippi, on the eleventh of July.)

[45] Italian-Americans suffered many labor abuses through the years (undoubtedly volumes could be written on the subject), and going without pay was not uncommon. I am reminded of one particular instance in Wisconsin, where Italian laborers were paid in worthless pieces of paper that were said to have been redeemable at the company's home office (located, of course, in a different city). When the Italians went to collect, neither their money nor the company office was there for them—they were deceived. (See "Italian Farmers in Cumberland" by John Andreozzi, *Italian Americans in a Multicultural Society*, Jerome Krase and Judith De Sena, eds., New York: Forum Italicum, 1994, pp117-118.) Italians were taken advantage of in other countries as well. In Brazil, for example, in 1906, a traveling inspector named Adolfo Rossi reported on the many abuses Italian laborers and their

families were subjected to by plantation owners and their overseers. Abuses included women and girls being attacked and the flogging of workmen (wages were also withheld in many cases.) Italian laborers replaced black slaves on the Brazilian plantations (or fazendas) after the latter were emancipated in 1888; and, apparently, the "old slave system," as Robert Foerster put it, "still lingered on in the fazendas." (See Foerster, pp. 284, 294-296.)

[46] One of the eighty was a publisher of a pro-labor Italian newspaper. (See Mangione and Morreale, p. 187.)

[47] Also in 1904, a man named William Cato was lynched in Statesboro, Georgia; he is listed as black. This deserves to be looked into as well. (See Katz, p. 60; "Georgia Lynchings" http://users.bestweb.net/~rg/lynchings/Georgia%20Lynchings.htm, "Before the Needles" website.)

[48] This information might prove Gambino wrong when he stated that "Italians were second only to blacks in numbers of lynch victims in the years 1870 to 1940." (See *Vendetta*, p. 135.) Obviously Cutler's data did not stretch to the 1940s however.

[49] In 1906, the average pay an unskilled Italian worker received for a 10-hour work day was $1.46; unskilled Irish workers received $2.00 on average. (See La Sorte, p. 65.)

[50] In Germany, in 1907, "legitimation cards" were issued to immigrant workers for the first time. The names of the immigrant and his employer were inscribed on the card. Anyone who sought work without a "due discharge" etched on his card would be expelled from Germany. The German government did this in order to establish the kind of total control over foreigners that it could not *(yet)* exercise over German natives. This policy operated on the premise that "the immigrant has only a pecuniary interest in coming and must accept his employers' terms or stay away." ("Slave labor or nothing" was surely a choice some immigrants had to make.) By December of 1908, this system covered "all industry and all immigrant workers"—it was called *Deutsche Arbeiterzentrale*. Each nationality was given a card of a different color. The tens of thousands of Italian workers affected by this new policy were issued green colored cards; and for each one they had to pay a fee of two marks. It is easy to see why Italian government officials, writers, and the immigrant workers themselves, ardently opposed such treatment—they were regarded as cattle. (See Foerster, p. 162.) With a super-police state rising to power in Germany two and a half decades later, one is forced to ponder whether or not past policies, such as the issuing of "legitimation cards," helped (even if unintentionally) to *legitimize* the omnipotence of a tyrannical central government and the destruction of civil liberties.

[51] It is easy to see similarities here with the discrimination many Southeast Asian peoples suffer at the hands of northeast Asians. For example, on account of their darker features, Filipinos are frequently excluded from "Asian" circles by people of Chinese, Japanese, or Korean background.

[52] When the Italian Consulate investigated thirty cases of alleged Black Hand crimes, all but one was found to be explicable by other means. (See Gambino, *Blood of My Blood*, p. 282.)

[53] Foerster estimated that a hundred or more Italians were killed in the disaster.

(See *The Italian Emigration of Our Times*, p. 389.)

[54] Less than a year after the Tampa lynching, a man named Jerry Gusto was lynched in Columbia County, Florida; he is listed as black and was lynched with five other blacks. (See "Florida Lynchings," http://users.bestweb.net/~rg/lynchings/ Florida%20Lynchings.htm. "Before the Needles" website.) The NAACP source lists the men as "Six Unknown Negroes." (See Katz, p. 56.) This would be an interesting case to look into.

[55] Gambino was wrong, however, when he wrote that the Lawrence strike was "unsuccessful." (See *Blood of My Blood*, p. 116.)

[56] In Chicago, "the police said that forty-five unsolved murders that year [1913] were the work of the Black Hand—and offered no evidence to back the assertion. At one point the Chicago police arrested fifty Italians at random. A court fined them each one dollar and court expenses on trumped-up charges of disorderly conduct, and released them." The entire Italian community in Chicago was presumed guilty of the crimes, and the fines 45 of them paid were intended to scare the Italians into being "good." This stimulated more distrust for the law. (See Gambino, *Blood of My Blood*, p. 283.) In order to protect itself, Chicago's Italian-American community had established, by the previous year, some 400 mutual aid societies. (See Gambino again, p. 111.)

[57] Two days before the strike, on February 23, 1913, a man named Marion Cantri was lynched in Clarendon, South Carolina; he is listed as black. (See "South Carolina Lynchings," http://users.bestweb.net/~rg/lynchings/South%20Carolina%20 Lynchings.htm, "Before the Needles" website.)

[58] See "The Ludlow Massacre: Monument," http://www.umwa.org/ history/ ludlow2.shtml, UMWA website; see also, "the Ludlow Massacre" http://www.pbs.org/wgbh/amex/rockefellers/sfeature/sf_8.html, PBS Online/WGBH.

[59] In *Blood of My Blood* (pp. 116-117), Gambino implies that 11 of the victims were Italian; and in *La Storia* (p. 268), Mangione and Morreale state that 12 were of Italian background. For pro-Hispanic bias, see the online article by Don Hermosillo, "Hispanic Contributions to World History" http://www.neta.com/~1stbooks/tragic2.htm. It is clear that Hermosillo deliberately altered the names of the Ludlow victims to increase the number of Hispanics killed.

[60] See the following web-pages: "1914 No. 5 Eccles Mine Explosion" http://www.rootsweb.com/~wvcoal/ecles.html; "List of Men Killed in the 1914 Eccles Explosion: Page One of Three" http://wwwrootsweb.com/~wvcoal/ecles1.html; "List of Men Killed in the 1914 Eccles Explosion: Page Two of Three" http://www.rootsweb.com/~wvcoal/ecles2.html; "List of Men Killed in the 1914 Eccles Explosion: Page Three of Three" http://www.rootsweb.com/~wvcoal/ecles3.html.

[61] I am using "Piazza" as the surname given in the Yale Law Journal, as opposed to the *Marion Evening Post's* "Piazzi," because the press at this time had almost always misspelled Italian last names; "Piazzi" is also not as common a name as 'Pi-

azza." In *Blood of My Blood* (p. 119), Richard Gambino incorrectly stated that this lynching occurred in 1910.

[62] The following lynching deserves further investigation to determine whether the victim was of Italian, black, or other background: On August 12, 1914, "Oli Romeo" was lynched in St. Tammany County, Louisiana. See "Louisiana Lynchings": http: users.bestweb.net/~rg/lyunchings/Louisiana%20Lynchings.htm, "Before the Needles" website; see also Katz, p.73. Both sources list Romeo as black.

[63] *The Italian*. Dir. Reginald Barker. Perf. George Beban, Clara Williams. Prod. Thomas Inc, 1915.

[64] The dates given in the *Yale Law Journal*, of and before the lynching, are wrong (June 11th and 12th) —they conflict with the dates reported in the *Marion Daily Republican* (June 9th and 10th). Richard Gambino, in *Blood of My Blood* (p. 119), gave an incorrect date for this lynching as well—1911.

[65] Italian church goers were segregated against in other places as well. For the religious segregation of Italians in Poughkeepsie, see "Our Parish History" http://www.mtcarmelparish.com/our_parish_history.htm. There, Italians were "allowed" to worship in the basement of Saint Peter's church. Also see Moises Sandoval's online article about how "Italians worshiped in the dark, humid basement" of a church in St. Paul, Minnesota; "Huddled Masses: The History of Our Immigrant Church," http://www.uscatholic.org/2000/07/hm0007.htm, Claretian Publications. Sandoval quotes Father Nicola Carlo Odone as saying that it was humiliating for the Italians "to have to meet under the feet of a different people [i.e. the Irish] which looks at us from above with contempt." One Italian-American had this to say about the contempt and racial prejudice that the Irish Catholic clergy harbored for Italians: "They thought we were Africans" and "they looked down on us" (see Orsi, p 56).

[66]Indeed, conditions Italian migrants endured in countries other than the United States were often worse. On the thousands of Italian children employed in France's glassworks industry, and on Italian women forced into prostitution in France and having to put up with substandard living conditions there, see Foerster, pp. 137, 144-148. To understand the plight of the children, see p. 145, where it was reported that in 1867, "during the world exposition in Paris, 1544 Italian begging children were arrested." On the grotesque living conditions awaiting the Italian migrants in Germany, see pp. 165-169. Of the hardships Italians endured in Switzerland and the prejudice they were subjected to, see pp. 180-186. (From what I have personally heard from travelers abroad, Italians are still regarded with great contempt in Switzerland, as they continue to take the kinds of low paying, menial jobs that the non-Italian Swiss refuse. The Italian film *Bread and Chocolate* acknowledges this. Likewise, Switzerland's northern neighbors also tend to regard their Mediterranean and Middle Eastern citizens with equal disdain.) Foerster wrote that, in Austria-Hungary, "Much more than in any other great country of Europe, there has been an active political and racial depreciation of the [Italian] immigrants…" He goes on to say, "The Italians…have shown little tendency…to let themselves be absorbed…. Intermarriage with native peoples has been uncommon" (p. 199). Thus the Italians

refused even harder to assimilate when harshly oppressed. For the brutal living and working conditions that Italian boys and girls faced in old Austria-Hungary, see p. 201. Conversely, Italian immigration to other parts of southern Europe, North Africa, and the Middle East was characterized much less by prejudice and discrimination (see pp. 206-222). There are probably two important reasons for this: these regions shared a similar "Mediterraneanness" which was more hospitable and compatible to the Italian way of life, and less Italians immigrated to these parts (because real opportunity lay in the more industrialized nations). Italian immigration to South America was very successful because not only were countries like Argentina and Brazil familiar on account of their Romance (or *Italic*) languages, but they were familiar in *all* aspects of "Latinity"—these countries were culturally suitable to the Italian immigrants, Roman Catholicism was the predominant religion, they were located in a warm climate (as Italy was), and unlike North Americans, many of the people in Latin America shared Mediterranean ethnic roots with the Italian newcomers and thus *looked* like them. This is why, throughout the nineteenth century (when Italians began emigrating *en masse*), South America received more Italian immigrants than North America. Only in another Latin country could the son of an Italian immigrant rise to become president. It is no wonder then that people of Italian descent are still a dominant group in South America's "southern cone" (see pp. 223-320). (The president of Uruguay stated on Vatican Radio, not too long ago, that it is difficult to find a Uruguayan who lacks Italian blood.) Nevertheless, when Italians first arrived in South America in considerable numbers they could easily be classified as a *dominated* people. In Brazil (as in the United States), Italian laborers replaced the slave class when the latter was freed in 1888. As early as that year of emancipation, it was reported that Italian immigrants were subjected to "great suffering and privation," and were kept in a state of bondage and inferiority while living on the Brazilian plantations (or *fazendas*). Police abuse and a host of other indignities afflicted the Italians as well (see pp. 294-295). Interestingly, before the *original* slave class was freed, it was said that the Italians were leading advocates of abolition—the *mascate* (i.e. an Italian itinerant trader) frequently established friendships with blacks on the plantations, and often encouraged them to escape (pp. 280-285). By 1906, four-fifths of Brazil's plantation hands were Italian; see pp. 289-290. (In the 1980s, the acclaimed Brazilian telenovela *Terra Nostra* depicted Italian life on the *fazenda* during the period of early immigration.) Overall, I found Robert Foerster's book, *The Italian Emigration of Our Times*, to be very helpful as far as data in concerned, yet somewhat supportive of existing prejudices against Italians: namely that they are dirty, ignorant, and prone to violence. I also noticed his apparent bias in favor of *Northern* Italians. In this regard, Foerster does not differ from his contemporaries.

[67] Ironically, as they died by the thousands overseas during World War II, Italian-Americans were being denied their civil rights, by the thousands, here at home. More on that later.

[68] These last two sources can be found online: "Italian Immigrants in Springfield" by Kaitlin Moredock, http://www.lib.niu.edu/ipo/ihy991219.html (taken from

Illinois History: A Magazine for Young People, December 1999); "The Life of an Italian Immigrant in the Early 1900's" by Cecilia P., http://www.wfl68.frnkln. k12.il.us/fchs_Lh003.htm.

[69] The online article written by Cecilia P., a West Franklin native, stated that the riot was kindled when a couple of Sicilian boys allegedly killed the brother and friend of a non-Italian girl who refused to date them. The two victims were of course the"kidnapped boys" mentioned in Higham's book. Yet Lagumina's *Wop!* (pp. 199-200) gives the name "Amiel Calcaterra" as one of the boys who was killed. Obviously then, he could not have been a "non-Italian."

[70] See "California Lynchings," http://users.bestweb.net/~ rg/lynchings/ California%20Lynchings.htm, "Before the Needles" website, Rob Gallagher (website manager).

[71] See also Higham's notes on p. 395: Calvin Coolidge, "Whose Country Is This?" *Good Housekeeping*, LXXII (February, 1921), 14.

[72] See Appendix III in the back of the book.

[73] Also see, "Immigration Restriction Act of 1924, May 26, 1924," http://nkasd.wiu.k12.pa.us/vhs/discush1924.html.

[74] For the dates of the anti-Klan outbreaks, see Higham's notes on p. 391. It should be known that the few outbreaks mentioned were all located in Northern states, where the Klan's influence has historically been less powerful and where hyphenated Americans have tended to settle in large numbers. Grave retaliation would have surely befallen the ethnics had their anti-Klan violence been in localities south of the Mason-Dixon line.

[75] I noticed conflicting data in *La Storia* pertaining to the date on which Sacco and Vanzetti were executed. "June 1, 1927" is the date given on page 299, and "August 22, 1927" is specified on page 301. It is my understanding that the latter is correct.

[76] Not much is known about this lynching. See "Florida Lynchings," http://users. bestweb.net/~rg/lynchings/Florida%20Lynchings.htm, "Before the Needles" website.

[77] It should be noted that at the beginning of the movie *Scarface*, the audience is asked what it will do about gangsterism in society, strongly hinting that vigilantism or mob justice is what is needed. At the end of the movie, the leading character "Tony Camonte" (played by Paul Muni) is sentenced to die by hanging in the state of Illinois. Interestingly, however, Illinois replaced the noose with the electric chair ten years before this film was released—the hanging of "Tony Camonte" could thus be a subtle yet symbolic way of advocating the lynching of Italian criminals. While it is true that levels of violence, at this time, increased among organized crime members of Italian descent, the number of Italian-American criminals compared to the total Italian-American population was still infinitesimally small. This did not stop the press from spreading the following racist rumors: "There was about ninety guineas knocked off all over the country" during a mob war in the autumn of 1931. Years later it was discovered that there was only one murder between September and November 1931 that *might* have been mob related. (See Mangione and

Morreale, pp. 253-254.)

[78] In Philadelphia, Italian street vendors, minding their own business, were physically accosted by disgruntled African-Americans. (See Stefano Luconi's "A Troubled Political Partnership: Italian Americans and African Americans in the New Deal Democratic Coalition," *Are Italians White? How Race Is Made in America*, Jennifer Guglielmo and Salvatore Salerno Eds, New York: Rutledge, 2003, p. 136.)

[79] For fear of speaking Italian, see "Wartime Violation of Italian American Civil Liberties Act," 106th Congress, 1st Session, on H.R. 2442, Oct. 26, 1999, http://commdocs.house.gov/committees/judiciary/hju60413.000/hju60413_0.htm, pp. 109 & 116; for people afraid of being "too Italian," see ibid., p. 118. To read the personal accounts of Italian-Americans, see Stephen Fox's *The Unknown Internment: An Oral History of the Relocation of Italian Americans during World War II*, Boston: Twayne Publishers, 1990.

[80]For a propagandized look at how "beneficial" life was at Fort Missoula (not taking into account the violation of the Italians' and Italian-Americans' rights), see Umberto Benedetti, *Italian Boys at Fort Missoula, Montana 1941-1943*, Missoula: Pictorial Histories Publishing Co., 1997.

[81] For a list of the names of those taken in this initial roundup, see *Report to the Congress of the United States: A Review of the Restrictions on Persons of Italian Ancestry During World War II*, Washington D.C., United States Department of Justice, Appendix C, November 2001.

[82] For a list of the names of those interned, see the U.S. Department of Justice source, Appendices C, D, and E.

[83] See Richard Aquila, *Home Front Soldier: The Story of a GI and His Italian American Family During World War II*, Albany, NY: State University of New York Press, p. 42. In his book, Aquila confirmed that job and housing discrimination, as well as middle class prejudice, was still rampant against Italian-Americans during the war years. It is likely that it was even more widespread than during the Depression due to Italy's enemy status.

[84]See the DOJ source's "A List of Wartime Restrictions on Persons of Italian Ancestry as a Result of Executive Order No. 9066," Appendix K, pp. 1-3. To read the names of many of the people of Italian ancestry who were arrested for "curfew, contraband, or other violations," see Appendix F, pp. 1-13.

[85] Mangione and Morreale tell us in *La Storia* (p. 341) that while 5% of the total Italian-American population served in the military during WWII, after the attack on Pearl Harbor "10 percent of the Italian aliens had husbands or sons in the American armed forces, and the number was steadily increasing." And while Mangione and Morreale fix the number of Italians who served at 500,000, Gambino estimates that a full 1.5 million enlisted; see *Blood of My Blood*, p. 321.

[86] Other notable Italian-American war heroes included Major A. Martini, another "fighter ace" who shot down 22 Nazi planes over Paris, and Henry Mucci, the leader of a successful mission that freed from a Japanese prison camp 500 survivors of the infamous "Bataan Death March"; see "Knock-knock!`Who's there?' —`It's

the FBI!'" by Richard A. Capozzola, http://www.italianinfo.net/knock-knock.htm. See also "Chronology," http://www.italianinfo.net/chronology.htm. For the story of an Italian tenement in Yonkers pestered by the FBI, even though all the Italian inhabitants had sons and brothers fighting overseas, see http://www.italianinfo.net/knock-knock.htm.

[87] Interestingly, when President Roosevelt was asked if he planned to intern all Italian aliens after war had been declared on Italy, his reply was: "I'm not worried about Italians. They're just a bunch of opera singers." (See Mangione and Morreale, p. 25.)

[88] All of my sources concur that Attorney General Francis Biddle was a just man who opposed the violation of Italian-American civil liberties: Mangione and Morreale, p. 341; Pisani, p. 207; Fox, pp. 186-187; U.S. DOJ, Part I, Sec. C, p.3/ Part II, Sec.A, p.8/Part II, Sec.B, p.14/Part II, Sec.C,p.23/Part II, Sec.E, pp. 38-39.

[89] Evacuations of Italian-American fishermen from designated areas on the West Coast was still occurring in the Fall of 1942; see "Wartime Violation of Italian American Civil Liberties Act," 106th Congress, 1st Session, on H.R. 2442, Oct. 26, 1999, http://commdocs.house.gov/committees/judiciary/hju60413.000/hju60413 _0.htm.

[90] See also R*acial Violence in Britain in the Nineteenth and Twentieth Century.* Ed Panayi, Panikos. "The Anti-Italian Riots, June 1940." Llucio Sponza. London: Leicester University Press, 1996.

[91] For more on the Italian-Canadian experience, see the documentary: *Barbed Wire and Mandolins.* Dir. Nicola Zavaglia. National Board of Canada, 1997.

[92] For proof that Italian sugar-cane workers were of the lowest caste in Australia (next to the Aborigines), see: "Italians Were Replacements for Slaves," by Antonio Maglio, http://www.tandemnews.com/printer.php?storyid'1992TandemNews.com, (downloaded May 17, 2003). Though not as bloody, anti-Italian sentiment in Australia dates as far back as its American counterpart. The same year 11 Italians were lynched in America (1891), the Australian government recruited 335 Italians from the Veneto to replace the Melanesian sugar-cane harvesters who were considered "half slaves." Sugar-cane harvesting was the lowest type of work one could find in Australia; most men would not have survived the tremendous hardships that this job offered, but the Venetians had. In fact, the Venetians were such good workers that, shortly after they replaced the Melanesians, some eight thousand Australian farmers petitioned the government to stop sending them (the petition was rejected, however). Even "the powerful Workers' Union denounced the fact that the Italians, willing to work harder than the slaves and to accept low wages, would in the long run take jobs away from Australians." It was the same old story of "union-hating Italians" looking to take over "white" jobs and then the *world!* Feelings of enmity between White Australia and the Italian community thus grew and endured for an entire century to come. Gaetano Rando, a historian of Italian emigration, stated that the Australian government was "fundamentally racist" in its attitude towards Italians and others. He went on to say that, "The constant inflow of Italians was seen with apprehension by that part of the population that worried about safeguarding ra-

cial purity and social harmony. The Labour Party and the trade unions were afraid of the repercussions on unemployment of those arrivals. The press fueled worries and fears." As early as 1883, the Australian newspapers maligned Italians as "grossly ignorant," bringing with them "jack knives and contagious diseases"—similar phrases appeared in American newspapers at this time; hence common Anglo fears. (The phrase "dirty dagoes" was also popular—*and still is*—in Australia.) Once, when a ship carrying 1,090 Italians docked, the Australian papers made the ridiculous claim that Italy was invading—and this was at a time (during the late 19th and early twentieth centuries) when Italian emigration to Australia was virtually non-existent compared to Italian emigration elsewhere. Before World War II Italians were indeed a rarity in Australia—only 36 were recorded as living in all of Western Australia in 1891, and by 1921 there were only a mere 2,000. (See "From the Apennines to the Bush: Temporary Migrants from Tuscany and the Western Australia's Italophobia, 1921-1939," Adriano Boncompagni, http://www.fga.it/altre italie/19_saggi1C.htm , Altreitalie.) The venomous hatred against Italians living in Australia *had to be* motivated by two factors: economic and racial. And since there were not too many Italians competing with white natives, the hatred was most probably race based at its core. Naturally the press' racist propaganda led to a negative public opinion of Italians, which in turn led to violent acts such as the Kalgoorlie-Boulder riots. Kalgoorlie was an outpost mining-town (not dissimilar from the ones in our own American West) and was the site of anti-Italian rioting on two separate occasions—the first occurring in 1919 and the second in 1934. (See "Divisions and Solidarity: The 1934 Kalgoorlie race riots revisited," Sarah Gregson, http://www.anu.edu.au/polsci/marx/interventions/Kalgoorlie.htm, Marxist Interventions.) The one in 1919 was triggered when "a 22 year old returned soldier, Thomas Northwood, was fatally stabbed by an Italian, [and other] returned servicemen led riots against southern Europeans, organizing a march of outraged townspeople to various Italian-owned businesses in the area. Single Italian men were given an ultimatum to leave the town or face ejection and, as a result, many migrants fled." For an account of the 1934 riot, see "From The Apennines to the Bush," by Adriano Boncompagni (cited above). Boncompagni describes the situation: "An Italian bartender accidentally killed a local Anglo-Australian sports hero. This accident sparked the resentment of many Anglo-Australian miners against the Italians residing in Kalgoorlie, which culminated in two days of riots. A raging crowd of miners devastated and burnt many shops and private [abodes] of Italians and other southern Europeans in Boulder and Kalgoorlie and pushed hundreds of Italian migrants to shelter in the surrounding countryside." In addition, Gregson found that "Most discussions of the Kalgoorlie riots demonstrate the undoubted prevalence of racist attitudes in the town, revealed in frequent references to claims that southern Europeans were disrespectful to women, scabbed on the job, caused mine accidents, lived in filthy conditions and sent all their earnings out of the country." Boncompagni lists the same stereotypes as fueling the hatred of Italians. And, like me, Boncompagni believes that the common "Italophobia" which exists intercontinentally in Anglo-Saxon societies could very possibly date back to Medieval England with all the ignorance that stemmed from that dark epoch.

[93] For more on Italians interned in English-speaking countries, see: *Enemies Within: Italians and Other Internees in Canada and Abroad*, Eds. Franca Iacovetta, Roberto Perin, Angelo Principe, Toronto: University of Toronto Press, 2000.

[94] See "Austrian 1st Mountain Division War Crimes in the Second World War," http://fl6.parsimony.net/forum27945/messages/945.htm, The World At Arms (downloaded May 19, 2003). Approximately 9,500 Italian soldiers were massacred by the Austrian 1st Mountain Division on the Greek island of Cefalonia. Part of this atrocity was depicted in the movie *Captain Corelli's Mandolin* (2001). It is not surprising that the part of the German army that carried out the slaughter was "Austrian" when one reads of the World War I atrocities cited earlier in this book.

[95] See Appendix IV.

[96] Just like the 24 Italian-American witnesses at the hearings, J. Edgar Hoover denied for many years that a criminal organization known as "the Mafia" existed—that was until Hoover found out the FBI would be given large sums of money to investigate specific criminal groups. (See Mangione and Morreale, pp. 260-261.)

[97] An early demonstration of Afro-Italian solidarity was reported in 1896, when a large number of blacks attended the burial of the Italians that were lynched in Hahnville, Louisiana; see Mangione and Morreale, p. 212.

[98] See *New York: A Documentary*. Dir. Ric Burns. Narrators: George Plimpton, Martin Scorsese, Eli Wallach. Steeplechase Films, 1999. To see what the policy of urban renewal did to a New Haven enclave, see "Death of a Neighborhood," Rob Gurwitt, http://www.motherjones.com/mother_jones/SO00/urban.html, MojoWire Magazine, downloaded May 22, 2003. See also Michael Novak's *The Rise of the Unmeltable Ethnics*, New York: Macmillan, 1972.

[99] For the upper-class' negative opinion of Italian politicians, see Lagumina, pp. 307-309.

[100] To prove that the old saying "what goes around comes around" is true, two Italian-Americans, Supreme Court Justice John J. Sirica and New Jersey Congressman Peter Rodino, were instrumental in helping to "de-throne" Nixon. See Mangione and Morreale, p. 404.

[101] *The Godfather*. Dir. Francis Ford Coppola. Perf. Marlon Brando, James Caan, Al Pacino. Paramount, 1972.

[102] Although *The Godfather* did soil the modern image of Italian-Americans (and led to the creation of many more mob movies), I believe subsequent films such as *Goodfellas* (1990) and *Casino* (1995) were more damaging due to their extremely debasing portrayals. *The Godfather* in book form was unquestionably the most damaging piece of literature for the Italian-American community—within five years of its publication, over 150 "Mafia-related" books were written. (See Mangione and Morreale, p. 263.)

[103] A friend of mine who went to a New York City high school in the 1960s said the main reason he dropped out was because his non-Italian teachers did not understand him, and were even hostile. My own father remembers, in grade school, the anti-Italian ridicule he was subjected to by members of the school's faculty. These

grievances seem to have been quite common years ago; and according to the testimony of younger acquaintances, anti-Italian sentiment in the classroom is not at all a thing of the past—apparently many "liberal" teachers have turned Italian bashing (or the neglect of Italian students) into a politically correct art form.

[104] As we found out earlier, Al Smith was the first Italian-American male to run in a presidential race.

[105] This is not a direct quote.

[106] It turned out that officer Hoskin had Lorenzo's younger brother, Rocco, at the police station for driving while intoxicated.

[107] Not knowing where to turn at the time, I myself contacted a well known Italian-American disc-jockey over the phone, hoping to garner support for a protest march—he essentially said we would look like a bunch of "assholes" and hung up.

[108] See, Jennifer Guglielmo and Salvatore Salerno, *Are Italians White? How Race is Made In America*, New York: Routledge, 2003, p.1.

[109] It is my conviction that many modern civil rights "industry" organizations have instilled a sense of hopelessness in the black community, and that the resulting pessimism makes blacks feel as if they cannot succeed.

[110] Social Darwinist theories put forth by the likes of Herbert Spencer and William Graham Sumner also gained popularity, as they justified the exploitative nature of American capitalism and the nation's burgeoning imperialism.

[111] The torch of this kind of ignorance has also been passed in recent years to Germany, the Netherlands, and the Scandinavian countries—all make bitter use of the word "wog" when discriminating against any person who happens to possess a degree of color in their societies.

[112] A similarly derisive term ethnic Canadians (particularly Italo-Canadians) use to describe Anglos is "mangia-cake" (pronounced manja-cake). My Italian-Canadian cousins, who are relatively recent émigrés to Canada, first exposed me to this interesting term.

[113] For example, I personally detest the term Native Americans; my reasoning is such that all people born and bred on American soil are "Native Americans," The term also reminds me of the pain my immigrant ancestors experienced when "native American" was a code word for "superior white man" But even so, I totally respect an indigenous person's choice to identify himself or herself as a "Native American."

[114] Strangely enough, many Cambodians even resemble littoral Mediterraneans with their large round eyes, brownish skin and short, thin statures. They are quite distinct physically from the other peoples of Southeast Asia.

[115] Personally, I do not like the term "Latino" because I have found it to be exclusionary. Even though the original Latin tribe and language were native to Italy, and though no nation on earth possesses more Latinity, Italians are not considered "Latino" in modern American society.

[116] It is no historical secret that Scandinavian Visigoths and Celts dominated the Iberian Peninsula for centuries. Verily the Northern European presence in the Spanish people's genes is so strong that up until recently the *World Almanac* described Spaniards as a "Mix of Mediterranean and Nordic types." (See, *The World Almanac*

and Book of Facts 2003, New York: World Almanac Books, p. 839.)

[117] See, Giuseppe Sergi, *The Mediterranean Race: A Study of the Origin of European Peoples*, New York: Humanities Press, 1967.

[118] Some of these groups are actually calling for the secession of the American Southwest, drawing attention to the fact that states, such as New Mexico, Arizona and Texas, used to belong to Mexico. An even better claim would come from American Indian groups like the Navajo, whose ancestors inhabited that region thousands of years before the Mexican government's founding.

[119] "Soprano Sting Operation Railroads Physician," Press Release, Order Sons of Italy in America, Frank Sinatra Lodge 2621, Englishtown, New Jersey, Aug. 27, 2001.

[120] "Re: Involvement," http://messages.clubs.yahoo.com/clubs/i...=italian ameri cans &sid=163090542&mid=2474&n=1, Nov. 27, 2001.

[121] "Re: Involvement," http://messages.clubs.yahoo.com/clubs/i...=italian ameri cans &sid=163090542&mid=2469&n=1, Nov. 27, 2001.

[122] "Columbus Day Began in Colorado. AIM Would Like the Holiday to End Here, Too," by Lisa Levitt Ryckman, *Rocky Mountain News*, Sep. 8, 2001.

[123] "Transform Columbus Day," http://www.transformcolumbusday.org/faq. htm#first%20amendment downloaded Jul. 18, 2004.

[124] "Transform Columbus Day,"http://www.transformcolumbusday.org/alliance statements.htm downloaded Jul. 18, 2004.

[125]This quote comes from: "Sicilian Culture: Famous Quotes from Sinatra," http://www.sicilianculture.com/dialect/sinatra.htm, downloaded Jan. 5, 2004.

[126] See, the Italic Institute of America's "On Image & Defamation: Report to the Membership," by the Executive Council of the IIA, Nov. 2002.

[a] A man named Ernest Lacore was hanged in Will, Illinois in 1894, however I have withheld his name from the list because I am unsure about his ethnic background.

[b] Also in 1888, a man named Nocollo Fimenello (probably *"Nicolo"*) was executed in Colorado. Although his name sounds Italian (and very well could be), I have not included him in the list because the website identified him as "Hispanic." See, http://users.bestweb.net/~rg/execution/Colorado.htm.

[c] On July 30, 1896, a man named "James Casharego" was executed in Sebastian, Arkansas. If his name was misspelled it is possible that he could have been of Italian background; nonetheless, I have left him off the list. See, http://users.bestweb.net/~rg/execution/Arkansas.htm.

[d] In June of 1917 a man named Charles Victoriano was hanged in Jefferson, Louisiana; his surname sounds Italian, but after doing the research I found that "Victoriano" is primarily a Hispanic name. Also in 1917 a man listed as "black," by the name of "Mockey Palucca," was executed in Orangeburg, South Carolina. In my research I found that two other "blacks" were executed bearing the Italian-sounding names "Oscar Cicero" and "Jesse Cora"; they were executed in 1903 and 1910, respectively. On some of these execution lists, at the "Before the Needles"

website, it appears that a number of Italians had black partners in crime. This was not uncommon during the late nineteenth and early twentieth centuries; for example, see *Bloody Williamson: A Chapter in American Lawlessness*, by Paul M. Angle, Chicago: University of Illinois Press, pp. 109-110.

[e] Benigno was convicted of murder-robbery. A non-Italian accomplice did not receive the death penalty, however, thus angering Cleveland's Italian community. See, "Cleveland's Sly-Fanner Murders" by Allan May, http://crimemagazine. com/sly-fanner.htm.

[f] It is clear that these six men received an unfair trial; see *Spirit of Vengeance*, by John Baiamonte, Baton Rouge: Louisiana State University Press, 1986.

[g] The first person executed in the state of Florida was Benjamin Donica in 1827— it is possible that he was of Italian background.

[h] Zangara tried to assassinate President Franklin D. Roosevelt

[i] Also in 1937, a man named Clemens Matura was executed in Texas. I have not included him in the list, however, because I am not sure about his ethnicity. See "Before the Needles," http://users.bestweb.net/~rg/execution/Texas.htm.

[j] Renna was falsely labeled "Hispanic" on the "Before the Needles" website; see http://users.bestweb.net/~rg/execution/New%20York.htm.

[k] A man named Leo Lera was executed in Texas in 1943, but I have left him off the list because I am unsure of his ethnic background.

[l] Earlier in 1948, a man named Irvin Matteo was executed in Louisiana—he is listed as a black man. See, http://users.bestweb.net/~rg/execution/Louisiana.htm.

[m] Because I am unsure about the ethnicity of one "Albert Sala," executed in Nevada in 1946, and because his surname seems to have both Spanish and Italian roots, I am withholding his name from the list.

[n] In 1951 a man by the name of Grant Rio was executed in the state of Washington; see http://users.bestweb.net/~rg/execution/Washington.htm. I have withheld his name from the list because, again, I do not know whether he was of Italian or Hispanic background.

Index

African-Americans, 38, 44, 49, 53, 58, 63, 96, 110, 119, 125, 133, 137, 143, 154, 160, 167, 194, 218, 233, 239, 245

Age of Exploration, 18, 183

Anglo, 16, 17, 18, 23, 25, 41, 45, 46, 63, 64, 65, 85, 86, 94, 97, 103, 110, 113, 119, 137, 139, 140, 144, 155, 156, 157, 158, 161, 167, 179, 182, 186, 193, 233, 234, 235, 236, 247

Asia, 143

assimilation, 4, 13, 63, 105, 120, 128, 136, 139, 140, 141, 142, 160, 162, 191

Atlantic, 24, 48, 58, 177, 180, 183

Bensonhurst, 119, 120, 142, 166

Black Hand, 46, 72, 74, 76, 81, 84, 91, 106, 241

Brazil, 240, 243

Brooklyn Standard Union, 21

Bush, 156, 247

CA Workingmen's Party, 15

Cabot, 57, 237

Caboto, 192

California, 14, 16, 19, 43, 65, 77, 91, 92, 99, 100, 101, 105, 177, 199, 205, 207, 209, 211, 212, 213, 214, 216, 217, 239, 244

Canada, 66, 103, 104, 123, 169, 246, 248

Caruso, 57, 79, 201

Catalina, 213

Cesar, 19

Charles, 53, 57, 91, 110, 200, 203, 209, 210, 213, 221, 230, 234, 250

Chavez, 19

Chicago, 19, 29, 60, 74, 96, 117, 150, 159, 219, 230, 232, 241, 251

Chicano, 19, 155

Chinatown, 15

Chinese Exclusion Act, 16

Chinese-Americans, 4, 9, 14

Cicero Riots, 63

Colombo, 111, 112, 165, 181, 182, 190, 228

Columbus Day, 4, 7, 102, 121, 126, 128, 165, 175, 176, 177, 178, 179, 180, 181, 183, 185, 186, 227, 229, 230, 250

Congress, 16, 86, 98, 107, 135, 227, 230, 231, 232, 245

criminality, 47, 80, 119, 129, 187

Cripple Creek, 69

Croton Lake, 80, 81, 201, 222

Cuba, 155

DiMaggio, 99

Draft Riots, 23

East Harlem, 87, 96, 105

emigration, 238, 247

England, 80, 248

English, 18, 22, 45, 56, 59, 69, 70, 72, 75, 78, 86, 87, 103, 116, 118, 119, 140, 144, 148, 160, 162, 183, 186, 248

Erwin, Mississippi, 67, 239

Ethiopia, 96

Europeans, 16, 18, 38, 81, 86, 93, 95, 125, 141, 144, 151, 157, 235, 247

Executions, 5, 52, 92, 195, 196, 197, 205, 206, 214, 215, 217

Farmingville, 20, 21

Florida, 71, 92, 95, 105, 159, 209,

211, 214, 215, 217, 239, 241, 244, 251
Fort Missoula, 98, 245
France, 50, 62, 64, 142, 183, 198, 203, 204, 219, 233, 236, 237, 238, 242
French, 55, 58, 75, 108, 142, 183, 235, 238
Garibaldi, 52, 187
Germans, 55, 62, 72, 75, 99, 101, 103, 144, 147, 148, 153, 169, 183, 184, 235, 238, 240, 248
Germany, 14, 83, 103, 169, 174, 183, 184, 235, 240, 242
Godfather, 112, 114, 117, 120, 122, 129, 133, 222, 231, 248
Goodfellas, 120, 121, 123, 222, 231, 248
Guinea, 189
Hahnville, 63, 248
Harvard, 61, 89
Hernandez v. Texas, 19
Hispanics, 4, 10, 17, 18, 19, 21, 22, 51, 65, 117, 119, 125, 136, 145, 147, 148, 154, 155, 156, 159, 161, 162, 165, 170, 186, 218, 237, 238, 241
Hosokawa, 16, 17, 220
identity, 37, 45, 115, 136, 137, 138, 140, 142, 143, 148, 149, 151, 154, 157, 158, 160, 161, 186, 188, 192, 233
Identity, 4, 138, 157, 159
immigration, 14, 16, 20, 22, 23, 39, 40, 44, 45, 46, 47, 48, 50, 51, 57, 59, 68, 74, 90, 91, 92, 93, 105, 107, 140, 142, 143, 146, 147, 150, 157, 162, 175, 233, 235, 243
Immigration Act, 39, 92, 93, 95, 223
Immigration Restriction Act of 1924, 16, 223, 244
India, 143, 144, 148, 161

Indies, 181
internment, 17, 98, 99, 103, 104, 149, 152, 174, 175, 181, 182
involuntary servitude, 71
Irish-Americans, 4, 22, 23, 24, 97, 125
Italian American Civil Rights League, 111, 112
Italian American Foundation, 109, 126, 163
Italian-Americans, 1, 3, 4, 6, 7, 13, 17, 24, 37, 38, 44, 51, 52, 57, 58, 60, 64, 66, 73-75, 78, 85, 86, 90, 91, 93-97, 99-110, 112-121, 125-130, 133-137, 142, 143, 146, 148, 149, 150, 151, 152, 154, 157, 160, 161, 162, 164-167, 170-176, 178, 179, 181, 182, 185, 186, 187, 189-194, 217, 219, 237, 239, 244, 245, 248,249, 250
Italy, 6, 16, 28, 30, 39, 40, 44, 45, 46, 47, 51, 54, 58, 60, 62, 67, 73, 74, 83, 88, 89, 95, 96, 97, 98, 103, 104, 108, 112, 114, 119, 126, 141, 142, 155, 160, 161, 163, 164, 165, 166, 167, 168, 177, 183, 188, 225, 230, 234, 235, 236, 238, 243, 245, 246, 247, 249
Japanese, 4, 9, 10, 13, 16, 17, 67, 69, 81, 98, 99, 101, 102, 103, 104, 143, 149, 152, 181, 184, 241, 246
Japanese-Americans, 4, 16, 17, 101, 102, 103, 181
Jewish-Americans, 4, 11, 13, 24, 25, 38, 125, 163
Jews, 24, 25, 26, 27, 54, 58, 92, 94, 108, 115, 124, 151, 153, 155, 167, 170, 171, 172, 173, 174, 183, 235
Johnston City, 84
Katz, 55, 67, 86, 220, 237, 238,

239, 240, 241, 242
Ku Klux Klan, 50, 73, 93, 95, 226
La Bianca, 110
Latimer Massacre, 63, 221
Latinity, 18, 243, 249
Latins, 6, 18, 186, 192
Lawrence Strike, 78, 79, 80, 224
Lee Avenue Court, 21
Lincoln, 23
Little Italy, 30, 74, 96, 104, 108, 164, 225
Louisiana, 25, 42, 54, 55, 63, 64, 65, 67, 69, 72, 81, 92, 100, 149, 198, 200, 205, 206, 207, 208, 209, 211, 213, 214, 219, 233, 236, 237, 242, 248, 250, 251
Lower Manhattan, 30, 77, 164, 233
Ludlow Massacre, 26, 69, 82, 83, 223, 225, 241
lynchings, 6, 12, 15, 25, 47, 52, 56, 57, 58, 62, 64, 67, 69, 76, 77, 84, 89, 94, 95, 106, 129, 133, 143, 166, 174, 185, 194, 225, 233, 236, 237, 238, 237-240-244, 241, 242, 244
Mafia, 4, 46, 57, 59, 81, 110, 112, 114, 118, 133, 165, 168, 169, 186, 222
Maine, 53, 195, 196
Massachusetts, 61, 65, 77, 88, 92, 94, 100, 105, 109, 152, 197, 203, 204, 205, 209, 213, 214, 215, 216, 217
Media, 113, 121, 219, 225, 228
Mediterranean, 46, 67, 81, 91, 107, 137, 138, 139, 142, 143, 145, 152, 156, 158, 160, 161, 162, 172, 183, 184, 186, 192, 221, 233, 234, 235, 242, 250
Mexican-American, 19, 113, 155, 220
Mezzogiorno, 28, 39, 44, 46, 88, 191
Minnesota, 18, 73, 242

Molly Maguires, 23
National Origins Act, 50, 92, 141
New Orleans, 6, 15, 47, 53, 54, 55, 56, 57, 58, 62, 72, 100, 106, 129, 133, 166, 233, 236, 237
New Orleans lynching, 57, 58, 133
New York Times, 57, 74, 80, 105, 107, 120, 234
North Carolina, 50, 60, 70
Operation Wetback, 19
Pacific, 65, 99, 102, 121, 125
Palmer Raids, 191
Panic of 1876, 14, 15
Pearl Harbor, 16, 98, 245
politics, 118, 140, 157, 158
Portugal, 143
Portuguese, 142, 156, 209
poverty, 20, 23, 39, 46, 47, 48, 53, 56, 66, 73, 91, 95, 120, 136, 154, 170, 178
prejudice, 19, 44, 47, 53, 57, 67, 119, 169, 191, 233, 235, 236, 242, 245
Puerto Ricans, 19, 21, 161, 182, 237
Race, 4, 46, 86, 92, 107, 146, 162, 220, 221, 226, 234, 245, 250
Racial Beliefs, 4, 143
racialization, 141, 158
Restrictions on Persons of Italian Ancestry, 17, 230, 245
Riverhead, 20
Roman Catholic, 17, 113, 141, 161, 243
Rome, 6, 86, 92, 136, 137, 148, 192
Sacco and Vanzetti, 13, 86, 88, 89, 90, 94, 100, 209, 244
Sachem, 20
Salazar, 19
Scelsa v. CUNY, 121
segregation, 49, 50, 77, 236, 242
September 11, 87, 126, 169
Simpson and Yinger, 16, 17
Sirica, 248

Son of Sam, 117, 227
Sons of Italy, 112, 126, 163, 165, 166, 168, 188, 230
Sopranos, 123, 128, 129, 133, 166, 167, 168, 169, 186, 227, 228
Spain, 59, 142, 162, 182, 183
Spaniards, 77, 235
Spanish Crown, 18, 181
sports, 190, 192, 247
Spring Valley, 62, 63, 157
Supreme Court, 19, 126, 191, 248
Tallulah, 64
Tampa, 75, 76, 77, 92, 220, 230, 241
Tom Tom, 59
Tontitown, 63, 64, 239
Truckee, 15
Turks, 142, 151, 157, 184, 235
Uncle Sam, 18, 102
Venetians, 192, 246
Virginia, 45, 59, 68, 70, 92, 207, 212, 214, 229, 237
Washington, 53, 55, 59, 61, 65, 92, 109, 147, 195, 198, 199, 205, 207, 209, 220, 230, 233, 245, 251
WASPs, 23, 24, 25, 41, 44, 54, 107, 137, 156, 160
West Virginia, 59, 68, 70, 83, 92, 207, 212, 229
West Virginia,, 59, 68, 92, 229
Wetback, 19
White Anglo-Saxon Protestant, 18, 25, 63, 85, 144, 233
whiteness, 6, 45, 46, 63, 146, 156, 160
Willisville, 83, 84, 229
Wog, 4, 158
World War II, 17, 39, 44, 73, 90, 97, 98, 101, 103, 104, 106, 118, 128, 132, 142, 181, 182, 184, 191, 219, 227, 230, 237, 244, 245, 247
Yale, 84, 85, 110, 220, 230, 242
Yellow Peril, 16, 65
Zoot Suit Riots, 19